1984

COMPUTER-MEDIATED
COMMUNICATION SYSTEMS
Status and Evaluation

HUMAN COMMUNICATION RESEARCH SERIES

PETER R. MONGE, Editor

Monge and Cappella:
MULTIVARIATE TECHNIQUES IN
HUMAN COMMUNICATION RESEARCH 1980

Cushman and McPhee:
MESSAGE-ATTITUDE-BEHAVIOR
RELATIONSHIP 1980

Woelfel and Fink:
MEASUREMENT OF COMMUNICATION
PROCESSES 1980

Kerr and Hiltz:
COMPUTER-MEDIATED COMMUNICATION SYSTEMS:
STATUS AND EVALUATION 1982

COMPUTER-MEDIATED COMMUNICATION SYSTEMS
Status and Evaluation

Elaine B. Kerr

Computerized Conferencing and Communications Center
New Jersey Institute of Technology
Newark, New Jersey

Starr Roxanne Hiltz

Department of Sociology
Upsala College
East Orange, New Jersey
and
Computerized Conferencing and Communications Center
New Jersey Institute of Technology
Newark, New Jersey

1982

ACADEMIC PRESS

A Subsidiary of Harcourt Brace Jovanovich, Publishers
New York   London
Paris   San Diego   San Francisco   São Paulo   Sydney   Tokyo   Toronto

ACADEMIC PRESS, INC.
111 Fifth Avenue, New York, New York 10003

United Kingdom Edition published by
ACADEMIC PRESS, INC. (LONDON) LTD.
24/28 Oval Road, London NW1   7DX

Library of Congress Cataloging in Publication Data

Kerr, Elaine B.
   Computer-mediated communication systems.

   (Human communication research series)
   Includes index.
   1. Information networks.   2. Computer networks.
3. Electronic mail systems.   I. Hiltz, Starr Roxanne.
II. Title.   III. Series.
TK5105.5.K47   1982   001.64'404   82-8841
ISBN 0-12-404980-X   AACR2

PRINTED IN THE UNITED STATES OF AMERICA

82 83 84 85   9 8 7 6 5 4 3 2 1

To our friendship:
Now twenty-one years and still growing

To our children:
Jonathan, Katherine, and Paul

And to Murray Turoff:
Who got us both into this

Contents

---

[1] Coauthored with Murray Turoff.
[2] This section is an edited version of Peter and Trudy Johnson-Lenz, "Consider tl Groupware: Design and Group Process Impacts on Communication in the Electron Medium," in Hiltz and Kerr (1981).

3. Acceptance and Usage of Computer-Mediated Communication Systems

4. Impacts of Computer-Mediated Communications upon Individuals and Groups

5. Appropriate Research Methodology

6. Summary and Conclusions

Preface

The idea seems simple enough at first glance. Communications or information entered into a computer from one terminal can be retrieved immediately or at a later time from any other terminal linked to the central computer.

It is the applications and impacts that are startling, and the acceptance of the technology that is problematical. Essentially, computer-mediated communication means that large numbers of people in business, government, education, or at home can use the computer to maintain continuous communication and information exchanges. It also requires that people accept fairly radical changes in the way they work and even in the way they think, if they are to reap the potential benefits.

More than a replacement for the telephone, mails, or face-to-face meetings, computer communication is a new medium for building and maintaining human relationships. It is faster and cheaper than alternative methods for linking geographically dispersed people in working groups. But more importantly, it tends to expand greatly the human and information resources to which one has constant and convenient access.

This volume has its origins as a report for a National Science Foundation-sponsored project (Hiltz and Kerr, 1981). In expanded and reworked form, it synthesizes current knowledge about computerized conferencing systems, electronic mail, and office information–communication systems. It should be of interest both to students and researchers studying this new form of electronic communication and to organizations that are planning the installation of electronic mail or other computer-mediated communication systems and that need to be aware of the information gleaned from the studies presented here. The book is organized into four main sections, focusing on the following issues:

1. What are the important considerations in designing software or choosing a system from the many available options and capabilities?
2. What factors determine whether such systems are likely to be accepted or rejected?
3. What are the likely impacts of such systems upon the individuals, groups, and organizations which use them? It is not the economic costs and benefits, but the social problems and "payoffs" in the form of enhanced performance and organizational efficiency that should be the main considerations in deciding whether or not to use a computer-mediated communication system.
4. Given the conditional nature of many of the possible impacts, no system should be implemented without formal evaluation and feedback from users to guide the implementation. The major kinds of evaluational strategies that have been successfully employed are described in this book.

To date, implementations of this technology have taken the form either of proprietary electronic mail systems, with little or no assessment and reporting of the results, or of relatively small-scale field trials with associated evaluations, generally published as organizational research reports and not available in the open literature. For this project, we attempted to gather all of the acquired knowledge and insights gained from existing evaluations by using the researchers as a panel of experts to systematically report their findings within a common conceptual framework. We also used a panel of system designers to rate the importance of the many optional features an organization or individual can choose from the technology. The result is a synthesis of the "state of the art," designed as a reference for anyone contemplating the use of computer-mediated communication systems.

Acknowledgments

The initial phases of this project were financed by a grant to Upsala College (IST-8018077) from the Division of Information Science and Technology of the National Science Foundation. The opinions and conclusions reported here are solely those of the authors and do not necessarily represent those of the National Science Foundation.

Peter and Trudy Johnson-Lenz wrote the section on "groupware" that appears in Chapter 2, and Murray Turoff coauthored the first section of that chapter. In addition, Valarie Lamont provided a first draft for the section on group determinants of acceptance, and Jane McCarroll contributed a first draft for the section on group level impacts. Their contributions to the planning and review processes are also gratefully acknowledged.

We wish to thank others who helped to make this book possible. From participation in the Electronic Information Exchange System (EIES) project to sharing of data on design and evaluation to critical reading of early drafts of the manuscript, the following have provided invaluable assistance in one or more capacities: James Bair, Robert Bezilla, John Bregenzer, David Brown, Richard Dalton, James Danowski, Morley Greenberg, Edward Housman, Kenneth Johnson, Hubert Lipinski, Clifford Lynch, Joseph Martino, Richard Miller, Jacob Palme, Robert Parnes, Charlton Price, Ronald Rice, John Senders, Elliot Siegel, Sarah Spang, Richard Stern, Don Tapscott, and Stuart Umpleby.

We are grateful to Harold Bamford for his support and encouragement throughout the project. We would also like to thank Upsala College, and particularly President Rodney Felder and George Fenwick, for support that assured completion of the project when it greatly exceeded initial time estimates.

CHAPTER 1

Introduction

INTRODUCTION

Research in a new area is like an assault on the wilderness: Skilled observers are first sent forth to explore promising new territories and gather information. Next comes the phase of gathering this information together to systematically map what is known of the terrain. The information in this book can be likened to the mapping of available knowledge gained from exploratory studies of computer-mediated communication systems. Having identified the opportunities and the dangers, we are in a better position to conclude that the new technology is "safe" for permanent settlers who are less adventuresome or perhaps less foolhardy than the pioneers who first explored it.

This book was stimulated by the desire to capture and document what was learned from the completion of the operational trials of the Electronic Information Exchange System (EIES), and to compare these findings with those of other computer-mediated communication systems: conferencing systems, electronic message systems, and general information–communication systems designed to support "knowledge workers" (managers, administrators, and professionals who retrieve, process, and communicate information). In our post-industrial economy, or "information society," there is an expanding population of such white-collar and service workers who can potentially achieve significant productivity gains from the use of these communication systems.

Following are examples of current applications:

1. Hewlett-Packard's internal message network handles more than 25 million messages a year.
2. Small science and technology advisory offices in many states try to respond to questions bearing on proposed new legislation. The same inquiry frequently occurs in several states, producing duplication of effort. By joining an electronic information exchange, they share their "inquiries" and "responses" and build a common knowledge base to aid them in their work.
3. Half a dozen authors located throughout the United States jointly write a major report. Each can read, edit, and make comments about the others' work as soon as it is entered.
4. Middle managers in a major corporation take a "continuing education" course; much of the "class" is conducted on-line.
5. College-educated professionals in many fields resign from their nine-to-five office jobs and work full-time from their homes, as free-lance consultants on nationwide communication networks.
6. A group of cerebral palsy children in New Jersey establishes "computer pen pals" across the world.
7. Approximately 250 individuals, representing most of the utilities which currently operate nuclear reactors, use a computer-mediated communication system to share technical data on a daily basis.

This small selection from hundreds of groups currently working on dozens of systems represents only a sample of the uses of this new technology.

OVERVIEW OF THE MEDIUM

Computer-mediated communication systems use computers to structure, store, and process communications. Users compose text items by typing on terminals linked to a central computer, either directly or by telephone lines and a packet-switched network such as Telenet or Tymnet. The terminal may have a typewriter-like device that produces printed "hard copy," or it may have a television-like screen, called a CRT (Cathode Ray Tube).

Geographically dispersed groups are able to communicate at a speed and cost superior to telephone, mail, and face-to-face meetings. A permanent written transcript is maintained of the proceedings. The medium is asynchronous, meaning that time and space are minimized as barriers to interaction and that people can participate at the time and pace most convenient to them.

This is a new form of enhanced human communication, made possible by the proliferation of terminals, the development of time-sharing digital systems, and the reduced costs of computer time. Based on a hybrid of computer science, communication theory, and information science, its potentials are now beginning to emerge with a core of user experience and related evaluational studies. We present here the current state of the art.

Although the basic configuration resembles a written version of the telephone conference call, there are important differences, in addition to the self-determined participation rate. Because text items are retained in the computer until deliberately deleted, they may be copied to others or merged into larger documents, and they allow latecomers to catch up with the proceedings.

These systems typically include some or all of the following components:

1. *Messages* may be sent to an individual, a number of individuals, or a defined group, and may be open or blind copied. In some systems there is the option of using a regular signature, a pen name, or anonymity. Those to whom messages can be sent may or may not be restricted. Messages are retained in the computer and delivered when the recipient signs on line. Confirmation of the time and date of delivery is usually provided to the sender.

2. *Conferences* are a common writing space for group deliberations. Upon accessing a conference, users are brought up to date in the proceedings. Membership is controlled by a moderator. Participation is usually asynchronous but may at times be conducted in "real time." Conferences may be a few weeks to several years in duration, and the size may range from 2 to more than 50 members. Some conferences may be "public," or open to all members of a given system.

3. *Notebooks or Files* are personal spaces useful for drafting or coauthoring material which later will be submitted to other parts of the system, and for storage of items such as customized programs and documents.

4. *Bulletins or Journals* are spaces for the generation and submission

of reports, newsletter items, and formal papers. Special software may allow refereeing by anonymous reviewers, and abstracts can permit recipients to access the full text only if it is of interest.

5. *Text Editor* allows users to revise or modify material while preparing it or afterwards.

Advanced systems may also include mechanisms for such tasks as searching and retrieving, indexing, voting, merging text, delayed entries, alarms, reminder files, and calendars. They may also be integrated with data bases and decision support or other analytical tools.

METHODOLOGY: HOW THE DATA WERE GATHERED

Background

The EIES field trials are among the most intensely evaluated of recent information science endeavors, with formal evaluational efforts built into each of the seven official operational trial groups. In addition, the Hepatitis Data Base and White House Conference on Library and Information Services user groups contained formal evaluation components.

One product of these group experiences and accompanying evaluations was a final report for each of the nine groups, plus the overall cross-group evaluation. These separate reports contain major differences in what was measured and reported, and they do not facilitate the comparative overview of different approaches to evaluate this information exchange medium or the different experiences of each of these groups.

Other computer-based communication systems have been evaluated in the past. The most extensive studies, in addition to the EIES trials, were by Johansen, Vallee, and their colleagues for the PLANET system. In addition, Bair (1974) and Edwards (1977) conducted extensive research on NLS, and some evaluative data have been published for a number of other systems. By reading the various individual reports, however, it is not possible to reach any conclusions about the relative influence on the findings of the group and application, the features of the specific systems used, or the evaluation methods employed.

This book presents the comparative findings and methods, including their implications for needed future research.

Procedure

A study group, composed of 18 researchers working in this field and representing 12 separate research projects, was convened in New Jersey in July 1980. Invited to attend were all known scholars who had published evaluational findings. Because of expense or time conflicts, some could not attend; however, their participation was solicited in the group's post-meeting activities, through EIES, mail, or telephone.

The major findings for each of the operational trials and other evaluational projects were summarized, with the focus on the similarities and differences discovered among them. The participants were then divided into study groups to generate the lists of factors about which data would be systematically collected. The lists were reviewed and refined by the working groups on EIES and transformed into questionnaires, which were "data report forms." These forms and working papers were distributed via EIES and the mail to gather additional input from others working in this communications area, so as to collect comparable data for as many projects as possible.

Synthesizing Expert Opinions: A Modified
Delphi Approach

While some of the operational trials or case studies of computer-mediated communication have been extensively documented in the literature, there are many about which only sparse accounts are publicly available. This is particularly true of the acquired wisdom of designers, who tend to prefer to work on new enhancements of their systems rather than to document and critique the successes and failures of software that has already been implemented. Another problem is that even the published studies do not use a common framework, so that it is difficult to compare the results or construct a basis for generating cumulative results for future research.

Conversations within the "invisible college" of scholars working in the evaluation of this technology indicated that many had observations not documented in the open literature. Their opinions, based on their studies, were a form of expertise available to be tapped. A modified Delphi approach was chosen to gather and synthesize this acquired knowledge.

Delphi is a method for collecting and utilizing the opinions of experts. It may be characterized as:

> A method for structuring a group communication process so that the process is effective in allowing a group of individuals, as a whole, to deal with a complex problem. To accomplish this "structured communication," there is provided:

some feedback of individual contributions of information and knowledge; some assessment of the group judgment or view; some opportunity for individuals to revise views; and some degree of anonymity for the individual responses (Linstone and Turoff, 1975:3).

This project can be considered a "modified Delphi" because the last condition was absent. This was considered necessary for the group to understand the context of the differing opinions or observations. In all other respects, it was a Delphi. Common data reporting instruments were designed and mailed to systems designers (for the systems module), group leaders or managers (for the task module), and evaluators (for the acceptance and impacts modules). The results were tabulated, summarized, and returned to the respondents, who were invited to comment on observed differences or to change their ratings if the comparative data and discussion altered their opinions.

Factors in Computer-Mediated Communication Systems

The conceptual framework used to integrate this study is a model of a closed system with multiple feedback loops. By expanding and building on the list of factors generated by Vallee et al. (1974b:22), the determinants of acceptance and usage of computer-mediated communication systems can be categorized as characteristics of the *system* itself, including terminals and other equipment available to users, characteristics of the *task* or activity being performed on line, attributes of the *individual* user, and attributes of the *group* or organizational context. The interaction of these factors determines the level of system *acceptance*, which includes both the amount of use and the users' subjective attitudes of satisfaction or dissatisfaction. *Evaluation* of these systems may produce feedback to the designers, which can change the nature of the system itself and the tasks or applications for which it is subsequently employed. The evaluation methods used will to some extent filter the observed *impacts* upon attitudes and behaviors of the individuals or groups.

There are of course societal inputs which may intrude upon this system of variables, such as government regulations and changes in the economy. Such influences external to the system and its user community are defined as outside the limits of this study.

We gathered data for each system or study, using the modified Delphi method described above. The "task" data have been eliminated from this presentation of the results, since we were unable to progress much beyond a purely descriptive level of analysis in dealing with task attributes.

DESCRIPTIONS OF THE SYSTEMS
AND GROUPS STUDIED

Below is a brief description of the nature of each of the studies included in this book. The EIES groups are listed first, followed by the other systems. The person or persons who reported the data for that group are indicated after the group name. A completely descriptive manner of presenting the results in this book might be to say "Jane McCarroll, reporting the results for the Devices for the Disabled group on EIES for our questionnaire, states that. . . ." However, since these reports are referenced hundreds of times, we used the shorthand of either the last name of the person reporting the data or the short name of the group to indicate our questionnaire data. (We say, for example, "McCarroll states" or "JEDEC reports . . . .")

EIES Groups

EIES (Electronic Information Exchange System)

EIES was designed by Murray Turoff. It includes messages, conferences, notebooks, and a large number of special structures and advanced features. Its development and initial years of operation were financed by the National Science Foundation's Division of Information Science and Technology. Grant applications were solicited and competitively awarded to scientific groups wishing to use the system (NSF 76-45). Each group was required to produce an evaluation of its experiences. Four of the groups (Devices for the Disabled, Futures, General Systems Theory, and Social Nets) were small scientific research communities with no specific goals other than improving their informal communications. The remaining groups tended to have specific goals or tasks that they wished to accomplish in addition to improving their communications.

Devices for the Disabled

Jane H. McCarroll headed this multidisciplinary group which consisted of those concerned with the research and development of devices for the disabled (see McCarroll, 1980).

Futures (Bregenzer)

The Futures Research Group was coordinated by Joseph P. Martino and evaluated by John Bregenzer. It was composed of researchers from the multidisciplinary futures community who were concerned with planning, forecasting, and anticipating the future. Examples of such research include the development of structural and cross-impact models, the generation of scenarios, and the conduct of Delphi sequences (see Martino and Bregenzer, 1980, 1981; Bregenzer and Martino, 1980).

General Systems Theory

The General Systems Theory group, coordinated by Stuart A. Umpleby, consisted of a small research community attempting to integrate a number of scientific disciplines under the rubric of a systems approach to theory (see Umpleby, 1980).

Hepatitis

Elliot Siegel coordinated a group of experts in the field of viral hepatitis, collaborating with the National Library of Medicine to validate and update a hepatitis data base intended to facilitate information transfer to health practitioners (see Siegel, 1980).

JEDEC

This group, facilitated and evaluated by Peter and Trudy Johnson-Lenz, utilized EIES to develop standards for the Joint Electron Devices Council (see Johnson-Lenz and Johnson-Lenz, 1980b).

LEGITECH (Lamont)

Coordinated by Chandler Harrison Stevens and evaluated by Valarie C. Lamont, LEGITECH connected a large number of researchers concerned with scientific and technology issues of their various state legislatures. A special self-filtering communication structure called "Topics" was designed for their use (see Lamont, 1980; Stevens, 1980; Johnson-Lenz and Johnson-Lenz, 1980d, 1981).

Social Nets

The Social Networks group, led by Linton C. Freeman, included scholars from a variety of academic disciplines concerned with studying the nature of social networks (see Freeman and Freeman, 1980). Although two members took part in the face-to-face workshop meeting and contributed to the project, data reports were not completed for this group.

WHCLIS

The White House Conference on Library and Information Services, coordinated and evaluated by Elaine B. Kerr, utilized EIES for the planning of that national conference (see Kerr, 1980).

Workload (Senders)

"Mental Workload" can be described as the study of human factors in complex person–machine systems, such as the cockpit of a jet plane or the control panel of a nuclear power plant. Most of the members of this multidisciplinary group were engineers or psychologists. A group conference was concerned with the definition and discussion of the effects of physical, emotional, and mental stress on the decision-making behavior of people working with high-technology equipment. In addition, it had the goal of producing an on-line "electronic journal." The group was the least satisfied of all of the small research communities studied by Hiltz (1981). Although the software for the journal was completed, only one article was ever published. There was a lively discussion at the time of the Three Mile Island incident, but the group conference never seemed to achieve closure on topics. Hiltz observed that facilitative leadership seemed to be missing. The group's nominal leader spent comparatively little time on line, and no one else assumed a leadership role. One of the evaluation reports completed for the effort (Guillaume, 1980) reports a similar conclusion:

> The types of activity and interactions observed and the continuing lack of social and procedural interactions suggest that the failure to produce a journal was not a result of the hardware and software aspects of the system, but rather a result of the failure of the group to recognize and apply appropriate maintenance and task functions which would have facilitated the work of the group. These functions were particularly necessary because of the initial ambiguous attitudes regarding the usefulness of the system. . . . The failure, then, was a result of a breakdown in group processes (p. 27).

Other Systems

PLANET (Miller)

This is a very simple conferencing system. The user need not learn many commands, wait for line prompts, or use carriage returns. It is the easiest of these systems to learn to use. The other side of this coin is that there are few features. Lines or items, once entered, cannot be edited, and users can communicate only with those in the same conference or discussion group. PLANET has been studied with a wide variety of user groups, particularly geologists and other scientific or research groups (see Johansen et al., 1978a, 1979; Vallee et al., 1975, 1978). It is now licensed for commercial use to Infomedia Corporation, headed by Jacques Vallee. At the Institute for the Future, current research and development are focused on HUB.

HUB (Spang)

The HUB system adds three other forms of computer-mediated communications to an unstructured conferencing capability similar to PLANET: graphical communication through a shared visual space, communication focused on the operating of computer programs through its program workspace, and communication focused on the creation and editing of a document in its document workspace (see Lipinski et al., 1980:159; Adler and Lipinski, 1981). User groups have included corporate planners and computer scientists in academic and military settings.

COM

This is a conferencing system designed by Jacob Palme and developed at the Swedish National Defense Research Institute (see Palme, 1979; Palme et al., 1980). It currently has about 375 active users; most are researchers at various technical institutes. Evaluations have been conducted by an anthropologist (see Adriansson, 1980; Palme, 1981).

CONFER

CONFER is a conferencing system designed by Robert Parnes which currently operates on Amdahl computers at the University of Michigan and Wayne State University. More than 1500 users have been informally observed during a period of 5 years, including a wide variety of students, staff, and faculty at the two universities, and outside user groups of both a not-for-profit and commercial nature. Since CONFER is a special applications program running under the Michigan Terminal System (MTS), users may also access a large number of other computing facilities under MTS, including text processors, data bases, statistical packages, and programming languages (see Parnes et al., 1977; Zinn, 1979).

PANALOG

Edward M. Housman of GTE Labs is the designer of this conferencing system. A research effort, it has more than 100 users from all walks of life: teenagers, scientists, hearing-impaired people, artists, technicians, executives, etc. Only one user at a time can be on line (see Housman, 1980; Seabrook, 1978).

NLS (Bair)

The On Line System, designed by Douglas Englebart to augment knowledge work, is now called AUGMENT and marketed by Tymnet. NLS is a general office support system. It is well suited to document production, particularly when used with with an intelligent terminal and a special "mouse" device for editing. It includes three communications capabilities: the exchange of messages asynchronously, or in real time, and the exchange of files. An early evaluation of NLS was conducted by Bair (1974) and serves as the main basis for his input to this study. Another evaluation of NLS in nonmilitary business settings was conducted by Edwards (1977).

OICS (Tapscott)

This is an acronym for the Office Information Communication System. This extensive project, conducted by Bell Northern's Software

Research group, headed by Don Tapscott, employed a pilot system built especially for the study. It is a fully integrated office system, which has as one of its components the COCOS electronic mail system, developed by BNR, allowing users to compose, send, forward, reply to and file electronic messages. For paper correspondence, there is a program which automatically generates formatted letters and memos. There is also the capability for short synchronous messages.

Several text editors are available for text processing, and a line-oriented editor with a terse user interface was chosen most often (Tapscott, 1981:7). There is also a text formatting program for document production, including pagination, tables of contents, and an automatic spelling check using three dictionaries as data bases.

An information retrieval subsystem provides data bases for any type of information; a project bibliography and conference and seminar schedule were among those used during the pilot study. There is also an administrative function subset, with features such as phone lists, cost tracking schedules, and personal logs.

Finally, analytical tools include simple calculations such as those which could be done with a desk calculator, a variety of statistical applications including graphical output, and data processing facilities.

The study is a "quasi-experimental" field study. Nineteen "knowledge workers," consisting of seven managers, eight professionals, and four administrators, were given electronic work stations and the use of the system, and were compared with a control group of 26 persons. Data collection included a pretest questionnaire, monitor statistics on use (which averaged more than 3 hours per day), and post-test interviews and questionnaires.

MACC @ MAIL (Brown)

This system originated in 1976, when the fledgling EDUNET organization financed an effort by the University of Wisconsin to develop an electronic mail system for communication among its network members. It was then called Telemail. Later users included members of "Theory Net," an "invisible college" in the area of theoretical computer science, sponsored by the National Science Foundation (Landweber, 1979). The system has been used fairly steadily. For instance, during a 2-week monitoring period in early 1980, there were 387 registered users, of whom 202 were active, and about 150 sessions per day. An on-line EXPLAIN command can be used to obtain explanations of the available commands as well as a tutorial. Based on experiences, there are plans to enhance the system, including the addition of a conferencing-like capability (Roberts, 1980).

USC-MSG (Danowski)

This system was included as another example of a fairly simple message system. Its full name is MSG and LINK on TENEX at USC-ECL. The study included here involved 38 residents of a retirement community (see Danowski and Sacks, 1980). USC-ECL is the Educational Computing Laboratories at the University of California.

WYLBUR (Lynch)

The electronic mail system at the University of California's Division of Library Automation is implemented through a series of extensions to the widely used WYLBUR text-editing system (see Lynch, 1980). It is included as a third example of an electronic mail system. This implementation of MAIL with WYLBUR was developed by the Division of Library Automation of the University of California. There are at least two other implementations of a MAIL system using WYLBUR, at Stanford University and at New York University.

THE CONTEXT OF COMPUTER-MEDIATED COMMUNICATION SYSTEMS

This study does not begin to include all the existing computer-based communication systems. There are many commercial electronic messaging systems without published evaluations, and many proprietary systems used within single organizations. More than a thousand employees are linked by electronic mail at Continental Bank; more than 5000 use electronic messages on ARPANET; Texas Instruments has a worldwide network of 8000 terminals that handles more than 4 million messages annually. In addition, just about every major office products company has developed or announced plans for electronic mail services, including Tymnet's OnTyme, Telenet's Telemail, and Datapac's Envoy 100. Satellite Business Systems, Xerox ("XTEN") and AT&T ("Advanced Communication Systems") have announced the forthcoming availability of these systems. Datapoint, Wang, DEC, Prime, and IBM, among others, include this capability in their new "integrated" office systems being designed and introduced (Panko, 1980:1-2).

The largest publicly available multifunction system is The Source, recently purchased by *The Reader's Digest*. Conferencing systems include a private network within Proctor and Gamble; a conference system operating at the University of Wisconsin and originally developed at the federal Office of Emergency Preparedness by Murray

Turoff and others; the Florida Education Computing Network Conference System (Mailman *et al.*, 1981); and the KOMEX system in Germany (GMD, 1979).

Our criterion for inclusion in this study was production of a published evaluation. However, because of limitations in travel funds for workshop participants and in the available time of some of the invited participants, not all systems that have been evaluated were actively involved in the exercise of pooling their findings.

It should be clear at this point that the studies and systems covered in this report by no means constitute a representative sample of computer-mediated communication systems. Given our criterion of a published evaluation and the rapidly changing nature of the emerging technology, the sample is unavoidably small. The results, however, should be more than merely suggestive of the directions that the medium will take in the future. As the prototypes in terms of both development and assessment, these systems will likely continue to serve for some time as the models for future elaboration.

CHAPTER 2

System Design

INTRODUCTION

All computer-mediated communication systems share certain characteristics. The most fundamental, in terms of their effects upon human interaction, are that communication takes place by typing and reading, and that sending and receiving may occur at different times because the computer stores the text. The "style" (the electronic personality of the system projected by the interface) and capabilities of these systems vary widely, however. The purpose of the synthesis of design choices presented in this chapter is to familiarize the reader with the range of capabilities and characteristics that currently exist, and to summarize the "collective wisdom" of current designers in order to establish design guidelines and choices for future systems.

A system can be conceptualized as including a number of separable clusters of characteristics. Its core is the set of software capabilities and qualities defining what it can do and how it interacts with users. These software characteristics can in turn be divided into those dimensions common to all interactive computer systems and those peculiar to computer-based communication systems. A short hierarchical list of system characteristics, showing the interrelations of software characteristics, appears as Table 2–1.

TABLE 2–1

System Factors

A. Interactive Systems—General Interface Factors

Learning
  Accessibility
  Comprehension
  Guidance and self-documentation
  Informative
  Segmentation
Adaptability
  Control
  Flexibility and variety
  Leverage and simplicity
  Modifiability
Behavior
  Humanization
  Regularity and predictability
  Responsiveness
Error Control
  Forgiveness and recovery
  Protection
  Security
  Reliability
  Closure

B. Computer-Mediated Communication System Factors

Atmosphere
  Sense of community
  Evolution
  Human help
Communications
  Communication richness
  Special-purpose communication structures
  Indirect communication channels
  Document distribution
  Voting
Text Processing
  Text editing
  Text formatting
  Document formatting
  Text mobility
  Text retrieval and linkages
  Virtual text referencing
  Active and adaptive text
Specialized support software
  Integrated data structures
  User simulations
  Marketplace structure
  Privileges and protection

Table 2–1 (continued)

C. Other System Factors

Operational practices
  Evaluation and feedback
  Pricing
  Privacy
  Ownership
  Access policies
  Training and documentation
Hardware
  Capacity of central unit
  Storage
  Communication bandwidth
  Reliability
  Availability
  Network intelligence
  Distributed processing
Equipment characteristics
  Accessibility
  Human factors engineering
  Terminal intelligence
  Appearance of printed material from terminal
  Terminal interface characteristics

We used an expert panel of computer scientists involved in the design of the systems included in this study to rank and discuss the relative importance of various software features and to report the extent to which they are now included in their systems. Presenting the results of this survey constitutes the bulk of this chapter. Table 2–2 lists the short definitions of software characteristics presented to the panel.

However, a system is more than the sum of its individual parts; ideally, it is a set of procedures and capabilities supporting a group in its work on line. The idea of designing a total system as "groupware" is treated in the second part of this chapter.

Another set of characteristics can be thought of as "implementation." On what type of computer is the software implemented? How many ports are there? Is it linked to a digital packet switching network? How is the system priced and paid for? In what form is the documentation? What kind of training and user support are provided? Implementation characteristics can change; for example, more ports can be added. The designers were asked to describe these characteristics of their systems, and the data are presented in the Appendix.

The total system also includes the equipment available to the individual user: a terminal may be hard copy or CRT, portable or not,

TABLE 2–2

Definitions of System Factors

Interactive Systems—General Interface Factors

A. Learning

Accessibility: The knowledge and effort needed by users to gain access to a system.

Comprehension: The ability of users to understand as a whole what the system is capable of accomplishing, before having to learn how to do it.

Guidance and Self-Documentation: The ability of the system to provide guidance or training to the user as and when required.

Informative: Providing clear information for users on what they are being asked to do in terms of operations or errors.

Segmentation: The ability of the user to learn only the minimum in order to carry out a specific task.

B. Adaptability

Control: The ability of users to feel in control of the computer, while making sure they understand what they are doing and where they are in the interaction.

Flexibility and Variety: The ability of users to tailor the system to their own style of interaction in carrying out tasks.

Leverage and Simplicity: The ability of users to execute significant computer operations with a minimum of interface effort (minimization of the number and length of user-supplied entries).

Modifiability: The ability of users to adapt the system to serve their needs.

C. Behavior

Humanization: Treating the user as an intelligent human being rather than as a slave of the computer.

Regularity and Predictability: The ability of a user to anticipate the actions of the computer and to expect consistent responses to operations and functions.

Responsiveness: The ability of the system to respond quickly and meaningfully to user requests to carry out various operations and functions.

D. Error Control

Forgiveness and Recovery: The ability of the system not to penalize users unnecessarily for mistakes and to provide mechanisms to easily recover from errors.

Protection: Protection of the system from damage by a user interaction.

Security: Ability to protect the users' data from errors unintentionally or intentionally generated.

Reliability: The ability of the system to function without error or loss of data. Also, the frequency and length of instances of the system being unavailable during scheduled operation.

Closure: Informing users when an operation has been successfully or unsuccessfully completed.

Computer-Mediated Communication Systems — System Factors

A. Atmosphere

Sense of Community: The ability of the system to provide features, such as membership and interest directories, which allow users to form communities of interests as needed.

Table 2–2 (continued)

Evolution: The ability of the system to change through feedback from its user community.

Human Help: The ability of the system to supply human help directly to users.

B. Communication Capabilities

Communication Richness: The richness of the communication options offered, such as conferences, messages and document access, and the variety of communication features associated with the options, such as confirmations of deliveries, notifications of access, use of pen names, status reports of readership, footnote and commenting or voting features.

Special Purpose Communication Structures: The ability of the system to supply or be adapted to supply special-purpose communication structures for activities such as facilitating, providing protection from information overload by filtering, allowing participation by very large groups through rules of order, incorporating systems such as personalized calendars which allow direct or indirect communications among the users.

Indirect Communication Channels: The ability to set up indirect communication linkages among individuals and groups, such as informing a group of authors what the readers are looking for and not finding in key word searches.

Document Distribution: The features which allow the distribution of documents to interested parties.

Voting: Provision of voting scales which may be associated with items for responses by others, with feedback to participants.

C. Text Processing

Text Editing: The direct modification of text during the composition process.

Text Formatting: The ability to have the computer set up the formats for text such as paragraphing, tables, spacing, margins, etc.

Document Formatting: The ability to format a document by paging and incorporating such things as headings.

Text Mobility: The ability to move text around the system, such as from a message into a personal notebook.

Text Retrieval and Linkages: The relationships, indexes and linkages set up to relate items of text to one another, and the possibilities of dealing with nonlinear type documents, as in "hypertext."

Virtual Text Referencing: The ability to reference and incorporate existing text items in new text items in a virtual manner.

Active and Adaptive Text: The ability of text to incorporate programs or functions that are executed as part of the delivery mechanism to readers. This includes the ability of text to contain forms or surveys for the reader to respond to and to make conditional on various factors or specific responses what the reader actually sees.

D. Specialized Support Software

Integrated Data Structures: The ability of the users to communicate data in other than free text and the ability of the computer to recognize data items and who has authored them. It is usually assumed that such structures maintain the identity of the creators or suppliers of the data and allow authorship control over the segments of the data structures the user is responsible for. An example of this might be a budget planning system.

User Simulations: The ability of a system to develop tailored programs to simulate aspects of users' communication behavior, and thereby augment their

Table 2–2 (continued)

communication capabilities by acting as an intermediary. A simple example
would be a background task to carry out a search while the user is off line.
Privileges and Protection: The ability of the system to preserve the access privilege
structure provided by the author of material and to deal with read, write, edit,
and utilize access both on the part of the sender and receiver. In some
instances it is necessary to allow a function triggered by a user to access
material for utilization that was supplied by another user. However, the user
making use of this material would not necessarily have reading privileges for
that material. An example is being able to ask of someone else's calendar if he
can meet on a certain date and time. This is "utilize" access and is different
from the more standard forms of access usually provided on interactive
systems. The ability of the user to understand the forms of access and to make
use of them as well as to be able to track their use by others on his or her
material is a further aspect of this factor.
Marketplace Structures: Software designed to facilitate payments based on the
provision and use of information. For example, the ability of a user to
advertise and price information and to collect revenues for its use.

"smart" or "dumb," etc. This local equipment mediates between the
system and the user. A review of human-factor considerations in the
design of terminals appears in Hiltz and Kerr (1981). We have chosen
to exclude from this discussion consideration of the ever-changing
choices of equipment for linking the individual to the system, but we
must be aware that it is part of "the system" as perceived by users.

In covering the software characteristics, our approach is to use two
dimensions simultaneously to order the discussion. First is the division between the general characteristics of interactive systems and
those peculiar to computer-based communication systems. The second
is to categorize the characteristics in terms of the relative importance
accorded them by the designers and the extent to which there is agreement or disagreement about their relative importance. Table 2–3 presents an overview or summary in terms of the mean importance ratings
and the amount of agreement or dispersion in these ratings. There is
considerable overlap between the two dimensions: General characteristics of interactive systems tend to fall disproportionately into the
high importance and high agreement cells of the table, while ratings
of system characteristics dealing particularly with the capabilities of
computer-based communication systems tend to fall into the moderate
to low importance cells, as the result of exhibiting more disagreement
among the designers.

The discussion which follows does not follow the order in the table,
but rather groups these factors into related clusters.

TABLE 2-3

Summary of Ratings of System Features

Importance	Agreement[a] (SD = 1.0 or less)	Disagreement[a] (SD = 1.1 or more)
High Importance (x < 1.5)	Accessibility (1.2) Text editing (1.2) Humanization (1.3) Guidance and self documentation (1.3) Control (1.3) Forgiveness and recovery (1.3) Responsiveness (1.4)	
Moderate Importance (x = 1.5–2.0)	Reliability (1.6) Text mobility (1.6) Segmentation (1.7) Text retrieval and linkages (2.0) Closure (2.0)	Protection (1.6) Evolution (1.6) Informative (1.9) Communication richness (2.0) Sense of community (2.0)
Less Importance (x = 2.1 or more)	Human help (2.1) Text formatting (2.3) Document distribution (2.6) Integrated data structures (2.8) Virtual text referencing (3.1)	Regularity and predictability (2.2) Leverage and simplicity (2.3) Privileges and protection (2.3) Flexibility (2.6) Active and adaptive text (2.6) Modifiability (2.7) Special purpose structures (2.8) Indirect communication channels (2.8) Voting (2.8) Marketplace structures (2.8) Comprehension (3.0) User simulations (3.0)

[a] Means are shown in parentheses.

SYSTEM SOFTWARE FACTORS (Coauthored with Murray Turoff)

A computerized conferencing or message system is an interactive computer system. There is a considerable literature on system factors and their relationship to system acceptance, including Martin (1973), Walker (1971), Bennett (1972), and Shneiderman (1980). More specific reviews relating to message and conferencing systems are found in Uhlig (1977), Vallee (1976), and Hiltz and Turoff (1978b). Much of this "wisdom" is based on introspection, the reflections of designers and implementors of "successful" systems, and field trials, rather than controlled experimentation. Although field studies usually involve polling users about their reactions, users seldom have the opportunity of comparing alternative designs for achieving the same objective. Rarely are field trials matched in any way other than having users of different systems sometimes respond to the same questions. Introspective studies are often suspect because "success" is usually equated with usage when the users have had no choice or basis of comparison. And system designers have an understandable bias. Over the years, few social scientists have investigated this area, and it is only recently that more attention has been paid to comparative studies (Shneiderman, 1980).

As a result, the factors that have been chosen are the ones that repeatedly occur in the literature. This gives them some foundation and recognizes that they can be very important if not minimally satisfied. The difficulty comes in assessing factors in combination and determining which factors may be more fundamental or may be independent measures of an interface. In fact, we are unable to find any studies that attempt to quantifiably assess the interactions among the factors. Given this situation, our discussion of factors cannot escape from a degree of subjective evaluation. This survey is based upon the responses of designers and their degree of consensus.

The system factors defined in Table 2–2 are divided into those which apply to interactive systems in general and those which seem to have unique relationships to computerized conferencing or message systems. Most specific interactive systems oriented to a particular application produce a subset of factors that appear to be crucial to the nature of that application. The procedure followed was to administer the list of factors, with the short definitions included, to the system designers who were to rate the factors on two dimensions: the extent to which they are important for systems of this type if the "ideal" system were to be constructed, and the extent to which they were incorporated into the design of their current system. We will focus on the importance ratings here. The instructions were to try to rate no more than about 25% of the factors as "very important" on a scale of 1 to 5, since it would not have helped us to be told that everything was "very important." What we wished to uncover were differences in points of view about the relative importance of factors. It should be noted that several of the designers objected to the list provided on the grounds that it seemed to reflect the biases of the EIES designer, Murray Turoff, who compiled it. An opportunity was provided on the last page to list and describe other omitted system factors which they felt were equal to or more important than those given.

GENERAL INTERFACE CHARACTERISTICS

With the exception of text editing, all of the system characteristics for which there is near unanimity on high importance consist of factors applicable to any interactive computer system. We will deal first with the characteristics in the top left cell of Table 2–3, which can be considered the systems design equivalents of "motherhood and apple pie," according to the ratings of our panel. We will then turn to the factors given moderately high ratings, and finally to those which are considered less crucial.

Accessibility

Accessibility is generally recognized to be important by almost all designers working with populations of non-computer-oriented users. It is also one of the issues most ignored by designers of systems software. Complaints about standard sign-on protocols through industry-provided executive software or various communication nets are rather commonplace. In itself accessibility rarely seems to be a determining factor in acceptance, except in extreme cases of individuals who are already highly negative and looking for further excuses not to use the system. While it is a factor often expressed historically, it might better be considered a component of the more general area of "humanization" discussed below. The less a user must do to access the specific task or system, the better. With the proliferation of more intelligent terminals and microcomputers, this problem is being solved by sign-on procedures stored in the terminal's software which automatically execute the steps needed to access a task. While most computer manufacturers have discovered this as an issue to address, some of the interconnection schemes from one nation's digital network to another require users to supply addresses of more than 16 characters.

Accessibility in practice is of course also a function of the availability of terminals. Ideally, terminals would be ubiquitous—on everyone's desk at home as well as at work.

The designers are nearly unanimous in their opinion that accessibility is very important. Seven rate it as "1", "very important," and two rate it as "2", "important." Judgments about what is easy and what is difficult are illuminated by the comments. For instance, the COM designer rates his system as only a "3" because remote users must use a phone and modem rather than simply turning on a switch, and CONFER's Parnes likewise gives the system a "3" because of the difficulty of the Telenet interface. Yet the @MAIL designer, Dave Brown, gives his system a "1" when it requires a telephone, modem, and the unfriendly Telenet interface for remote users to access. There is evidently some disagreement about precisely what constitutes easy accessibility. From the comments of most of the designers, it seems that an ideally accessible system would require merely setting one switch on a terminal and entering an identifying name and password.

Control, and Forgiveness and Recovery

"Control" is the user's sense of being in control of the system rather than the system dictating the interaction. One aspect of this is providing mechanisms with which users can easily escape or change their minds about procedures in which they find themselves. Control also means they should be allowed to delete items such as messages or conference comments if they change their minds. Some message systems are set up like the post office in that writers lose control of their material after it is sent. In most systems, control problems usually result from not providing users with an understanding of how to master the machine and the poor operation of interactive questions which appear to "bully" the user (Bennett, 1972). Control as a subjective feeling is probably also associated with "forgiveness and recovery." This is the extent to which the system forgives the user for making an error. The usual objective is that the user should not have to exert more effort to correct an error than it took to make it in the first place. Most current systems do not provide complete audit trails, so that the deletion of a text item usually means that it must be retyped. However, most attempt to provide a secondary confirmation question before completing a requested deletion. Individuals who integrate a system into their daily tasks, spending long hours on line, find forgiveness a crucial factor, since when working under pressure they tend to have a higher than normal error rate. In contrast, new users are likely be slower and more careful. It is therefore possible that forgiveness is a crucial factor for the experienced users, and in this sense tied to the concept of leverage and simplicity which makes forgiveness a more challenging design problem.

The panel of designers is nearly unanimous in believing that control is a crucial characteristic for computer-based conferencing systems. All rate it as "1" or "2" in importance. The comments indicate that it is particularly important for inexperienced users. The close tie to the concept of forgiveness and recovery is indicated by the fact the the mean rating and standard deviation is exactly the same for the two system characteristics.

Guidance and Self-Documentation

"Guidance" is the degree to which a system allows users to learn as they use it. Because users prefer "trial and error" learning (Bennett, 1972), the most effective form of guidance is selective help messages which can be triggered for printout at any point in the interaction. It is also possible to have the system demonstrate to the user how to interact with it by mimicking an interaction supplied from a stored file. The dynamic aspects of an interactive system are much easier to show by illustration than by descriptive writings. Comprehensive write-ups are usually too wordy for most users to tolerate and are more often used as references to answer specific questions from experienced users.

The designers are nearly unanimous on the crucial importance of this characteristic. The only exception is the WYLBUR mail system, whose designer feels that such on-line guidance to enable users to learn without studying print is useful mainly for casual users, and that it is better to rely on print. More specifically, Lynch feels that at least for a mail system, one should be able to read just a few pages of documentation, and then use the system; one should not need on-line help. Most of the other systems report the successful use of "help," "explain," or "?" commands to allow users to access documentation or tutorials on line.

Responsiveness

"Responsiveness" is the ability of the system to react quickly to user actions. It may be better to have slightly slower and regular response rates than highly irregular ones for a given operation (Martin, 1973).

Users are willing to wait longer when they believe their requested operations take more effort, although their beliefs may be different from the reality of what is time-consuming for the computer.

All the designers have made efforts to keep response time rapid. During busy periods, however, it tends to decline or become erratic on most systems. CONFER, for instance, reports that response is virtually instantaneous if system activity as a whole is low; however, during busy periods, it may take as long as 5 seconds for the system to respond with a prompt. EIES tries to deal with the problem by assigning priorities according to the nature of the operation being carried out, with composition receiving the highest of four priority levels and therefore the fastest response time, and searches receiving the lowest priority level.

Humanization

The term that has recently emerged to encompass a number of these factors, with the additions that the system should be polite and respectful to users and that transactions should be courteous, is "humanization" (Sterling, 1974, 1975). This includes a number of values about the protection of private information. In terms of computerized conferencing systems, it is associated with protecting pen names and anonymity in those systems which provide them. It suggests that the system should relieve the user of unnecessary chores and should address ethical issues such as the ownership of information.

Six of the nine designers rate "humanization" as being of the highest importance; the other three give it a "2". However, what is "human" seems to be interpreted differently. CONFER, HUB, and PLANET emphasize the use of simple English words for commands and prompts, while WYLBUR implicitly disagrees that the use of full English is the "natural" human tendency by emphasizing the availability of multiple command abbreviations rather than full English language words. The designer notes that full words are available, but users stop using them fairly quickly. MACC @MAIL mentions its "friendly" documentation and EIES its human user consultants available for help. As the PAN-ALOG designer states, "All feel the user should be treated as a human being . . . ," but the problem is that what seems friendly and natural to the novice may begin to seem verbose and burdensome to an experienced user.

Leverage and Simplicity/Modifiability

"Leverage and simplicity" suggest that experienced users wish to perform powerful operations with less direct interaction with the system, and need a longer lever with which to execute tasks. This can be provided by allowing them to define their own commands or providing general high-level commands for all users. As a system becomes more complex in terms of its options, this measure becomes associated with its modifiability. This is the extent to which it can be tailored to reflect the user tasks as opposed to the basic system design. Highly tailored message systems which reflect the corporate memo form have been modified to reflect user tasks. More general systems attempt to provide this degree of modifiability within a larger framework. It is easier for users to accept a system which appears on the surface to fit their task environment. Designing a general system that can be tailored to a host of different user environments is not an easy system level task, and most of the initial message and conferencing systems do not have this degree of modifiability.

Both these characteristics elicited much disagreement about their relative importance and yielded relatively low mean ratings. The highest ratings for the importance of leverage came from the most complex systems (EIES, HUB, and OICS) where they are perhaps most necessary. There is fairly close agreement in this case between the extent to which a system is reported as having the characteristic and the relative importance assigned to it. This is also true of modifiability: The designers of modifiable systems feel that it is important. For instance, HUB, which responds with a "4" on importance and a "5" on the inclusion of modifiability, comments that its "basic structure cannot be changed. Assembly language complex to modify." However, there seems to be some difference of interpretation in what "modifiability" means. It was defined as "the ability of users to adapt the system to serve their needs." The WYLBUR representative reports that "if the system meets needs, there is little need to modify it (an implementor operation, as opposed to tailoring, which the user does.)" However, the possibility of "tailoring" is included in the concept which we labeled "modifiability."

Flexibility and Variety

"Flexibility and variety" give users the ability to adapt their own interaction styles to the system. One way of accomplishing this is to provide different interfaces, such as both commands and menus. Even when given a fairly homogeneous population of users in which the optimum interface can be predicted, there will still be a minority who prefer a different mode of interaction. Another aspect of flexibility is the user's ability to be at one level in the system regardless of the task being performed. In other words, any command may be executed at any time from any system state. This gives users the greatest ability to control their sequence of actions. Certainly these design choices influence the sense of control that users feel.

Flexibility is closely related to the concept of modifiability and the ratings are similar: relatively low, but with considerable disagreement, as some designers assign it a high degree of importance. The COM designer, Palme, feels that there is a risk that too much flexibility will give novices too much complexity, and the MACC @MAIL designer feels that such features are expensive and little used.

Informativeness

An "informative" system is one in which error messages or other information delivered to users pinpoints the state of the system. For example, an error message may inform users what kind of error has been made, rather than simply announcing that an error has occurred. Because this can mean a 30% or more additional programming effort for a reasonably complex system, it is sometimes neglected.

The importance of a system being informative is given a moderate rating overall, and with considerable disagreement. This is because one system, PANALOG, gives it a rating of "5". If this response were excluded, it would rate quite high, since all the other ratings are "1" or "2". There is the problem, however, of the fine line between being "informative" and being bothersome or "verbose" by annoying users with too much information about what a program is doing or can do.

OTHER FACTORS: INTERACTIVE SYSTEMS
DESIGN

We now turn to other interactive system characteristics that are rated as somewhat less important or have less consensus as principles.

Reliability

"Reliability" is the ability of the system to maintain data, in this case communications, without loss. For fostering human communication this is a crucial item in that no system that loses communications will be used. Most designers are well aware of this point and it does not seem to have been a problem in any of the systems to date.

All of the designers except Housman of PANALOG rate reliability as a "1" or "2" and use measures such as back-up files to ensure minimal data loss in the event of a system crash. Housman maintains that the PANALOG users accept occasional message losses, especially with apologies.

Protection and Security

"Protection," sometimes referred to as "bulletproofing," means protecting the system from possible damage by users. This can be somewhat difficult in a time-sharing environment. The impact is that damage to the system by one user may hurt others. Some Source users, for example, threatened to destroy system directories unless price increases were rescinded.

The complement of protection of the system from the user is the security of the user's data from damage or mistakes made by the system. For instance, can whole files be wiped out by a bug or crash? Can errors occur whereby unauthorized persons obtain access to materials which were not directed to them?

The importance of protection is rated moderately high overall, but there is disagreement. As in several other instances, it is caused by the response of the PANALOG designer, who gives this characteristic a "5"; all others rate it at the top or next to the top level of importance.

The same rating pattern occurs for the closely related concept of security: Seven of the nine designers give it a "1" and one rates it a "2". The PANALOG designer gives it a "5", thereby reducing its average importance. The HUB system automatically encrypts files to increase security. However, in the case of power or hardware failures, system errors may damage or delete files.

As the COM designer notes, privileges which may be useful in some instances also provide a possible loss of protection from a mistake made by the privileged user; for instance, giving deletion privileges to conference organizers or moderators means that they can mistakenly delete items or whole transcripts.

Closure

"Closure" is the notification to a user that an initiated operation has been completed. It should come often enough to free short-term memory before proceeding to the next task. The nature of computerized conferencing and message systems usually leads to rapid closure by successive prompts and confirmations that messages have been sent. As a system becomes more complex the nature of closure becomes more sensitive. In a very sophisticated system a user can trigger tasks to be accomplished while doing something else or even while off line. The issue then arises as to when to notify a user of closure or nonclosure, if, for example, a message has not been delivered. Beginning users seem to want more closure than do more experienced users (Shneiderman, 1980). Closure is probably not independent of the measure of "control" discussed below.

The desirability of closure is a very controversial issue among the designers. The HUB designer, who rates it a "4" on the 1 to 5 scale, states that it becomes very tiresome and is needed only if you have a "flaky" system that might not always carry out the expected procedure because of a crash or software bug. Therefore, messages are not acknowledged as sent on HUB, and complex tasks are acknowledged by the receipt of the next prompt in the sequence rather than by any confirmation that the preceding step has been accomplished. It should be remembered that HUB includes a modeling system; certainly it would be tiresome to have every step of a set of computations confirmed. The next lowest rating, a "3", is given by OICS, which is also not a conferencing system, but a general management and office support system. On the other hand the designers of the three large American conferencing systems, CONFER, EIES, and PLANET, all give closure a "1" in importance. And the designers for the message systems give it a "2". In other words, the perceived importance of closure seems to be related to the main function of a system, that is, whether it is group conferences, messages, or other professional or office support function.

Segmentation and Comprehension

In discussing the concept and problems of segmentation in Electronic Message Systems (EMS), Panko and Panko (1981) present an argument that may be generalized to other types of computer-mediated communication systems and other classes of users:

> Looking at managers, the largest segment consists of people who want to delegate all terminal work. The next segment works at the terminal but only in a limited way, being content to learn only a few features. The next segment consists of people who use the system aggressively . . . . EMS should provide good support for all levels of users. In the simplest segment, for instance, a secretarial support system is needed, or perhaps a message system very much simpler and more automatic than any of today's systems. For the complex users, extensive power could be supplied.

> It may . . . be possible to define a simple core set of commands that users could learn quickly. Later, other commands or clusters of commands could be added as desired. While many people have conceived this notion, implementation has proven surprisingly difficult, because one never knows what a given user will wish for next . . . .

Unfortunately, many programmers have adopted a philosophy that works against market segmentation. At the heart of this strategy is a belief that indirect users and simple users are in some sense bad people who must be educated to see the light and use the system [to its] full complexity . . . .

Since programmers often control development, it is usually difficult to do anything but expand the system to meet the needs of [the] most complex users. Medium users are left to reel through an open-ended set of commands with many error states and subtle assumptions. Light users, the most numerous in managerial circles, are pretty much left to fend for themselves (pp. 10–15).

In other words, the Pankos are arguing for segmentation of the system into different levels of complexity for different "market segments" of users.

Comprehension and its tradeoff with segmentation is one of the more controversial design issues leading to major differences among systems. To a large extent it is not a major factor for elementary message systems with a small number of alternative commands. For instance, the WYLBUR-MAIL designer comments that "Our experience is that once a user masters a small subset of commands (which is very quick), he picks up commands as he needs them with very little trouble. One key to this is to have a consistent syntax." Comprehension means that users fully understand all the functions a system could perform even though they may not necessarily know how to perform them all. The level of effort to completely understand a rich system might be far more than beginning users are willing to expend. This problem can be overcome by segmenting the system into small functional pieces that users learn only as needed. The danger of complete segmentation is that users may never realize that the system is capable of doing more than what was initially learned. JOSS (developed by Shaw and Baker at the RAND Corporation in the early 1960s) was so well segmented that even some experienced computer people viewed it as a calculator-type system after only half an hour's exposure and never realized it had fundamentally the power of FORTRAN. In other words, after a brief exposure it was written off as a very simple and not too powerful system. Many of the tradeoffs between these two objectives are made in the initial material and training provided new users and the mechanisms for later learning. However, for complex systems, exposing users to a menu rather than a limited set of commands makes them more aware of options that they may not yet need, but might later find useful. In most conferencing systems, simple messaging is usually taught first, since this allows people to quickly begin to communicate and gives them an initial sense of accomplishment and comprehension.

In rating the importance of comprehension, none of the designers feel that it is very important, and some of the comments indicate that, as defined, it is a liability rather than an asset. For instance, Palme, who gives comprehension a "4" for importance and a "3" for inclusion in COM, seems to feel that it is a good thing that his "system appears limited to novices who need not see advanced features." On the other hand, the companion concept, segmentation, is generally rated as "1" or "2" in importance, with the exception of OICS, which rates it a "3". The key part of the system, presented to all users even when the more complex capabilities are hidden, seems to vary quite a bit. For instance, for HUB the "conferencing module is the core; other services are learned as needed." By contrast, in MACC's @MAIL system, the core commands of course concern the basics of sending and receiving messages. Brown notes that the user can get along with only two commands, "TO" to send a message, and "PRINT" to print an incoming message.

Regularity and Predictability

"Regularity and predictability" mean that the system does not behave in unexpected ways. In terms of the current generation of systems, most of the irregularity is generated by the digital packaging systems which tend to eject users from systems or occasionally misdirect communications. As a general rule, most irregularity occurs at the interface between systems. Sometimes this can occur in the same computer when the conferencing package is composed of a host of separate systems.

The reason for the lack of consensus on the importance of this characteristic is again attributable to a deviant response from the PAN-ALOG designer, who gives it a "5". Seven of the nine rate this characteristic as a "2" in importance and most rate their systems as "2" on the 1 to 5 scale for inclusion. However, there is a difference in interpretation underlying the apparent agreement on importance. About half the designers responded in terms of predictability or regularity for response time, rather than in terms of the predictability of what the system will do, which was how the characteristic was defined.

Summary

These design factors are applicable to all interactive systems as well as to computerized conferencing systems. It is impossible to satisfy all of them in terms of one optimum global design. Instead, the designer is faced with formulating some sort of workable compromise reflecting the nature of the system's use and the user population. Many of these items have inherent conflicts or represent some sensitive balance between two conflicting objectives.

Too much guidance can give users the feeling they are not in control. Frequent closure can reduce their ability for a high level of leverage. Full comprehension can significantly reduce the opportunity for segmentation. With a very modifiable system it is difficult to have generalized routines to make the system informative. Making the system totally forgiving can reduce the flexibility and variety of the interface. Finally, there are numerous internal design tradeoffs, such as that of responsiveness, regularity, and accessibility versus reliability, protection, and security. In general these factors can be divided into three groups: those concerned with learning or extending one's knowledge of the system—guidance, forgiveness, segmentation, informativeness, and closure; those concerned with use of the system—control, comprehension, leverage, modifiability, and flexibility; and those concerned with the environment in which the internals of the system operate—accessibility, regularity, reliability, responsiveness, security, and protection. Humanization largely represents an attempt to incorporate many of these factors into one grouping and to add the ethical component of ownership and privacy of materials.

FACTORS SPECIFIC TO COMPUTER-MEDIATED COMMUNICATION SYSTEMS

The following factors have unique relationships to computerized conferencing and in some cases messaging systems. The variability in their importance ratings by the designers is to be expected, since these systems are less than 10 years old, while interactive systems have been in existence for about 20 years. The user populations of message systems now have exceeded 100,000. Conference system populations are still in the tens of thousands, and interactive systems have probably exceeded 1 million users if specialized business information systems are included. At this stage of development, agreement as to the proper mix of factors or their significance for various applications and circumstances cannot be expected.

Text Handling

Since users are composing text, most systems have at least a crude text-editing capability. In some cases time-sharing systems utilize a text-editing package, and in others a powerful text-handling system is integrated into the system itself. There are also some aspects of text handling that seem unique to situations in which one is communicating text items among different individuals. The following classification of text-handling features tends to reflect the levels of capability one can consider incorporating into a communication environment.

"Text editing" in this context is the simple literal or explicit correction of text during composition or afterwards. The design of text editors can be optimized based upon bandwidth and terminal type; the best editor for a slow-speed hard copy terminal may be very different from that for a high-speed CRT. Ultimately much basic text editing will be performed off line at the terminal since the cost of logic to accomplish this is becoming cheaper than the communications cost between the terminal and computer. There are many alternative editor designs and more are being developed with the growth of the microcomputer market. Concerning the relative acceptability of different editors, people seem to prefer the one they learned first and are quite reluctant to exert the effort to master a new one. The situation is analogous to the use of standard typewriter keyboards; new, more optimum keyboard layouts have not been able to penetrate the mass market.

The importance of a good text editor (although the definition of what is "good" lacks consensus) is the only feature of computer-mediated communication systems about which the designers are unanimous: It is rated at the top of the list, along with accessibility. However, the nature and capabilities of what is available vary tremendously, from full text editing capabilities on systems like OICS (which includes the UNIX editor) and WYLBUR (which is basically a text editing system to begin with, with the message capability as an add-on); to HUB, which allows text editing only on the line currently being written; and PANALOG, which offers mainly the backspace and rubout. COM is taking the approach that will probably become more prevalent in the future: the introduction of a choice of editors, so that users may choose the one best suited to their terminal (hard copy or CRT) and level of experience.

The more sophisticated forms of text handling do not seem to be crucial for the initial acceptance of these systems. On EIES it takes about 100 hours of experience before there is a shift to writing documents larger than one-page conference comments or messages. However, there is good reason to believe that sophisticated text handling features are important for long-term acceptance within an organizational context. The early EMISARI system allowed its users by the virtual referencing capability to compile weekly status reports incorporating earlier communications, and this was felt to be necessary to the day-to-day operation of the system.

No text handling features, other than basic text editing, are given consistently high ratings of importance. But text mobility and the related concept of text retrieval and linkages do receive consistently moderately high ratings.

"Text mobility" is the ability to transfer or copy pieces of text, for example to incorporate part of a message into a report, for other than the text's original purpose. Associated with this is virtual text referencing, which allows the user to reference an existing piece of text in another without copying the original. In other words, a single item can be used in many different locations merely by referencing it. This facilitates the ability of groups to coauthor drafts and controls the responsibility for text items. It can be crucial to supporting accountability in formal organizations.

Most systems facilitate text mobility with copy commands or saved files which can be moved to other locations and reentered. All except the PANALOG designer rate this capability as "1" or "2".

Text retrieval and linkages are necessary to facilitate the easy compilation and reading of large documents. Our definition referred to "the possibilities of referring to nonlinear type documents" (see Table 2–2). Readers of books are not limited to reading them completely, front to back, in sequence. In "hypertext," readers can choose which parts to read and in what order, flip back and forth, and specify if they wish to see more on a particular topic or proceed to something else.

The PLANET system gives this the lowest rating; as a "simple" system to use, it retains simple linear transcripts. The PANALOG designer, who rates this capability as top importance, describes an interesting variation: The system traces the linkages among conversational messages and can trace all the "ripples" of any message.

"Text formatting" is the ability to vary the format of text without disturbing the literal copy. This is performed by specifying margins, page sizes, and options such as right justification and columns. Both authors and receivers of the material may need separate text formatting capabilities operating on the same text item. Text formatting becomes important when formal material, reports, and larger documents are being communicated. One difficulty is that such formatting is done for a hard copy and may actually be annoying for a reader on a CRT, for whom "page numbers" and "new pages" may be annoying.

"Document formatting" is the ability to control the format of a set of pages and treat that set as one complete document, providing automatic headings and pagination. Most of these features are common to any system that handles some kind of text inputting and they are not particularly different for computerized conferencing systems.

"Document distribution" is a form of communication. How to distribute larger documents and their abstracts so that they reach those interested and do not foster information overload is a fundamental design issue. Usually this is accomplished by communicating abstracts and providing a way for readers to access the complete document. The system often notifies the author when the larger document has been read.

"Active and adaptive text" means that one can allow programming capabilities as part of the text itself. For example, a text item could query its readers and use their responses to determine the flow of more text. This ability to mix programming and text can in the long run impact upon writing styles and the nature of documents. However, few systems yet provide this in terms of an easily learned and controlled feature.

Evolution

"Evolution" is the concept that an interactive system grows by initially establishing a simple system, and then providing mechanisms for user involvement and feedback from which to advance the system design. This approach is more common with interactive systems which provide cognitive support rather than merely routine data retrieval (Walker, 1971). The technology is so new, and the possibilities for alternative functions and capabilities so numerous, that an approach of feedback, evaluation, and incremental implementation of new features is desirable. The problem is that users are then faced with a system that changes as they use it. The success of this approach is tied to the ways in which changes are presented to users and whether they feel they have adequate input to the process. It is also based on the view that users cannot adequately understand what they might do with a new technology such as computerized conferencing until they have an opportunity to experience it.

The PLANET system does not have built-in evolutionary mechanisms, and its designers and implementors have frequently stressed the need for a stable system rather than a constantly changing one that confuses users. They give evolution a "4". The other designers give it a "1" or "2" rating. COM's Palme does warn, in a similar vein, that "too much change can discourage users," especially if the system evolution is guided by the expressed needs of the most advanced users, who may request changes that are detrimental to the acclimation of new users. By contrast, PANALOG's designer says that system evolution is simply "fundamental"; HUB's designer reports that the system has been evolved largely through user feedback, with the third "evolution" currently being installed; the WYLBUR MAIL system's designer comments that "some of our best ideas have come from users"; and CONFER's Parnes reports that his system is "constantly maturing because of user-input actively solicited" by him. In sum, the desirability of system evolution based on user feedback is rather controversial.

Communication Richness

"Communication richness" refers to the ability of the computer to offer a variety of ways of delivering material that are not conceivable by mail or telephone. Even elementary message systems can incorporate features such as tailored approval by reviewers before a message is forwarded to its final destination. The original EMISARI system allowed messages to be sent to data, which meant they would be delivered to those retrieving the specific data items. In terms of current systems, CONFER has a unique footnoting capability for its conference comments, and some message systems regulate message sending by job position. EIES has the ability to send messages to key words that individuals have tagged as "interests," with the resulting communication being delivered to those selecting that interest. As yet there is no clearcut pattern to these options except that they provide mechanisms by which the content can be the address, and the delivery therefore can be highly conditional on the state of the system and its user population. This is a high-level merging of the conditional capabilities of a computer system with those of a communication system.

The desirability of communication richness in computer-mediated communication systems is far from agreed upon, with the ratings ranging from "1" to "4". The mail systems, which offer only one or two structures for communication, are firmly opposed to offering a variety of structures. Interestingly, no one claims that his system now completely embodies the concept of communication richness. The conferencing and general purpose office support systems tend to rate it most highly and to embody the concept most fully in their designs. COM's designer, who reports that his system includes most of the "rich" features mentioned in our definition, indicates they are not actually used with any great frequency; the simpler structures instead carry the bulk of the communications. He feels, furthermore, that if the features which provide "richness" and variety of options increase the system's complexity, they may do more harm than good.

Sense of Community

The "sense of community" was first noted by Ulric Neisner (1964) in his early study of programmers associated with the MAC system. He observed that in the relatively fast development atmosphere of one of the first interactive systems, the only way users (in this case, programmers) were able to keep up was with informal communications within the close community that developed. The idea of formal user groups for major pieces of software has been accepted by industry, and others have observed that the relative success of user communities seems to be correlated with how much they exchange information on the use of the system and their willingness to help each other. In fact, a conferencing system is used at the University of Wisconsin to support user communities of different major software systems; each system is the topic of a different conference. In a number of other systems, conferences or message files are devoted to discussions of system problems or used as sounding boards for new features.

The conferencing systems tend to rate the sense of community high, and to provide mechanisms such as open on-line directories with biographical entries so that users may more easily locate others with similar interests. In some systems (CONFER and PLANET) the attempt to build a sense of community is limited to specific conference activities, and users cannot easily browse through a list of all system members.

A compromise is reached in COM and EIES. For COM, all users must enter a short personal description, but it may include no more than their address. To provide for privacy, there is a facility for protected conferences, meaning that all information about the conference is invisible to outsiders. Palme notes, however, that "this facility is used very little by our users, so it does not seem to be very important." On EIES, some groups have simply chosen not to have their members fill in their directory descriptions, and conference moderators choose whether or not to list conference descriptions in the public space containing conference abstracts. On the specifically office-oriented systems, HUB and OICS, a sense of community is not considered important. Although their designers do not comment, one can speculate that it is felt that "chit-chat" resulting from socializing on line is to be discouraged. Another explanation is that mail and office support systems for intraorganizational communication do not need facilities such as directories, since most of the people already know each other.

The atmosphere of a community can be further engineered by providing direct notification to participants of when a person enters or leaves a conference, as in PLANET, or by letting users find out where in the system a person is at a particular time. For instance, COM informs all users when a person connects or disconnects from the system and gives a list, when one enters COM, of who is currently connected. Palme notes that "you are also told in which conference a person is at the moment, which I also feel adds to the togetherness feeling you create. Some of our users however feel that this facility is an infringement of their privacy rights."

Such specific mechanisms are highly dependent on the scale and mode of use of the conferencing system. For instance, unless users frequently participate in a conference synchronously (at the same time), it makes no sense to make such a notification and it actually may be misleading. An example of the extent to which it may be misleading is that most of the EIES users who participate in many conferences have an automatic routine to scan them all and print new entries; they may not actually be at their terminals when the conferences are scanned, and a notification to others that they are "entering" and "leaving" would be misleading. Problems of scale also emerge in a large system. At any one time on EIES, there are likely to be 20 to 25 users on line, and during a typical 20-minute session, half will sign off line and be replaced by others. That would yield an annoying once-per-minute notification of comings and goings. In a system with thousands of users, which is now possible, such notifications would totally clog up the communication channels.

Human Help

"Human help" is the concept that users can get aid from persons dedicated to helping them by communicating their questions and requests on line. In those systems which provide this and other mechanisms for learning, it seems to be the most popular approach and ranks highest when evaluated by users. While it may be more costly than the alternatives, it apparently provides greater satisfaction. On EIES, feedback from users indicates that this is among the most popular aspects of the system for both experienced and inexperienced users. On some systems special software is provided to facilitate this function. User consultants, as they are called, mutually review their responses to user queries to establish consistency.

User consultants may be a vital element in system acceptance. As Bair in Uhlig et al., 1979 puts it:

> Although the best documentation and assistance may be available and frequent
> courses given, a continually available channel of communication with the [service
> providers] is necessary . . . . The feedback mechanism should enable users to ask

questions at any time, receive a response as fast as possible from an expert, and submit design suggestions which may eventually be implemented (p. 257).

Reporting the results of another case history of office automation, Open Systems (1981:7) concludes that to achieve high acceptance and participation rates, "you have to do a lot of 'hand holding' initially—like 24 hours of training (and encouragement) per person—from an outside group specializing in social psychology."

While evaluations indicate that human help is very important, especially if provided by nonprogrammers, as on EIES, the systems designers rate it relatively low. The modal rating for the availability of human help is a "2". Although WYLBUR reports that human help is easily and directly accessible, it is rated only a "4" in importance. Explaining this rating, Lynch notes that the bulk of questions are usually handled by users helping one another. This may be another difference attributable to the distinction between intraorganizational systems, for which many users are co-located, and network systems linking people who are geographically dispersed.

The other below average rating is for HUB, which reports that each group on its system does have a contact person to help. Thus, the value of human help available both on and off line is somewhat controversial and is an issue that could merit a cost–benefit study. It could be, as Open Systems implies, that it is the nature of the human help that is important: that helpers need to be trained in facilitating social system change, as well as in the mechanics of a specific system, speaking the users' language rather than the designers' language.

Privileges and Protection

Privileges and protection are very sensitive issues in communication systems. They are complicated by the use of indirect communication channels and the possibility of using information without being able to directly read it, as in group calendars. Also, editing privileges must be under the control of whomever is responsible for the original text, which may be either the author or the person who requested the text to be drafted.

Ratings of the importance of these capabilities range from "1" to "4". EIES, OICS, and PLANET rate it very highly, but CONFER gives it only a "4" and does not see it as a major part of these systems, although it is conceded that it may be valuable for particular applications.

Special Purpose Communication Structures

Special purpose communication structures tailor a specific set of communication protocols to a given situation. The concept of structured communications is discussed much more extensively in the "Groupware" section below, along with several examples of special purpose structures. A simple example of a specialized structure is "electronic mail" which mimics the current internal memo system even to the replication of memo formats. Both HUB and EIES are evolving specialized structures to facilitate group problem-solving. This is a reflection of the fact that even face-to-face meetings evolve structures for special purposes, from simple brainstorming protocols to legislative rules of order. However, a number of the structures that have evolved are not simple extrapolations of current face-to-face structures, but rather reflect the opportunities offered by the computer. The large group networking of Inquiries and Responses by the LEGITECH group on EIES is a case in point.

Although two of the designers rate the availability of special purpose structures, such as filtering, very high, WYLBUR states that it is simply "not important." Miller, reporting for PLANET, is of the opinion that "many 'software' implementations of 'filtering' and special structures are better performed by human beings." However, if "many" are, which are better done by software, at least in terms of cost? The circumstances in which special structures are necessary or useful is certainly a controversial issue, according to the responses of our panel of designers, and a prime area for further research.

Integrated Data Structures

"Integrated data structures," which are the merger of classical data base systems with computerized conferencing systems, are just beginning to emerge in the more sophisticated systems such as HUB and EIES. Most of the current applications are cases in which the contents of the data base have a degree of qualitative input to be maintained. Status reports by components of ongoing projects are a typical example. As yet there is no system in which a generalized data base system is merged completely with a computerized conferencing system. RE-SOURCES on EIES is an attempt in that direction for formatted textual data bases.

Five of the eight designers responding rate integrated data structures as only a "3" in importance; thus there is fairly high agreement that they are "not seen as a major part of a general conferencing system," as the CONFER designer puts it. However, OICS, which comes close to this capability and will soon have an on-line data base for a budgeting system, rates it as a "1". This may be a case where the value of a feature cannot be determined until it is implemented and its perceived benefits measured for a variety of applications.

Indirect Communication Channels

"Indirect communication channels" refers to the the ability to alert users to the information and communication needs of others without direct communication. An example is collecting the unmatched keys used in searches of conference files and supplying the list to those writing into the file. In the EMISARI system this was used on the Policy file by those scheduling the policy committee rulings. Patterns of communication and informal behavior can be processed by the computer to aid users. This area has been explored only in very primitive ways in the current generation of systems. An analogy is the use of library sign-up cards in the back of books. Before these were replaced by computer systems, people in organizational libraries could discover who else had read the same books, and this could result in establishing new communication paths, especially in research and development organizations. Because this implies certain dangers of invading privacy, it is a factor that can impede the acceptance of such systems. It is probably best to make the use of indirect communications a very explicit process of which users are completely aware, and to reach agreement with them for incorporating these types of new features.

Several of the designers did not understand the explanation of indirect communication structures that was given. With the exception of EIES, the designers all gave such a capability only a "3" or a "4", if they responded at all.

Voting

"Voting" provides a mechanism for formal feedback and promoting consensus within conferences. It can take the form of using scales already provided, such as 1 to 5 or 1 to 10 ratings on desirability or feasibility, a rank ordering of items (see for instance, Hiltz et al., 1981), or user-defined scales. EIES, HUB, and PLANET, designed as conferencing systems, provide a wide variety of scales, as does CONFER, which has created a technique called "Dynamic Value Voting" specifically for the computerized conferencing context. PANALOG provides simply a "YES, NO, or ABSTAIN" voting scale for issues, and COM allows voting but without any preconstructed scales, since they are felt to constrict answers too much. Systems designed mainly to support mail or offices without a group conferencing capability do not include voting, as might be expected.

There is a great deal of disagreement about the relative importance of voting, with the ratings of importance closely paralleling the extent to which voting is incorporated into a system.

User Simulation and Marketplace Structures

These are two special structures that could be incorporated into computer-mediated communication systems. Neither gained much enthusiastic support, or even a great deal of understanding, at this point in the development of these systems.

"User simulation" is the idea that the system can allow its users to set up models to work for them to obtain information and carry out communications. This has been accomplished only in a very primitive way, to date, in terms of users establishing profiles of keys with which the system monitors communication traffic to highlight items of potential interest. Other techniques of an artificial intelligence nature could be applied to facilitate this function.

Ratings of the importance of this feature spread all the way from "1" to "5", and there is no relationship between the current degree of implementation and the importance rating accorded. This is another example of a special structure for which there is too little development and experience with a variety of applications for any consensus to emerge among designers.

"Marketplace structures" make it possible to pay people for information or services provided on line. For instance, those who reviewed a draft paper could be credited for their effort. Or a charge could be made for the privilege of reading a report; this type of royalty would be paid by a reader to an author without the intermediary of a publisher.

Once again, ratings range all the way from "1" to "5". It is possible that those who rate it as completely unimportant do not understand the concept. The @MAIL system on MACC has implemented a system such that a reader can be charged for accessing a file, with the author receiving the credits. Certainly, if "electronic publishing" is to develop in the future, some such structure must be implemented, to motivate authors to use this method to distribute their work, in lieu of the royalties that would be received if it were published in more traditional ways.

Other Capabilities

In addition to the rather extensive list of possible software features offered our panel of designers, we asked, "What important characteristics of computer systems for human communication have we omitted? Please give a name and brief description for any important omitted system qualities or characteristics."

One characteristic was mentioned by two different designers and therefore should be added to a list of desirable software features. This is a "scanning" capability which would enable users to easily skim a condensed text version, index, or abstract of available items to locate and select those of interest without reading the full text of all items of possible interest.

Two other characteristics are suggested by one designer. First, there is "Interface Coupling." If several interfaces are provided, such as menus and commands, they should be coupled in a cognitively "natural" manner so that the transition among them is simple for the user. Second, there is "chair" or "moderator." If there are conferences, they should have a leader who has the power to keep the entries on the topic. This can be provided by software giving the leader the ability to edit or delete items considered irrelevant, or to add keys or other devices to help order and integrate the discussion. COM's designer, Palme, who realized that this item had been omitted, notes that their conference "organizers" are allowed to delete items or to move items to a conference more suitable to the subject of the item. "Deletion is very seldom used, moving items is seldom used but still valuable."

WYLBUR suggests "scratchpad files," which are defined as "the ability to create text and send it without naming the file." Such a problem would probably not occur to a designer who started with a communication system rather than a word processing system, since communication systems are not built around "files," at least at the level of user awareness. However, inconvenient though it may seem, many mail systems are tacked onto word processors, and require the user to save and name a file before sending it to someone—"a major nuisance," in Lynch's words.

PANALOG suggests "personal correspondence and tickler files." Such a capability means that users have their own set of message files, one of which is time-fused to return a designated message on an indicated date.

SUMMARY AND CONCLUSIONS

In terms of system software, such characteristics of all interactive systems as accessibility, humanization and responsiveness are most highly rated. Text editing capabilities are also rated by system designers as extremely important, because users without microcomputers spend most of their time on line entering text. There is quite a bit of disagreement about the relative importance or even desirability of many of the software features unique to computer-mediated communication systems, such as system evolution and communication richness (see summary chart in Table 2–3).

The design of interactive systems is more an art than a science, since specific designs represent trade-offs between conflicting goals and objectives. This includes both basic design principles, such as comprehension versus segmentation, and the constraints imposed by hardware and software. For example, some might view the "ideal system" as maintaining complete audit trails of all user interactions. This would permit complete "recovery" to any point in the user's interaction and might allow anticipative and adaptive features to the user interface. However, for the foreseeable future, the hardware costs are prohibitive for most systems.

Another factor making design difficult is the inability to separate motivational and psychological factors from the impact of design choices. The degree of motivation to use a system is probably the primary factor in determining its success. Even a poorly designed system will be used if there is sufficient motivation, and a well-designed system will not be used without positive motivation. In the latter case, users often blame design choices to disguise their negative attitudes toward using any computer system.

Within very wide limitations, the specific design choices have second-order influences upon use, acceptance, and impacts, and can be evaluated only if controlled by knowledge of the motivational factors. Because most system studies have not been able to address or control motivational factors, our current knowledge tends to be lore rather than validated hypotheses. However, there is a significant impact of design upon those user subsets with intermediate or uncertain motivational levels. This group is difficult to pinpoint because its members are usually less outspoken in their reactions to a system. As a result, the only possible way to formulate scientific evaluations is by a program of feedback and assessment that pinpoints and identifies their attitudes and behavior. Since communication-oriented interactive systems are now reaching out to populations that are not "computer literate," most future users will probably fall into this uncertain motivational category. It is from this population subset that a better understanding of design alternatives and their consequences may emerge.

The final complicating factor is that many design objectives must be evaluated within the specific context of the application and characteristics of the groups involved. Certainly, some of the disagreements observed here can be attributed to whether the system is very limited or relatively complex and rich. The importance of items such as "sense of community" may be an example of dependence upon group behavior, since one group might find features designed to support a sense of community favorable and another might not.

This use of the Delphi method functioned to organize the wisdom of a group of designers who, because of their affiliations, responsibilities, and biases, would not otherwise have been able to meet and cooperatively achieve these results. Consequently, these empirical findings have unique importance. The areas of disagreement provide guidance to the empiricists for careful experimentation and evaluation. For the theorists, there is the complementary challenge of discerning the relationship between the factors measuring the properties of interactive systems and the real objective of the cognitive processes that these systems are meant to support. The ultimate measure is the quality of the cognitive results produced by users in their applications of these systems. For computer-mediated communication systems, this remains the ultimate challenge in evaluating alternative designs.

A system for human communication is more than just a collection of software capabilities; ideally, it is "groupware," an integrated set of group processes and software capabilities melded to support the specific goals or tasks of a particular user group.

ADDENDUM

GROUPWARE: THE PROCESS AND IMPACTS
OF DESIGN CHOICES
Peter Johnson-Lenz and Trudy Johnson-Lenz[1]

The examination of design choices has so far considered software characteristics individually. However, any particular system is formed by a multitude of choices among alternatives. Chapter 3 will suggest that the system and group are an interacting entity; the same system may be accepted by one group and rejected by another, and may have very different impacts upon different groups. In this section, we will look at the design of a total system for a particular group and application in terms of the kind of evolutionary, participatory process that can best match group needs to software possibilities (see also Hiltz and Turoff, 1981, for an extended discussion of system design as an evolutionary process). After reviewing the processes and procedures available for the design of "groupware," design choices will be discussed in terms of specific examples of the variety of total structures that may result. The particular design characteristics of a given system and how an individual or group uses that system may result in sig-

[1]This section is an edited version of Peter and Trudy Johnson-Lenz, "Consider the Groupware: Design and Group Process Impacts on Communication in the Electronic Medium," Chapter 5 in Hiltz and Kerr (1981).

nificant impacts. By knowing about such specific impacts, a designer or facilitator can exert some control over the impacts upon users by making informed choices.

Structured Communication

There are two major aspects of the design of computerized communication systems: the user or human-machine interface and the communication structure. Although the first has been the subject of much research and experimentation, the communication structure or social interface has been much less studied. This determines how groups work together on different kinds of tasks in the electronic medium. Ultimately, structuring the communication process involves the design of social systems and may even result in new cultural forms within this highly adaptable, plastic medium (Bezilla and Kerr, 1979).

For a group to use a computer-based communications system effectively, it must have a set of explicit procedures to follow, which include the goals and tasks, who can communicate with whom and when, how decisions are made and disagreements resolved, and the sequence of activities to be followed. These procedures may also consist of norms or rules enforced by the group or the software. Taken together, they constitute a communication structure, without which the group's work will be neither effective nor efficient.

> Group work is about individuals bound together through communication to get something done, taking into account how people function together in a social system and taking into account how people relate to one another as individuals, using procedures to organize and systematize the work with leaders who help train group members and select procedures in group meetings . . . .

> Completing a task effectively involves *intentionally* designing the group's work so that the end product will help them achieve their purpose and *intentionally* working together in ways that insure effective interpersonal relationships. Seldom, if ever, do task or interpersonal aspects of group work just 'happen' if maximum group effectiveness is desired. Members must intentionally function in ways that cause them to happen effectively (Stech and Ratliffe, 1976:xiii, 199).

There are many different communication structures being used in the electronic medium. For example, computerized conferencing systems support both messaging (electronic mail) and conferencing. Each of these capabilities represents a different structure and consequently has different impacts. Even the particular structure of conferencing is different on various systems. The CONFER conferencing structure is more interactive than EIES, for example, while conferencing on PLANET is deliberately kept very simple. In addition new communication structures beyond conferencing have been developed. These include subsystems on EIES such as TOPICS which supports a variety of inquiry/response exchange processes, TERMS for collective glossary development, and TOUR which is an interactive hypertext system with participatory activities; each of these has been designed and implemented by the authors.

Groupware

A group working together in a computer-mediated environment, following certain procedures, can be greatly aided by supportive and facilitative software. However, this is only one component of structured communication. The other consists of the processes and procedures used by the group. The most effective use of the medium occurs when a group uses processes and procedures specifically designed to meet its needs, plus software which supports and facilitates those procedures. The group process without computer support may be inefficient and cumbersome. Software without a group which can make effective use of it is a wasted resource. Effective group work in the electronic medium thus requires both explicit and intentional group processes and procedures and the software to support them. This union of *group* process and *software* support we call *groupware* to distinguish it from either process or software alone. Furthermore, a particular software system can often support different processes, while a specific procedure can be followed using a variety of software tools. The most effective results are achieved when the groupware is carefully matched to the group's needs and preferences.

GROUPWARE Equation

GROUPWARE = intentional GROUP processes and procedures to achieve specific purposes

+

softWARE tools designed to support and facilitate the group's work

---

The design of computer-mediated systems is considered an art, and this is even more true of the design of groupware. Selecting the appropriate design elements in concert with a group's needs and processes requires sensitivity and a certain amount of intuition. It also requires a highly participatory design process with extensive communication between the designers and users.

An Overview of the Groupware Design Process

The process of groupware design begins with the articulation of group needs by making explicit its purposes, the process characteristics it wishes to follow, and the potential difficulties to be overcome. Usually, only a few people representing the group's interests are involved in this phase. In response, the groupware designer suggests specific structures and procedures. These are specified at first without regard for the computer system, since they must make sense as group procedures in and of themselves.

Unless the group's task is fairly simple and of short duration, its needs will evolve over time as its members gain experience with the communication structures chosen. Process evaluation may indicate the need for adjustments or replacements in the groupware structures. Thus, for ongoing group work, the design process must be dynamic and evolve with the group's needs and activities. An example of such a design process can be found in the case study of the evolution of the TOPICS system (Johnson-Lenz and Johnson-Lenz, 1981).

The taxonomy of group characteristics likely to affect the acceptance of computer-mediated communication systems, outlined in Chapter 3, should also be taken into account in selecting appropriate groupware to maximize both acceptance and desired outcomes.

Varieties of Procedures

Once the group's characteristics and processes are made explicit, the optimal procedures and structures can be chosen. A procedure is simply a method a group can use to accomplish its task. The impacts of the use of computerized communications for group work are determined in part by the choice of procedures and structures, quite apart from the specific design of the software to support these procedures, which has its own impacts.

Procedures may include some or all of the following choices of characteristics:

1. Individual work versus group interaction
2. Anonymity versus signed responses
3. Feedback of group results versus none
4. Aggregated versus unprocessed results
5. Voting versus none
6. Numerical processing versus none
7. Filtered information (selection mechanisms to access only selected items) versus unfiltered information

8. Synchronous versus asynchronous interaction
9. Sequenced versus free or unstructured interaction
10. One-time access to information versus continuous access
11. Patterns of communication: one-to-one, one-to-many, many-to-many, many-to-one

A variety of standard group procedures have been developed and used successfully over the years with groups having different purposes and characteristics. According to Stech and Ratliffe (1976:160–189), these include reflective thinking, rational management, brainstorming, nominal group process, Delphi, action research, parliamentary procedure, PERT chart planning, scheduling, budgeting, assigning, and product and process evaluation. Three other group procedures are policy capturing, developed by Kenneth R. Hammond (Hammond et al., 1975); interpretive structural modeling (ISM), developed by John Warfield (1976); and problem/possibility focuser generation, created by Robert Theobald (1966).

The procedure selection phase of the design process involves matching the group's processes with the appropriate procedures. This is still an art, since there is a sizeable variety of process characteristics and hence procedures to match them. There is also some disagreement as to which procedures are most appropriate for which situations, based on designer and facilitator biases.

Software Design Elements

Finally, to meet the group's needs, the groupware designer chooses specific software tools, which are also subject to design choices. The impacts of the use of computer-mediated communication for group work are determined in part by the choice of the computer system (hardware and software) and the design elements outlined below, but in many ways, these are the least interesting, most easily assessed, and most controllable impacts.

Just as groups, group process, and group procedures vary along a number of dimensions, the design of software tools consists of many elements. The designer's choices are a series of trade-offs among those software design elements. The preceding portion of this chapter addresses design principles at the level of concepts such as forgiveness, escape, generalizability and segmentation, and variety or flexibility of interaction. Consistent with these principles are choices among design elements, such as:

1. Menus versus commands
2. Simple commands versus a more complex and powerful interface

3. Friendly interface versus terse commands and diagnostics
4. Choice of words (metaphors) used in referring to the software and the commands
5. Tailorable interface which differs by users
6. Guided or tutorial versus terse mode
7. Human user support versus print or on-line documentation
8. Use of keywords for organization versus retrieval by item numbers only
9. Storage of text versus none
10. Automated delivery of waiting items versus none
11. Use of markers to keep track of what has been delivered
12. Use of graphics
13. Formats for entry of material and presentation of results
14. Human actions versus machine action for different functions
15. Choice of computational algorithms if needed.

Examples of Specific Communication Structures

Design elements are combined to form tools, structures, and systems, each with different characteristics and consequently different impacts. In addition, since one group's use of a particular structure may be different from another's, this will make evaluating the impacts of the use of a given communication structure even more difficult.

Below are descriptions of some generic software structures or systems used on EIES. Other systems have communications structures with slightly different characteristics.

Messaging: As the simplest form of electronic communications, messaging is often referred to as electronic mail. On EIES, the length of a message is limited to 57 lines, and may be sent to one or more people or to a defined group. It may be signed or sent anonymously or with a pen name, and either open or blind copied. The author receives a confirmation when it has been received. Messages are put into a member's delivery "queue" in the order in which they are sent, and are delivered in that order; there is no facility for sorting one's messages or rejecting some of them. They may be delivered automatically when users are on line or may be requested at the users' convenience. There is no automatic provision on EIES for special disposition of messages, such as filing for later reference, answering immediately, or forwarding to someone else. These actions can be taken, but the user must initiate them. Old messages can be retrieved from the system for about three months, although users may store particular messages on line for a longer time. A message may be modified by the sender and copied by anyone with access to it (sender and recipients). A message may be associated with one previous message, and keywords may be assigned to it for later retrieval or to indicate the subject matter.

Each of these characteristics is a design choice, and may vary for other systems, with consequent implications for both use (acceptance) of the system and its impacts. For example, the maximum length of a message may be quite short, such as the 10–line limit imposed on EMISARI (Turoff, 1972); or there may be no effective limit on size at all, as in other systems. The pen name or anonymity features can have important consequences for the group process, ranging from greater openness in expressing opinions to encouraging the trading of insults. Some message systems do not force delivery and do not give confirmations of receipt; these choices may have the effect of maximizing immediate convenience at the expense of facilitating group processes. (See Hiltz, 1982, Chapter 5, for a discussion of the advantages and disadvantages of forced message delivery.)

Conferencing: In a computer conference, all text items are retained in the order in which they were entered, forming a written, self-documenting transcript. The major advantage of using a conference rather than messages for group communication is that all the exchanges are kept in one place rather than being interspersed with other messages. The computer maintains a marker for each conference member. When members enter the conference, the system indicates how many new items are waiting and gives them the option of accepting any or all of them. Members may "browse" through conferences by looking at conference comment titles they have not yet received and moving their markers as desired. Any comment may be printed out, whether or not it has been previously delivered. On EIES, waiting comments are delivered in succession. In contrast, on CONFER the system asks the user for a one-line reaction or "vote" on each comment before proceeding to the next one and in this respect is more interactive. Conferences may be either asynchronous or synchronous.

Filtered Exchange: Since messaging and conferencing can quickly produce information overload, with a member of a 10–person conference potentially receiving nine comments for each one entered, there is a need for structures to automatically filter out those items not of interest. On EIES, the TOPICS subsystem has several features to reduce information overload. Topics or inquiries are introduced in a concise format, limited to three to five lines, and only these short inquiries are delivered to all members of the exchange. Members are given the opportunity to select those topics or inquiries of interest to receive additional background information and associated responses entered to date. The user's selection of topics also governs which responses in the exchange will be delivered in the future. There are a series of delivery options so that users can access topics and responses in "batch," by keywords, by topic, and so forth, depending on their needs and preferences. Finally, a keyword index and retrieval mechanism allows Boolean searches.

Another set of features on EIES for reducing information overload is SUBMIT and READ. A user may compose a long text item or set of items with a shorter abstract which is sent to others as a message or entered in a conference. Those recipients interested in the entire text item, based on the abstract, then READ it with a single command. This is similar to the short topic raisers and selection of items of interest in the TOPICS system, except that there are no length restrictions on SUBMITted abstracts.

Another example of filtered exchange on EIES is the INTERESTS feature. Users indicate their interests by keywords and thus "join" on-line interest groups. Members may then message each other or form conferences, with the subject of the items acting as the "address."

Relational Structures: Discussions within conferences and TOPIC exchanges are generally linear in form, with items arranged sequentially and chronologically. Information can be arranged with similar ideas grouped together, however. In the TOUR system, up to nine branches can follow each item for related material. "Tourists" can read the material in sequences of their own choosing, based on the branches selected. In addition, there are participatory activities within the tour, including response/tallies for anonymous ratings or questionnaires, and discussions or miniconferences about the material itself. There is also a relational keyword index and retrieval system so that users can retrieve those items of primary interest without taking the tour. A special command mode also allows users to move around the tour at will.

Voting: Voting capabilities are useful to view a group's opinions or determine if consensus is emerging. In EIES conferences, an author can make any item votable and specify scales on which users are to vote. The built-in scales were designed to support Delphi voting, and there is also an option for a user-defined scale. Feedback of the results can be restricted until there are a specified number of votes. Voting is anonymous, and vote changes are allowed.

Dynamic value voting routines are available on CONFER which include computational support for ranking exercises, and feedback of the best fit of the group ranking.

Decision-Support Tools: An area open for research and development is the design and implementation of decision-support tools in a computerized communication environment. These are procedures which aid a group in the phases of decision making: problem definition, solution generation, criteria setting, solution selection and implementation, and group process assessment.

The experiments to compare computerized communications with face-to-face decision making are a combination of decision-support tools and on-line data collection. One version involves a synchronous session in which subjects attempt to reach consensus on their rankings of 15 items. The experiment is conducted with or without feedback of individual and group rankings, and with human or computer leadership in which decision-support tools are used (Hiltz et al., 1981).

The TERMS system is a tool for the collective development of glossaries of terms and definitions. Members enter terms, definitions, and comments, and may vote on these definitions.

Examples of Groupware in Action

The examples of communication structures described above were all developed to meet particular needs of users. They are structures, systems, procedures, and tools composed of and optimizing various design elements to provide specific features and capabilities. However, groupware also includes the ways in which tools or software support are employed to further the group's process and help the members achieve their goals. To evaluate many of the impacts of the use of computerized communication for group work, one must consider the groupware: the group, its perceived needs, process, sequence of activities, choice of procedures, and structured communications. To illustrate, below are several examples of different uses of the same software structures by various groups. The impacts are different for different uses.

Conferences: There have been hundreds of conferences on EIES, all using the same software, ranging from an informal encounter group, to a participatory soap opera in which pen names were used almost exclusively to a conference on "superliteracy" in which one phase was entirely anonymous. Several conferences have been devoted to software specification and design, with strong task orientations and sometimes specific and urgent deadlines. Similarly, a conference for designing a workshop process and materials for a series of face-to-face meetings had a focus, a deadline, and was of short duration. Other longer-range planning conferences have lasted for many months, and still other conferences without a clear task focus moved from one subject to another, based on conferees' interests.

These are by no means representative examples of the range of conferences, but they do indicate that conferencing can take many forms and have different impacts. One impact of conferencing for the encounter group or the soap opera was that it allowed members to express feelings and different aspects of their personalities without fear of disclosure. However, this probably would not be an impact for those using conferencing for task work. Similarly, a group using voting might have a different perception of the ease of reaching consensus in a computer conference than one which relied on a more informal sense of the group's preferences.

TOPICS/POLITECHS: These can be used to support a series of mini-conferences, an inquiry/response process, or both. The Politechs-on-EIES Exchanges (currently Publictech, Legitech, Localtech, Brieftech, and Nettech) use the TOPICS system under the name POLITECHS and are coordinated by Participation Systems, Inc. The Publictech and Legitech Exchanges on EIES are examples of an inquiry/exchange process. Legitech is a private exchange for legislative researchers and resource people, focusing on inquiries and responses about proposed state legislation. In contrast, Publictech is publicly available on EIES and has a more diffuse focus, although its inquiries and responses generally concern scientific, technical, and public policy matters. It is the most open of the Politechs-on-EIES Exchanges from which more specialized Exchanges can be spun off as needed.

In contrast, a group concerned with personal and social transformation used the TOPICS system in the TRANSFORM exchange. It was a covenant space; that is, members agreed to a covenant of cooperation and sharing before admission, and needed a sponsor to introduce them to the exchange and its processes. Each topic introduced a miniconference on subjects such as the role of science fiction, myth, and imagery in transformation; the transformation of neighborhoods and communities; and the convergence of science and religion. There were also a number of group process and membership topics, including a collection of member biographies. The purpose of the exchange was to share ideas and information about personal and social transformation and to provide social and emotional support. Pen names and anonymity could be used, and response/tallies were available.

Evaluating the Impacts of Groupware

Groupware often involves combinations of processes and procedures in sequences to meet the group's needs. There are a variety of potential group processes and communication structures, and assessments of existing groupware have generally been informal or focused on only some of its aspects, so that there is no validated, empirically based evaluation of the impacts of various groupware designs at this time. Furthermore, it may be that different groups prefer different groupware approaches for what will appear to be arbitrary, situationally determined reasons, much as individuals prefer certain cultural norms and forms over others as a matter of taste.

Since the design, evolution, and evaluation of groupware are in fact those of social systems, effective groupware must include its users in the design and evaluation processes. Murray Turoff, designer of EIES, has observed:

> We are now beginning to realize that when we design a communication structure to operate within an interactive computer system for a group of humans, what we are really designing is a human system. It is an electronic social system where the properties or behavior of the group are a result of an inseparable combination of human psychology, group sociology and the characteristics of the design .... One advantage EIES has over other interactive systems is that it is primarily a communication system. Therefore, the human involvement in the process can be made an integral part of the system. In terms of EIES, this means that the design and implementation group, the user consultants, the evaluators and the user community at large form elements of both a formal and informal communication network governing the evolution of the system (Turoff, 1980a:113,115).

The Impacts of Effective Choices

Groupware begins with the group and its work. The groupware designer, working with group members, must sensitively choose processes appropriate for the group and its purposes and characteristics, procedures to support the group's process, and the communication structures and software tools which will make those procedures easy to follow. All of these taken together influence the impacts of the use of computerized communication for group work. If the overall process chosen is not appropriate, the group will be neither effective nor efficient. If the group does not support the process, it will not work. If the tools and procedures are inappropriate, either they will not be used or they will get in the way. How many of the apparent impacts of computerized communications are the result of inappropriate or outdated choices in the design and conduct of groupware? How many apparent impacts are specific to particular groupware? When evaluating the acceptance and impacts of computer-based human communication, consider the groupware. It makes a difference.

CHAPTER 3

Acceptance and Usage of Computer-Mediated Communication Systems

Initial exposure to this communication medium often occurs at small group demonstrations of a particular system or presentations at formal meetings. Afterwards, some onlookers feel excited and eager to try it themselves. Others frown, voice skepticism, or leave early; they want to have nothing to do with it. How can the same presentation of the same system produce such a range of initial reactions?

Among the people invited to make free use of EIES during the initial operational trials, about 40% never signed on at all or used the system so little (less than 5 hours) that they never really mastered it. Others became addicted almost from the beginning, signing on several times a day and claiming that it was one of the most productive, stimulating things they had ever encountered. Some users were not subsidized at all and made real economic sacrifices to pay the $100 or more a month they spent on EIES out of their own pockets. A few reported going into debt to maintain access to a communication system that they found essential and irreplaceable. Why is it that the same system is rejected as not worth the trouble to learn by some, and considered so valuable by others that they endure economic hardships to use it?

In this chapter, we will first present the conceptual framework developed to synthesize the findings of research projects that included any observations of the determinants of acceptance of computer-based communication systems. After summarizing the results of previously published research, we will examine each of the potentially important factors and present the results of our synthesis questionnaire, which produced acceptance data for six EIES studies and four other systems: NLS, HUB, OICS, and COM.

THE CONCEPTUALIZATION AND MEASUREMENT OF ACCEPTANCE

Acceptance is the degree of willingness of an individual or group to utilize computer-mediated communication systems. It is a subjective factor and not easily measured. Although it is often mistakenly equated with usage, usage can be considered a measure of acceptance only if:

1. Individuals are motivated to use the system. They have a task they consider important which can be performed on line.
2. They have convenient access to terminals.
3. They are completely free to use alternative systems for their communication activities.
4. The user understands what the system can do and how to operate it.

As a result, the degree of compliance pressure exercised and the reasons for nonuse must be considered when attempting to relate usage to acceptance. If people are directed either to use a system or lose their jobs, they will use it, but at a cost to their morale and productivity if their dissatisfaction continues. One consultant associated with a commercial electronic mail system strongly recommends that use by the "boss" will produce acceptance by others:

> We have used electronic mail when our bosses have . . . . Once the manager of a group begins to pass around information, meeting announcements or even work assignments by means of electronic mail, the people in that group become frequent users of the mail system (McQuillan, 1980:8).

In view of this, many of the research-oriented field trials of this technology may be more enlightening for understanding acceptance than the commercial applications, where users frequently have no real alternative or face high compliance pressure to carry out their tasks using the system provided.

The relationship between usage and compliance at the extremes can be represented in the diagram on the next page.

Degree of Acceptance by Compliance Pressure and Usage		
	Low Compliance	High Compliance
Low Usage	Low Acceptance	Active Rejection
High Usage	High Acceptance	Undetermined

Another useful distinction is between the operator of a system and the user, who may not be identical. The operator may be a secretary who is given instructions to input or retrieve materials. As Reichwald (1980) puts it:

> The circle of users . . . extends to all those who make a contribution to the discharge of their duties by having direct or indirect recourse to the technical facilities . . . in the situation of the operator, the technical features of the system are the primary factor that determines acceptance or nonacceptance, while in the situation of the user the contribution of the system to the performance of the tasks at hand . . . is the question that matters. Over and above this, however, it must be recognized that both the operator's and the user's willingness to work with the new system long-term is strongly influenced by the organizational consequences which the adoption of the system entails (p.5).

The interplay between objective "reality" and subjective expectations and impressions further complicates the process of conceptualization. The reality of the system—what it can do and how one goes about using it—may not be known. In particular, those not knowledgeable about computers may have mistaken expectations about the system or the situation which are the basis for their lack of use. For example, they may know that such systems are used by typing, but may not be aware of the need to wait for prompts before typing, or to prefix commands with a special symbol (such as " + " in EIES or "!" in COM) for the computer to recognize it as a command to be executed. The computer system may thus appear to be totally capricious and unresponsive, because it "doesn't work"; but training might turn this "system rejector" into a regular user. Secondly, the actual experiences that a user encounters may or may not be statistically typical of those of average users. For instance, someone who habitually tries to sign on only at the busiest midday time may encounter a much higher than average number of busy signals and much slower response time than is typical.

For these reasons, hours of use is not a completely valid measure of acceptance of computer-mediated communication systems. Ideally, one would supplement the amount of use as an indicator with subjective ratings of a system's acceptability and potential benefits. In practice, the amount of system usage is usually collected by an automatic monitor in terms of hours of use per person, and is the only indicator which is both easily collected and available for most of the research studies. In our data report forms, we preserved the distinction by asking separately about correlations with amount of use and with subjective satisfaction.

Acceptance is determined by many factors. Our approach is to delineate these factors in a morphology that is largely situationally independent. The factors will be discussed in the context of what is known about them and their influence on acceptance of the technology. To "know" in this context includes confirmed hypotheses as well as the acquired wisdom of those who have sought to design and evaluate the use of these systems.

We have categorized the determinants of acceptance and usage of computer-mediated communication systems into the characteristics of (1) the individual user, (2) the social group or organizational context, (3) the task, and (4) the system itself, including the equipment with which the system is used. Aspects of the system which may be important have been reviewed in the preceding chapter. Since any one field trial generally covers only one system and one main type of task, our evaluators could not report on correlations for these factors with degree of acceptance.

The list of potentially important factors developed for the individual and group categories is shown in Tables 3-1 and 3-2. This brief overview serves as both a warning of the complexity of the problems involved in pinpointing the determinants of acceptance and as an outline of the factors which will be examined in detail in this chapter.

The factors expressed under these categories are formed to be largely context-independent in that they can apply across a variety of systems and situations. Our approach is to discuss each factor in turn, since there is little data on the influence of the factors in combination. Even where there is hard evidence, we know only the limits of extreme values of factors leading to very high or very low acceptance. The difficulty in dealing with the intermediate range and the relationships among factors in this range is that the relative degree of importance of any factor can be highly situationally dependent. This has been demonstrated by observing that the same system can be accepted by one group and completely rejected by another.

TABLE 3-1

Characteristics of Individuals That May Affect System Acceptance

A. Attitudinal Variables
    1. Attitudes toward task
        a. Relative importance or priority
        b. Degree of liking or disliking of the task (pleasant/unpleasant, challenging/ boring, etc.)
    2. Attitudes toward media
        a. Attitudes toward computers in general
        b. Expectations about the specific system
            1) Anticipated usefulness
            2) Anticipated impacts on productivity
            3) Anticipated difficulty of use
        c. Attitudes toward alternative media (telephones, letters, travel, etc.)
    3. Attitudes toward the group (liking, respect, whether members are an important reference group)
    4. Expectations about how system use will affect relationships with the group
B. Skills and Characteristics
    1. Personal communication skills
        a. Reading speed
        b. Typing speed
        c. Preference for speaking or writing
        d. General literacy (writing ability)
    2. Previous related experience
        a. Use of computers
        b. Use of computer terminals
        c. Use of other computer-based communication systems
    3. Physical or intellectual disabilities
C. Demographic Characteristics
    1. Age
    2. Sex
    3. Educational level
    4. Race, nationality, or subculture
D. Environmental Variables
    1. Available resources, including secretarial support
    2. Position in the organization (or status in the informal group)
    3. Amount of pressure to use the system (from superiors and peers)
E. Psychological Variables
    1. Personality characteristics (e.g., Myers-Briggs Types of indicators)
    2. Basic values (Parsonian pattern variables)

TABLE 3-2

Group and Access Factors That May Affect System Use

I. Group Factors

A. Structure
   1. Size
   2. Degree of geographic dispersion
   3. Centralized versus decentralized control .
   4. Preexisting communication ties or network
B. Leadership
   1. Style
   2. Level of effort or activity by the leader
C. Cohesiveness
   1. Sociometric ties
      a. Have members met face to face?
      b. How many group members are known to each other before they begin communicating on the system?
      c. Have they worked together previously?
      d. Do they form cliques, have many "individualists," or are they an integrated group?
   2. Competitiveness
   3. Trust or openness among members

II. Selected Access Factors

A. Terminal access
   1. Own versus shared versus no regular access in office
   2. Availability of terminal to take home
   3. Type of terminal (CRT versus hard copy; speed)
B. Direct (hands on) versus indirect use

FINDINGS OF PREVIOUS STUDIES

Bair (in Uhlig *et al.*, 1979) notes that:

> The single most common cause of system failure is user rejection . . . . This does not imply that the system design and performance are not also major factors in rejection. However, the way the system was implemented has caused most failures by not overcoming the threatening nature of the complex and intrusive technology. In some cases, rejection by potential users occurred before the technology ever entered the organization (p. 243).

The most extensive description of active rejection behavior occurs in Bair's report on the Augmented Knowledge Workshop (NLS). A group of approximately 20 "knowledge workers" in an organizational unit were first invited to use the system on a voluntary basis. Acceptance was so poor that management ordered use of the system. This requirement was enforced by instructing secretaries not to type handwritten drafts without authorized exceptions, and by supervisors insisting that only work submitted on line would be reviewed. The circumstances surrounding this rather draconian measure are described as follows:

> The resistance to learning a new system as a way of doing one's daily knowledge work was higher than expected. Traditional work patterns were adhered to with a great deal of persistence by the population, a manifestation of the "rejection phenomenon." This occurs frequently upon the introduction of new technology; however, it was surprising in this context. It demonstrates that education and an understanding of the technology in general are not [sufficient] prerequisites for immediate acceptance . . . .

> Excuses for not using the system were exemplified by comments such as, "There isn't a terminal around," "I can't remember how to do it," "There isn't a good manual that I can understand," "I have too much work to do," etc. . . . .

> Individuals manifested a range of behaviors, from trying to ignore the whole thing to actively campaigning against it . . . .

> Ego threat was identified on the basis of verbal and nonverbal behaviors over a period of several months. When questioned about their work, subject's defensiveness was noted by facial flushing, elusive or aggressive statements, or reverse attack where the subject would say, "If I had nothing else to do like you, I'd learn to use it . . . ." Complaining within earshot of the observer usually centered around how busy [he or she was] and how important it was that he not be imposed upon (Bair, 1974:28-31).

As Bair insightfully observes, system acceptance involves changes in the most basic habits embedded in one's daily activities: how one thinks, composes materials, and communicates. Acceptance of a system involves not only learning new skills and habits, but extinguishing old habits as well. The successful introduction of a system thus requires not only good system design, training, documentation, and terminal availability, but also "social engineering."

FORUM-PLANET

The Institute for the Future's initial studies of this technology used the FORUM system, which was later modified to become PLANET. The second volume of their report summarizes their qualitative observations on the determinants of acceptance. The subjects were 10 small groups, ranging in size from 3 to 30 participants. Use is examined not only in terms of aggregate levels but also by variations in activity levels for individuals. The excerpted findings are as follows:

1. Physical Conditions
   a. Threshold of familiarity and skills: for computer conferencing to be used with ease, the system must become 'transparent"; that is, the physical and

mental attention needed for using the system must diminish so that the person can attend to communication itself.

b. Characteristics of the terminal: Some terminals are easier to use than others, and each has varying degrees of reliability.

c. Access to the terminal and phone link.

d. State of the computer and the network: When the network is loaded heavily, the time lag (response time) may be high . . . . The lag, of course, is frustrating and often confusing . . . . However, this frustration is minimal compared to that which occurs when the system crashes.

2. Personal Attitudes and Social Needs

a. Feeling of obligation to use FORUM: How much the individual feels obligated to use FORUM in contrast to communicating in some other mode or not communicating at all.

b. Desire to be "in touch": Some participants desired a high level of communication with the rest, while others found this unnecessary.

c. Work and lifestyle: Teleconferencing fits well into the lifestyles of some people, who prefer flexibility rather than rigidly scheduled work times and place.

d. Need to communicate information relating to role: Each person participates most in the area of discussion or conference which is most related to his or her perceived role in the group.

3. General Social Conditions

a. Physical separation: When Institute staff members were away on trips, they tended to make many more entries than usual.

b. Responses to questions: A specific or direct question almost always gets an answer from a participant.

c. Group task and structure: Very unstructured tasks and groups will have difficulty adapting to communication via FORUM (Vallee et al., 1974a:95-103).

Findings for Scientific Groups Using EIES

Hiltz's (1981) study of five scientific communities that used the EIES system for 18 to 24 months included a chapter on the determinants of amount of use. The findings are summarized:

Motivational variables are most strongly associated with level of use of the EIES system, rather than characteristics of the system itself. The most important reason given by users to explain limited use of EIES is that other, off-line professional activities must take higher priority. The relative priority of EIES-related and other professional work was by far the most important reason given both in the checklist on the follow-up questionnaire and in the post-use open-ended question.

The strongest observed correlate of the level of use is the *anticipated* level of use before experiencing the system at all. This variable is a conglomerate of individual attitudes and expectations, probably including relative importance to the person of communicating with others in the EIES group and amount of time available for such activities after the more mandatory job-related tasks are completed.

Measures of connectivity (preexisting communication ties with other group participants) also appear important . . . .

Access barriers as a class (including access to a terminal, trouble with Telenet and system unavailability) are the second ranking type of factor related to amount of use of EIES . . . .

Whatever explains preuse expectations or "receptivity" to this form of communication, the practical implications are clear. If prospective conferencing participants do not expect to use the system very much, it is probably a waste of resources to try to put them on line. Perhaps computerized communications resembles sex in this way: you enjoy it a lot more if you really want it before you get it, rather than having it thrust upon you (Hiltz, 1981:97-98).

Results of a Study of NLS

Gwen Edwards (1977) reports extensive data on the correlates of the amount of use of NLS, a computer-based text-processing and communications system. Her study was based on a questionnaire distributed to 250 NLS users in 13 organizations. Ninety four, or 38%, responded. Of these, 30% were managers, 42% researchers, and 28% support staff. Some of the researchers also had a supervisory role, as a total of 40% reported some supervisory responsibility. In looking at the correlates of usage, the dependent variable "general usage" was divided into three ordinal classes: "low" usage of less than an hour a day (28%), "medium" usage of one to three hours a day (31%), and "high" usage of more than three hours a day (41%).

Edwards reports that general attitudinal and access variables are most highly related to the amount of use of NLS. The strongest correlation was with having a terminal at home. Typing skills were found to be related only for those who had a negative perception of the system; there was no relationship between typing skills and amount of use for those with medium to highly positive perceptions. Edwards states that "Once the perceptual barrier is crossed, typing skill is irrelevant to usage." She suggests that "we can recommend that when implementing an Office of the Future system, it will be beneficial to convince potential users that they need not know how to type to make effective use of the system" (Edwards, 1977:43).

The other variables most strongly related to total use involve perceptions of the utility of the system:

1. The perception that use of NLS would improve one's professional image was positively related to the amount of use. This variable was not found to be a predictor for the scientists on EIES. A possible explanation is that the opinions of organizational peers are more important to one's future career than are the opinions

of peers located elsewhere, who do not influence tenure or promotion.

2. The perceived impact on productivity was measured with an identical question in the EIES study. The correlations were similar in direction but stronger for NLS.
3. Usage was related to the perception that NLS would increase the accessibility and visibility of one's work to others.
4. There was a moderate relationship with the user's initial perception of the system and subsequent general use. There was also a moderate relationship with training and the sophistication of the terminal.

Generally, correlations with communication use were similar to but weaker than those with general or total use. One exception is sharing a terminal, possibly because the concern with privacy influences communication use more than it does general usage.

THE PREDICTIVE POWER OF INDIVIDUAL CHARACTERISTICS

At this point, we will begin to systematically examine the variables included in this synthesis. The reasoning behind their inclusion will be explained, any relevant work on the factors reviewed, and the data for the studies presented.

The panel of evaluators was asked to report their findings according to the following scale:

"+ +": Strong quantitative evidence of a positive relationship
"+": Quantitative evidence of a moderate relationship or qualitative evidence of a positive relationship
"0": Evidence of no significant relationship
"−": Moderate to weak negative relationship shown by quantitative evidence, or qualitative evidence of a negative relationship
"− −": Quantitative evidence of a strong negative relationship

For predicting acceptance, then, "0" is not at all a neutral response. The key distinction is between the zeros, meaning the factor is not a predictor, and the other responses.

Attitudinal Variables

Given the findings of both Edwards (1977) and Hiltz (1981), it was expected that the relative priority of on-line versus off-line tasks would be a strategic variable. Of course, if and when all members of a professional network and all tasks could be accessed and performed on line, the distinction would no longer exist. At the present time, however, most users of these systems can access only a limited number of colleagues who are using a system for a specific task that forms only a subset of their work.

Assessment of the relative priority or importance of a task is only one dimension of attitudes that will affect how much time one is likely to spend on line performing that task. The other is its intrinsic attractiveness or interest. It could be that an on-line group activity is admittedly not very high on the list of the employing organization's priorities, but that the individual finds the activity enjoyable or rewarding for other reasons and therefore "makes time" for it.

Relative importance of the task was measured by some of the EIES evaluators. The Devices for the Disabled group reports a strong quantitative relationship with amount of use. Two other groups checked " + ", meaning qualitative evidence or a moderate positive relationship. These were Mental Workload and Hepatitis. In addition, we have a report from HUB of a " + ". The relationship with subjective satisfaction is generally reported to be at the same level, except for General Systems Theory, which reports no relationship for subjective satisfaction.

Combined with previous research reports, then, we can say that whenever the relative importance of a task has been studied, it has been found to be an important determinant of the amount of use of computer-mediated communication systems.

"Liking" for the task has results reported for five studies. The Hepatitis Knowledge Base evaluator reports quantitative evidence for a strong positive relationship for both amount of use and subjective satisfaction; for this group it is found to be even more important than the perceived relative importance of the task. On the other hand, for HUB there was no relationship found for amount of use and a weak positive relationship for subjective satisfaction. Devices for the Disabled reports a weak positive relationship for both aspects of acceptance, compared to the strong positive relationship for task importance. General Systems Theory reports the same level of predictive power as for task importance, and for WHCLIS there is some evidence of a positive relationship with subjective satisfaction. In sum, liking for the task seems to be generally important, but probably in most cases it is not as powerful a predictor as is the importance of the task. But in special circumstances where a user has many tasks that cry out for attention because of their importance (such as the Hepatitis researchers), the liking for the task may be a deciding factor.

Attitudes toward Computers

There are very mixed results for this variable. A strong positive relationship is reported for the Hepatitis group on EIES with subjective satisfaction, and a moderately positive one with amount of use. The OICS study reports a strong positive relationship with subjective attitudes toward the system. A moderate positive relationship is reported for amount of use and/or subjective satisfaction for the Devices for the Disabled group on EIES, HUB users, and NLS users studied by Bair. On the other hand, no relationship is reported for WHCLIS, and Hiltz (1981) found no overall relationship for the five EIES groups she studied. Whether the conflicting findings can be attributed to different indicators of attitudes toward computers, or to conditions or group characteristics which make this variable relevant, cannot now be determined.

Preuse Expectations about the System

This includes both general expectations about the system, such as the ease or difficulty of use, and specific expectations about its usefulness or impact on productivity. We are not sure how and when such expectations are formed, or how they may be influenced by training or publicity before users first sit down at the terminal and sign in. But users do report such expectations, and they sometimes have a powerful effect, influencing perceptions of the system and the amount of time and frustration which they are willing to invest in learning to use it.

For the EIES groups, the WHCLIS evaluation reports a strong positive relationship with the amount of use for both of these preuse types of expectations, and a moderate relationship with subsequent levels of subjective satisfaction. The LEGITECH evaluator found some evidence of a relationship with amount of use. The JEDEC evaluation reports a moderate relationship for both with amount of use. On the other hand, results for Devices for the Disabled show no relationship; and General Systems reports a weak negative relationship between anticipated usefulness and subjective satisfaction. Umpleby explains that those who expected little were pleasantly surprised, while those with great expectations felt some disappointment.

Turning to other systems, there are moderately positive relationships reported for HUB. The NLS study found a strong positive relationship between general preuse expectations and subsequent amount of use, and a moderate relationship between anticipated usefulness and subsequent use. The OICS study had only subjective satisfaction measures for correlation; there, both types of expectations were found to be moderately strongly related.

Both Bair and the Johnson-Lenzes point out specific aspects of expectations. The latter, in reporting the results of their study of JEDEC on EIES, found that interest in EIES itself as a communication medium was a very strong predictor. As part of their baseline questionnaire, JEDEC participants were asked an open-ended question about their reasons for participating in the project. Those who mentioned a belief in the potential of the communication medium itself as their first reason used the system much more than did others (Johnson-Lenz and Johnson-Lenz, 1980a:46). What Bair calls a "projected attitude" of not only liking the system at the beginning, but expecting that attitudes and liking will improve over time, was very highly correlated with the amount of use of NLS.

Attitudes toward the Group

Attitudes toward the group include such factors as whether one likes the members as persons, respects them as capable colleagues, and perhaps most importantly, trusts them and feels cooperative rather than competitive. For instance, the study of five scientific research communities on EIES (Hiltz, 1981) found that those scientists who felt that others in the group acted unethically and might "steal" one's contributions or ideas did not become heavy users of the system.

A related set of variables has to do with how a prospective user thinks that system use or nonuse will affect status within the group. We selected two aspects of this class of variables for inclusion in the data requests from the panel of evaluators: the perception of one's status relative to the group, and the perceived degree of pressure from group members to use the system.

Perception of Self with Respect to the Group

This variable has to do with the relative social status of the individual in the group. Does the user perceive the group as composed mostly of peers, of those with higher professional status, or lower professional status? It could be measured subjectively, as Hiltz (1981) did on a seven-point scale, asking for preuse perceptions of whether individuals felt they were ranked near the top of their field, about average, or were in a relatively unknown or newcomer status. It could also be gathered in terms of objective measures such as organizational rank of the members of a single bureaucracy, or citations to a scientist's work in a citation index.

It could be speculated that relatively lower-ranking members of a group would be motivated to use the system most, in order to make themselves more visible to the higher-ranking members and increase their status. However, Hiltz (1981) found no relationship between self-reported relative rank at preuse and subsequent amount of use of EIES for the five scientific communities she studied.

Unfortunately, none of the studies included in our survey covered measures of this variable.

Degree of Pressure to Use the System

One form of compliance pressure is to be ordered to use a system to enter or retrieve materials for others. The secretary usually fits into the high compliance pressure category, whereas managers and professionals usually choose whether or not to use a computer-mediated communication system for their work. Although there are of course many other differences between managers or professionals and secretaries, the amount of free choice versus compliance pressure may be one of the reasons why Panko and Panko (1981:18) found that whereas 71% of the managers and professionals using the system themselves had highly positive attitudes towards it, only 46% of the secretaries had highly positive attitudes.

For EIES, there were two groups for which measures of this variable were included in the studies. Hepatitis reported a strong positive relationship with both amount of use and satisfaction—that is, the evaluator found that the more pressure placed on the physicians to use the system, the more they used it and the more they liked it. On the other hand, no relationship was found for Devices for the Disabled. Bair included a measure of this variable in his NLS study, and reports a moderate relationship with amount of use. For HUB, a moderately strong positive relationship is reported for both amount of use and subjective satisfaction.

Once again, we conclude that the variable needs further study. Measures of different aspects or types of compliance pressure should be separated, and the conditions under which they are effective for increasing use and satisfaction determined.

Biographical Characteristics

Since many user groups do not include a wide variety of ages among their memberships, few studies have included age as a variable. When a relationship has been found, older users (above 50) generally tend to use the system least and have the lowest levels of subjective satisfaction. For instance, Open Systems (1981:7) reports that in an office automation pilot project at Hanscomb Air Force Base, "Workers over the age of 50 don't like the new approach and are worried about career aspirations because of it." There are, however, exceptions. For instance, among EIES general users, one woman in her 90s became an addict.

General Systems reports a moderately strong negative relationship between age and both amount of use of EIES and subjective satisfaction. Among other EIES user groups, no relationship is reported for Hepatitis and JEDEC, both of which were composed mostly of mid-career participants. A strong negative relationship is reported for the Swedish COM system between age and amount of use, and a moderate negative relationship between age and both use and subjective satisfaction for OICS. HUB trials found no relationship.

One possibility is that older users need lengthier or different kinds of training than younger users who are more likely to have previous experience with computer systems. On the other hand, it may be that older users are less likely to accept changes in their basic communication patterns, despite any special training efforts. But the fact that Danowski and Sacks (1980) report beneficial effects for aged users of a message system suggests that it may be worthwhile to invest in specially designed training sessions for older users to overcome any initial attitudinal or learning barriers.

Because most of these systems are used primarily at this time by male professionals and managers, there are generally not enough female subjects matched on other biographical characteristics for sex differences in acceptance to be statistically discernible. We generally have reports either that sex was not studied or that there was no relationship between the sex of the user and acceptance. But there may be a difference in style of use. Palme reports that women write more "letters," or private messages, and make fewer conference entries on COM.

With regard to level of education, we again have a limited range for most groups. Most users have had at least some college education. It may be that the minimum skill level of a high school graduate is required for these systems, but if a user group does not include lower educational levels, no relationship will appear between educational level and acceptance. No relationship is reported for JEDEC on EIES. For HUB, a moderately strong positive relationship is reported, but this is qualified by the comment that it refers to degree of education about computers, rather than general educational level. For COM, a moderately positive relationship is reported for level of use, and for

OICS, a moderately positive relationship for both amount of use and subjective satisfaction. We conclude that educational level, at least at a certain minimal level such as college education, may be a fairly important predictor of acceptance. However, the section below on "general literacy" provides evidence that children and others without a college education can use and like these systems.

Only one study included race or ethnicity as a variable. This may be because there are not a large number of persons representing other ethnic groups to use the variable, since most managers and professionals in Western nations are white males. HUB is the only system providing a data report, and it indicates no relationship.

Personality Factors

There has been little research on the relationship between personality factors and acceptance of computer-based communication systems. There is reason to believe, however, on the basis of qualitative observations and impressions, that basic personality characteristics and values do have predictive power.

Shneiderman (1980) reviews some personality traits and their conjectured relationship to programmer work styles:

> Assertive/passive. The assertive individual who is not afraid to ask pointed questions, is not intimidated easily . . . is often seen as the superior programmer type.
>
> Internal/external locus of control. Individuals with strong internal locus of control feel able to and seek to dominate situations. They feel they have the capacity to influence their world and control events. Individuals with external locus of control feel that they are victims of events beyond their control and are perfectly content to allow others to dominate them.
>
> High/low tolerance for ambiguity . . . . The early stages of program design and composition may require a higher tolerance for ambiguity . . . . Decisions must be made on limited data and there must be a willingness to take risks while proceeding on to the next decision (pp. 55-57).

Individuals who are assertive, have high internal control, and high tolerance for ambiguity probably will accept and use computerized communication systems more than those with the opposite traits.

In our synthesis questionnaire, introversion/extroversion and innovativeness/risk-taking were listed as variables under personality characteristics. WHCLIS reports a " + " for both personality dimensions. For the Hepatitis group, there was qualitative evidence of a positive relationship between innovativeness or risk-taking personality dimensions and acceptance of the system. HUB reports no relationship for introversion/extroversion but a " + " for innovativeness/risk-taking.

Bair's NLS study is apparently the only one which included scales generating quantitative evidence about the influence of personality characteristics. An "Organizational Climate Index" was used as a measure of personality and value characteristics. He reports finding strong positive relationships between introversion and both use and subjective satisfaction, as well as between innovativeness and both dependent variables.

Bair's earlier study (1974) reported that:

> Reactions seemed to correlate with the observer's assessment of personality type. Those who seemed to be closed minded were the most threatened by required use . . . . Also, those manifesting a high ego involvement with their work reacted more negatively than did others . . . . [Another] variable was one that is most obvious and generally true of any new tool—aggressiveness (generic use). The least aggressive subjects initially ignored the system. As the more inhibited persons saw their colleagues becoming involved . . . they responded to the pressure to become real AKWs ["augmented knowledge workers": people who could use the system well enough to enhance the effectiveness of their work] (p. 30).

In sum, we do not yet have enough evidence to know the full range of personality characteristics that may predict acceptance of these systems, or the most valid way to measure them in the context of user acceptance studies. However, the evidence to date indicates that personality characteristics may be important predictors and should be included in future studies.

Basic Values

The EIES evaluation of five user groups by Hiltz (1981) found weak support for a relationship between basic values and subsequent use. The preuse questionnaire contained sets of questions on two of the "pattern variables" used by Talcott Parsons (1951) and subsequent sociologists to characterize value patterns. These are "universalism–particularism" (whether scientists are judged solely by their work, or instead on the basis of who they are and personal relationships), and "affectivity–affective neutrality" (whether they are emotionally committed to their theories, or totally objective and emotionally uninvolved).

There are weak relationships which indicate a tendency for those responding at the "emotional commitment" end of the scales to use EIES more, and for those in the "balanced" area, between the relevancy and irrelevancy of personal attributes for judging scientific work, to use it more than those at either extreme. These results suggest possible relationships, but are not sufficiently strong or consistent to be conclusive.

Bair reports that for his NLS study, part of the Organizational Climate

Index measured basic values. This factor correlated at .62 with amount of use and .54 with subjective satisfaction, a strong positive relationship. McCarroll reports some relationship for the Devices for the Disabled group. She notes that if a user believes that information should be shared, then a greater obligation is felt to try a computer conferencing system as a way of implementing this value with actions.

We did not specify what we meant by "basic values" in our synthesis questionnaire, but simply asked for reports of any values that seemed to be correlated. None of the other studies included any value measures. Among those which might conceivably be related, in addition to the Parsonian "pattern variables" studied by Hiltz, are democracy and decentralization as opposed to authoritarianism or centralized control and decision making in organizations. Judging from the types of users who self-select to use EIES, the technology seems to have a strong appeal to those who value decentralization and participatory democratic decision making.

Communication Skills and Preferences

On the face of it, it would seem that since these systems are used by typing and reading, these skills should be related to system acceptance. However, this is not necessarily the case; as reviewed above, Hiltz (1981) found no relationship, and Edwards (1977) found typing speed correlated with subsequent amount of use only for those managers who initially had negative attitudes and expectations toward the system.

The findings are mixed. For Devices for the Disabled on EIES, there was no relationship between typing speed and amount of use or subjective satisfaction. The JEDEC study found no relationship between reading or typing speed and amount of use. However, the General Systems and Hepatitis groups found some evidence of a positive relationship between typing speed and acceptance measures, and the WHCLIS group data shows a strong positive relationship between typing speed and amount of use (Kerr, 1980, Table 14). For NLS users, Bair reports no relationship between typing speed and system acceptance measures; but for HUB, a moderately positive relationship is reported for both reading and typing speeds.

It would appear that within the context of certain types of tasks or an initial negative attitude toward a system, poor typing skills will be a barrier to acceptance. The fact that many studies show no relationship indicates that good typing skills are certainly not a prerequisite to acceptance of these systems. We need further specification of the conditions under which typing skills are related to acceptance, and of steps which can be taken to decrease the likelihood that poor typists will be reluctant to use a system.

Another aspect of communication skills is "general literacy," by which was meant facility with the written word. A person may not feel as skillful or persuasive when writing compared with when speaking, or may not have a sufficiently broad background to be able to assimilate the references and materials found though an on-line information exchange system. Unfortunately, practically no one included measures of this variable in a study. For the Hepatitis group on EIES, Siegel notes that since there was no variance, with all of the participants highly literate physicians, no observed relationship was possible. This is probably true of most of the user groups studied thus far. There is a report of a relationship for Devices for the Disabled on EIES. There, rather than interpreting general literacy in terms of facility with written English, the evaluator selected another dimension, the nature of research habits. She reports that those who generally make a practice of searching all available information sources when working on a problem are more likely to give the medium a serious try.

On the other hand, there are studies which indicate that high levels of literacy are not necessary in order to use and benefit from these systems. For instance, Danowski and Sacks (1980) studied a group of elderly subjects, most of whom probably had not attended college. And Kerr and Hiltz have current projects involving cerebral palsy and other young children. (See Kerr et al., 1979, for preliminary results; a more comprehensive evaluation is now in process.)

Previous Experience with Computers or Terminals

It might be hypothesized that those familiar with computers and computer terminals would accept computer-mediated communication systems more readily. For instance, it might seem logical that their initial learning time would be reduced. However, Hiltz (1981) found that there was no relationship between previous experience with computers or terminals and the time to learn the basic mechanics of EIES or to feel comfortable with the system. Only in the time reported to learn the more advanced features did previous computer experience make a difference. And Spang notes in her data report for HUB that previous use of a similar system may actually decrease the likelihood of accepting a different system with a similar function but new interface. Specifically, she notes that "If people are in the habit of using communication systems such as electronic mail, they find teleconferencing harder to accept." There is no standardization among systems, so that the commands or responses needed to perform a similar operation are different and users become frustrated by error messages given when a response from the familiar system is given to a new system. For example, in order to terminate a session, one might have to enter "logoff" for one system, "good bye" for another, and " – – " for a third. It could therefore be argued that "too much" previous experience could be negatively related to system acceptance.

Among the EIES groups, Devices for the Disabled reports no relationship. General Systems reports some evidence of a relationship, while Hepatitis and WHCLIS report a strong positive relationship. For JEDEC, the finding was that only one type of previous experience— using a computer terminal to play games—was positively related to the amount of subsequent use.

For the HUB system, there is both quantitative and qualitative evidence of a positive relationship between previous computer experience and both amount of use of HUB and subjective satisfaction with it. Since HUB includes a sophisticated package for modeling, previous experience might be particularly relevant. OICS, which has another fairly complex or sophisticated set of capabilities, also reports a strong positive relationship. Bair's study of NLS found a moderately strong relationship for amount of use, but what he terms a "surprising finding," a moderately negative relationship, for subjective satisfaction.

This leaves us with a thoroughly conflicting set of findings. For some groups and some systems, previous computer and terminal experience may contribute to acceptance, while for others, it is not related, or may even have a detrimental effect. What can be done to aid acclimation to a new system for those who have no previous experience at all and for those to whom the language and interface of another system is already second nature are important questions.

Some standardization of user interfaces would alleviate the problem of familiarity with one system hindering the learning of another. However, as we have seen in the Systems chapter, there is a great deal of disagreement among designers about optimal specifications for computer-mediated communication systems. It is likely to be some time before standardization among systems removes from the user the burden of remembering different "languages" for talking to different systems.

Access to Alternative Media

This variable refers to alternative means of communication with the on-line group, and their availability, cost, and feasibility. For example, is it possible to meet face to face without an unreasonable expenditure of travel time and money? How difficult is it for the members to communicate by phone? Are they generally at their desks when called, or is telephone ping pong the rule?

General Systems reports findings in the expected direction, that if there is "no access to alternative media, satisfaction increases." Hepatitis reports a similarly negative relationship with amount of use. OICS shows a " + " for subjective satisfaction and access to alternative media, but since this response form does not have any negative relationships indicated, we suspect that the " + " was used for a weak to moderate relationship of any kind. HUB reports a " + + " for both amount of use and acceptance.

Productivity and Work Patterns

It was hypothesized that high producers might be "workaholics" who would be more likely to enthusiastically embrace these systems as productivity-enhancing tools. However, the "productivity" entry on the acceptance module of our questionnaire seems to have been interpreted by some respondents as referring to a dependent variable rather than an independent one—that is, use of the system is reported as having increased productivity, whereas what had been intended by the item was the question of whether already highly productive people are more likely to accept such a system.

On a single cross-section, it is of course impossible to untangle cause and effect. Did highly productive workers use the system more, or did using the system make them more productive, or, probably, both? Whatever the direction of causation, those who do report a relationship generally find it to be either a strong positive one supported by quantitative data (NLS), or a moderately strong or qualitatively supported finding (JEDEC, OICS). The Hepatitis evaluator notes that a relationship was observed in the other direction: the group as a whole saw the use of EIES as boosting productivity on assigned tasks. The only exception is Devices for the Disabled, which reports no relationship.

Related to productivity are work patterns and duration. Is the person strictly a "nine to five" worker, or does he or she put in very long hours, including some night and weekend work? Those who work very long hours would be assumed to have higher levels of acceptance of or need for a computer-based communication system to support their work. In particular, it was assumed that those who do quite a bit of night and weekend work would especially appreciate the extension of support services to the 24-hour availability provided by such systems.

Work patterns are probably related to basic personality and lifestyle patterns. As Vallee *et al.* (1974b) point out:

> Teleconferencing fits well into the lifestyles of some people—they can do their job, make reports, and talk with colleagues wherever they are, regardless of time. They can work at home as well as at an office, and they can work at their own pace and time, which may be different from the standard 8:00 to 5:00 office job. For them, teleconferencing is a compatible and even liberating tool . . . .

> On the other hand, some people prefer· a scheduled, set work time and work space. Rather than finding it confining . . . they use it to focus their work attention and separate their job from the rest of their life (p. 99).

Length of the work day or work week as a correlate of acceptance was not included in most studies. Bair does report a strong positive relationship for NLS. Hepatitis reports a " + ". On the other hand, no relationship is reported for the Devices for the Disabled group.

The data are similar for night and weekend work as a correlate of acceptance, except that we have two additional studies supporting a relationship. The Devices for the Disabled group reports a positive relationship between night and weekend work and satisfaction with use of the system (though not with amount of use). And for JEDEC, if use of a terminal at home is taken as a proxy measure of use of the system nights and weekends, then there is a relationship with total amount of use that is significant at the .05 level.

In sum, the only way to untangle causality between work patterns and system use would be with a three- or more wave panel study that collected detailed data on productivity and work patterns before system use, after some system use, and after a great deal of system use. The available data do support the conclusion that high producers who work long hours and do some of their work nights or weekends are likely to use these systems more than their counterparts, and to be more satisfied with them as a means of communication.

GROUP FACTORS IN DETERMINING ACCEPTANCE

Size

In face-to-face communications, members of large groups tend to be more dissatisfied with group processes than members of smaller groups. Although resources expand with group size, allowing more efficient problem solving, there is a point of diminishing returns at which efficiency is reduced and consensus is more difficult to reach. The number of communication channels increases with group size, and large groups tend to break down into smaller ones. They tend also to be dominated by a few members, producing feelings of limited participation and decreased satisfaction for others (Kowitz and Knutson, 1980; Shaw, 1976).

These findings may not hold for computer-mediated group communications, in which the social dynamics are very different. If a group is too small, on-line activity is reduced, and the absence of new items when users sign on line can be a negative reinforcement discouraging use. On the other hand, too large a group generates so many communications that members are overloaded and unable to cope adequately; avoidance of the system may result.

Optimum size is a function of both the level of activity and the amount of structuring and filtering of the communications. For example, in the Topics subsystem on EIES, members are organized into "exchanges" and each exchange may have hundreds of Topics generating daily entries. However, members select only those topics of interest, so that most of the information is filtered out and does not overload the participants (Johnson-Lenz and Johnson-Lenz, 1981,Chapter 5; Stevens, 1980). In addition to or instead of special structures, larger groups may need stronger leadership or a different style of leadership than small groups. As Hare (1976:231)) points out, the larger the group, the greater are the demands placed on the leader for coordinating group activity.

Since most of the evaluations synthesized here involved only one group, it was not possible for evaluators to quantitatively test the effects of variations in group size on system acceptance. However, they could gather qualitative impressions of whether a group was too large or too small to function effectively.

Two of the largest EIES groups report a negative relationship between group size and amount of use of the system. General Systems Theory had more than 40 members at some points. It did not include any special structures to filter communications, and there was some complaint, especially by infrequent users, of receiving unwanted "junk mail" in the form of many waiting group messages when they signed on. LEGITECH, which grew to more than 70 members, reports a strong negative association. Although it had a special software structure, the evaluator reports that a small of number of members contributed almost all the text items. The more passive users may have been discouraged, or content to observe the information flow.

The evaluator for Hepatitis on EIES, which had about 10 members, reports a positive relationship between group size and both use and satisfaction. Apparently this group was near the lower limits of effective group size for this medium. The HUB evaluator observed a strong positive relationship between group size and both amount of use and subjective satisfaction, but no details are provided on the ranges of group size within which this relationship holds.

Degree of Geographic Dispersion

This refers to the distance separating the geographic locations of the members. It would seem that acceptance should increase with dispersion, since interaction is independent of location. But even those residing in the same geographic location may have communication needs similar to those who are separated. Particularly in large urban areas, they may not be able to meet regularly or reach each other on the telephone.

We asked the evaluators if they had any evidence to support the hypothesis that computer-mediated communication is best suited to geographically dispersed groups. HUB reports a strong positive relationship between the geographic dispersion of the group and acceptance of the system, and the Hepatitis group on EIES reports a strong positive association for amount of use and a moderate relationship for subjective satisfaction. Both the General Systems and the Devices for the Disabled groups on EIES report some evidence of a positive relationship for acceptance. Although not systematically queried on this topic, LEGITECH users did indicate that the presence of researchers from other states was an incentive to participate. And Bair notes that for NLS, "Although not addressed in the questionnaire, geographic dispersion was reported to (strongly) increase usage and satisfaction during extensive interviews and observations." Thus, the evidence completely supports the hypothesis that the more geographically dispersed a group, the more likely its members are to use a computer-mediated communication system and the more satisfied they are likely to be with it as a medium of communication.

Centralized versus Decentralized Control

This refers to the network for information exchange and decision making. At one extreme, a control locus regulates all information sent and received. The information flow is two-way between the control locus and members, but there is little or no direct exchange among the members themselves. At the other extreme, all members can interact freely and equally with each other.

Where speed and efficiency are important, centralized networks such as the wheel and chain patterns are superior to decentralized networks. For the solving of simple problems, centralized networks are more accurate, but complex problems are solved more accurately with decentralized networks. The most effective structure clearly depends on the group's needs.

Controlled experiments indicate that the medium of computerized communication seems to naturally support decentralized, egalitarian decision-making processes (Hiltz et al., 1980). Thus, it might be supposed that user groups which are decentralized or egalitarian in structure to begin with would adapt most readily to the medium. However, special "Groupware" may be employed to support centralized structures (see the previous chapter).

The results of the synthesis questionnaire support the conclusion that the medium can be adapted to either centralized or decentralized structures. The Hepatitis group on EIES had special procedures whereby all suggestions were first sent privately to the leaders for much of the project, with the leaders also controlling information on the outcomes of extensive voting. Siegel reports that this centralized process was positively related to both amount of use of the system and subjective satisfaction. General Systems also reports a positive relationship between centralization and amount of use. However, Devices for the Disabled reports a negative relationship, stating that "the more decentralized, the more tendency to use computerized conferencing."

Preexisting Communication Network

This refers to working relationships prior to conferencing, such as membership in a professional society or regular face-to-face meetings; these ties were probably the basis for forming the electronic group. Since prior ties imply a minimum level of familiarity among members, there should be fewer problems initiating and maintaining interaction on a new communication medium. The knowledge that one's peers are participating should increase acceptance. With no previous communication whatsoever, there are no ties upon which to build and possibly no felt need for communicating. But above a certain level, as, for example, with a group of co-located managers, existing communication channels may be so good that there is no felt need for improvement.

Bair's finding for NLS is that when the adequacy of the preexisting communication network is measured as an (unmet) "need to communicate," there is a strong positive relationship with amount of use and a moderately positive relationship with subjective satisfaction. However, the "need to communicate" is a composite variable rather than a pure measure of the nature and strength of preexisting communication channels. For OICS, there is a positive relationship with subjective satisfaction. HUB reports a positive relationship with both amount of use and subjective satisfaction. Among the EIES groups for which the variable was included—General Systems, Devices, Hepatitis, LEGITECH, and JEDEC—a positive relationship is reported for amount of use. For most of these studies, we do not know exactly how the nature and strength of the preexisting communications were measured. The measurement of such strength is reported for JEDEC (Johnson-Lenz and Johnson-Lenz, 1980a:62), which had quarterly face-to-face meetings. The strength of preexisting communications before system use was measured by how much the person reported communicating about JEDEC matters between these face-to-face meetings—not at all, a little, some, or a lot. Those who had communicated only a little between meetings also used EIES significantly less.

An explanation of the observed relationship is also reported for LEGITECH on EIES. Lamont notes that an initial core of users knew each other and had interacted before their use of EIES. They also wrote most of the comments in the group's policy conference, and seemed to be more satisfied with the system than those who had not communicated at all before their use of EIES. Finally, Umpleby comments that the same pattern was true for the General Systems Theory group: Those who knew each other before system use communicated more on line.

Leadership Style

Leadership functions include the "instrumental" task-oriented skills related to coordinating and motivating the completion of the group's task and the "social–emotional" functions of maintaining group cohesiveness.

Leadership style may be self-oriented (authoritarian) or group-oriented (egalitarian), with many degrees in between. An authoritarian leader's tendency to dominate the communication process is likely to decrease acceptance of the medium because of the reduced participation of others. The egalitarian leader appears to be effective in this medium. Generally, this leader encourages participation from all members, moves them to consensus and includes all those interested in the formation of policy. However, in the extreme, the members may be so equal that nothing is accomplished and the absence of a sense of direction confuses and frustrates members (Hare, 1976).

Hepatitis reports a strong positive relationship between leadership style and amount of use, and a moderate relationship with subjective satisfaction. All other studies which observed leadership style report a moderate relationship with amount of use: General Systems and the Devices groups on EIES, and NLS and HUB. General System reports no relationship for subjective satisfaction.

None of the studies report details on just what it is that constitutes an effective leadership style in this medium. A fruitful research project would be a content analysis of the "style" of communications used by successful and unsuccessful leaders of on-line groups.

Leadership Effort

This is easily measured by the amount of time spent on line. Ideally, one would also include the time spent off line thinking, planning, and communicating with group members, but this is less easily collected since the computer cannot automatically log off-line time. Some leaders are simply more active than others. The level of effort depends on the leadership style and the situation. Some may perceive a need for considerable interaction on their part, while others may feel that their activity could decrease participation by others.

The most active of the EIES leaders was in LEGITECH. By the beginning of June 1980, this leader had spent 1650 hours on line, about twice the amount spent by the next most hard-working or active leaders, who were in the Futures and General Systems groups. The LEGITECH evaluator reports qualitative evidence of a negative relationship between this very high participation rate by the leader and the amount of use and subjective satisfaction of the other group members. She notes that, in an attempt to bring a large number of researchers up to speed quickly and keep them informed of the status of the project, the leader contributed most of the conference items. Private message exchanges indicated that this decreased the enthusiasm of some of the other members to check in and contribute to the conference. What was perceived as "too much" leadership effort and activity "led first to information overload and then to a feeling of dissatisfaction." However, one unique aspect of computerized communications, compared to face-to-face meetings, lies in mechanisms to remedy such situations. Private messages served to define the problem and to allow the emergence of other leaders.

Other groups for which observations are available for leadership activity tend to report a moderately positive relationship between the amount of leadership effort and the acceptance of the system by the group members: the General Systems, Devices, and Hepatitis groups on EIES, and the HUB study. The only exception is Bair's study of NLS.

Based on the data, then, we can speculate that a kind of curvilinear relationship may exist between leadership effort and acceptance of a system by the other group members. Up to a certain point, the more the leader communicates on the system, the more the group members are likely to use it. But if the leader becomes extremely active, the other group members may feel deluged with information overload, or resentful of what appears to be domination of the proceedings.

Cohesiveness

Cohesiveness includes feelings of getting along, loyalty, pride, and commitment to the group. It is related to productivity, but only to the point at which extremely high cohesiveness is associated with low productivity. Vallee et al. (1975) refer to the relationship between motivation and participation in computer conferencing. Those users with high motivation and high personal stakes interact more often than do those who are less motivated.

We have divided cohesiveness into two main components: the types and density of social ties, and the affective or emotional components of these relationships among the members. Two aspects of the affective component have been singled out: the amount of competitiveness versus cooperation among the members, and the amount of trust.

Sociometric Ties: Type and Density

Social ties vary in their strength and intimacy, ranging from minimal familiarity with someone—having read published work or otherwise "heard of" the person—through working relationships and personal ties. Group ties may be diagrammed as a sociogram in which each person is a node and a line indicates a tie. With this system of representation, it can be seen if the ties divide the group into two or more distinct "cliques" or whether there is a single integrated group, and the proportion of isolates or those with no ties whatsoever can be observed.

It was hypothesized that groups with a greater density of ties prior to conferencing would use the system more. The most important kind of preexisting ties are probably minimal familiarity—having met or heard of someone—and existing working relationships. The former can be manipulated somewhat by having a face-to-face meeting prior to the use of the system, for groups in which the density of acquaintance is very low. This means convening the group in person before their first experience on line. For some groups, this is a structured part of the experience in which members can meet socially to discuss their plans for using the system. This variable can also be manipulated by having an explicitly social real-time "get together" on line at the beginning of a group's activities. Various EIES groups have successfully used this approach of on-line "cocktail parties."

One of the EIES groups (Social Networks) included in its evaluation a complete three-wave study of changing social ties, including one measure at preuse. Types of ties were measured at four levels of intimacy. Each participant was asked to designate those they had heard of or read publications by; those they had met or exchanged letters or phone calls or computer conferenced with; those whom they considered "friends"; and those with whom they had established "close personal" friendships. When the pre-use ties were diagrammed, two distinct friendship cliques were apparent, and there were many isolates who had no friends.

It was found that after using EIES, the density of all types of ties increased, there were fewer isolates, and the two distinct cliques became integrated into a more or less single friendship and collegial network (Freeman and Freeman, 1980). However, the study looks at density, cliques and isolates as dependent variables, or effects, rather than as predictors of acceptance. If comparable preuse measures were collected for all groups in the future, we might assess the effect of various levels of preexisting social ties upon subsequent acceptance of the system.

Those studies which did include some observation of the density of sociometric ties at preuse report that there is a positive relationship with acceptance. The studies reporting such data include Hepatitis, Devices, General Systems, and NLS.

Competition

Competition, as opposed to cooperation, is a group characteristic determining interdependent or individual activity by the members. Members of cooperative groups generally have higher morale, greater motivation and satisfaction with the task, and are more efficient and productive.

Hiltz (1981) included several questions on the overall amount of competition and the specific kinds of competition which characterized the various scientific specialty areas represented on EIES. Generally, there is no relationship between perceived degree of overall competition in a field and amount of use made of the system. However, "unfair" forms of competition are negatively related to system acceptance.

Only two groups report studying the degree of competition—HUB and the Hepatitis group on EIES. Both report a weak to moderate relationship. Thus, while competitiveness may pose some barriers to a group's acceptance and use of a system, it does not seem to be an important variable.

Trust or Openness among Members

One specific dimension of cooperation versus competition is the amount of trust group members feel toward one another and the degree to which they feel they can communicate openly. It would seem that the more trust among members, the greater the acceptance of the medium. There is really nothing but peer pressure to enforce the norm that ideas and information contributed by group members are the property of the author and are not to be used without permission.

Hiltz (1981) found that distrust of the motivations of others, as measured by the perception that some of the group members act unethically, almost invariably resulted in low use of the EIES system. The HUB and Hepatitis groups were the only ones indicating observations on trust, and both report a moderately positive or qualitatively supported relationship with acceptance measures.

OTHER DETERMINANTS

The data collection instrument also asked the researchers to list any factors which had been omitted from our list. Two potentially important determinants were reported: access to terminals and direct versus indirect use. These factors were added to a second round of data reporting for all studies.

Access to Terminals

The JEDEC study included several questions measuring access to terminals among participants, at their place of work and at home. It was found that:

> Those with their own terminals used the system far more. The observed difference between those who have their own terminal and those who must share one is significant at the .01 level. Sharing a terminal does not seem much better than having no access at all.

> The [data] showing average use level for those with and without home terminals further confirms this by showing that those with home terminals used the system much more . . . [In addition] participants were asked in the telephone follow-up interview to list obstacles to the effective use of EIES for JEDEC work. Seven people reported lack of a terminal as their first mention of an obstacle . . . all of these varied results seem to point quite clearly to the conclusion that convenient access to a terminal is essential for EIES use. Furthermore, anything that detracts from maximal access, such as not being able to take the terminal home or having to share it with another seems to result in a significant and substantial reduction in activity (Johnson-Lenz and Johnson-Lenz, 1980a:32-34).

Bair reports similar findings for the NLS study: a strong positive association between having a personal terminal and amount of use, and a moderate positive relationship with subjective satisfaction. Furthermore, he notes that the type of terminal is important, with the availability of high speed display terminals strongly predicting both use and satisfaction.

The final report on the study of NLS use at the Rome Air Development Center gives more detail on the importance of terminal access:

> Terminal availability is a crucial variable affecting the learning process. There is strong resistance to leaving one's work space to work in another or to physically carry a terminal to that area from some other work space. Ideally, every user would have his own terminal. This is not warranted by current usage levels here, nor is it feasible financially. However, it has become a problem to the point where it caused some people not to use the System (Bair, 1974:28).

For those who responded to this item, terminal access was unanimously reported to be positively related to amount of use. Having one's own terminal at one's place of work, as opposed to shared access with others, is particularly important; having a terminal to take home (or when traveling) is somewhat less strongly related.

Regarding the type of terminal, contrary to Bair's findings for NLS users, the Hepatitis evaluator reports that print capability was preferred to high speed CRT's, and that both were generally available to the participants.

Direct versus Indirect Use

Direct use refers to "hands on" use of the system, typing in and printing out all interactions. Completely indirect use means that usage is delegated to an intermediary such as a secretary who operates the system, typing in materials from handwritten notes or dictated drafts, retrieving and printing out waiting items, and delivering them to the group member. Generally, it is expected that interaction with a system primarily through an intermediary will be associated with lower levels of use and satisfaction. However, the availability of a secretary or other intermediary to enter long drafts or otherwise assume some of the mechanics of operating the system when there is a heavy workload or other problems might increase total use and satisfaction.

For WHCLIS, a strong correlation is reported between direct use of EIES (typing in material themselves versus delegating) and total amount of use of the system. On the other hand, Siegel found no relationship for the Hepatitis group.

TABLE 3-3

Summary Table of Acceptance Factors

Many Studies (5 or more)[b]	Few Studies (fewer than 5)[b]
Agree[a]	
Preexisting communications network (2 + +;6 +)	Task importance (1 + +;3 +)
Leadership style (1 + +;4 +)	Education (3 +;1 = 0)
Previous experience (4 + +;3 +;1 = 0)	Liking for task (1 + +;2 +;1 = 0)
Own versus shared terminal (3 + +;2 +)	
Expectations about system (3 + +;2 +;1 = 0)	Degree of pressure (1 + +;2 +;1 = 0)
Geographic dispersion (2 + +;3 +)	Innovativeness (1 + +;3 +)
Anticipated usefulness (3 + +;3 +;2 = 0)	Introversion versus extroversion (1 + +;1 +)
Terminal to take home (2 + +;2 +;1 = 0)	Basic values (1 + +;1 +)
Night or weekend hours (2 + +;3 +;1 = 0)	Perceptions of professional role (3 +;1 = 0)
Attitudes toward computers (4 +;1 = 0)	
	Type of terminal (2 +;1 = 0)
Disagree	Reading speed (1 +;2 = 0)
Typing speed (1 + +;3 +;3 = 0)	Previous productivity (1 + +;1 +;2 = 0)
Attitudes toward group (3 +;2 = 0)	Work hours/day or week (1 + +;1 +;1 = 0)
Age (1 − −;2 −;2 = 0)	Access to alternative media (1 + +;1 −)
Leadership effort (4 +;1 −;1 = 0)	Centralized versus decentralized (2 +;1 −;1 = 0)
	Size of group (1 + +;1 +;1 −;1 − −)
	Direct versus indirect use (1 + +;1 = 0)

[a] "Agree" means that 75% or more of the studies reporting results reported that the variable did predict acceptance (in terms of amount of use) and that there is agreement in the way in which the variables are related, positively or negatively.

[b] The numbers in parentheses summarize the observations. For example, "2 + +; 6 +" means that two studies reported a strong quantitative, positive relationship; six reported a qualitative or weak quantitative, positive relationship. A notation that "3 = 0" means that three studies found that the factor did not predict acceptance.

SUMMARY

There is sparse evidence about many of the determinants of acceptance of computer-mediated communication systems. The Futures study included none of the variables which we have reviewed; Mental Workload included only one; COM, only two, and several others, only a handful of the variables.

The evidence which we have collected and reviewed is summarized in Table 3-3. The two best predictors, based on existing evidence, seem to be a preexisting communication network which can create the demand for enhanced communication among the group members, and the nature of the leadership provided to the on-line group. Attitudes (expectations about the system and its potential usefulness), some previous experience with computer terminals, having one's own terminal, and the degree of geographic dispersion of the group are also predictors that have held across many studies.

CHAPTER 4

Impacts of Computer-Mediated Communications upon Individuals and Groups

INTRODUCTION

Almost 20 years ago, David Sarnoff predicted that computer technology would result in technological marvels and fundamental socioeconomic effects. In a speech to the 1964 Joint Fall Computer Conference, he stated:

> Tomorrow's standard computers and their peripheral equipment will instantly recognize a handwritten note, a design or drawing which they will store and instantly retrieve in original form. The computer of the future will respond to commands from human voices in different languages and with different vocal inflections . . . . The interlocking world of information toward which our technology leads us is now coming closer to realization. It will be possible eventually for any individual sitting in his office, laboratory, or home to query a computer on any available subject and within seconds to receive an answer . . . . This . . . will set in motion forces of change within the social order . . . . It will affect man's way of thinking, his means of education, his relationships to his physical and social environment, and it will alter ways of living (quoted in Theobald, 1966:41–42).

Summarizing Sarnoff's basic point, Theobald asserted that computer applications mean that we are passing from the industrial age into the "cybernetic age."

Sarnoff did not predict the use of computers for communication, and his predictions of particular technological breakthroughs that would aid such applications have not yet been realized. But to what extent do the predictions that computers would "alter our ways of living" hold true for observed impacts of computer-mediated communication systems? And are the observed impacts mostly for the better or the worse? This chapter explores these questions.

TOWARD A DEFINITION OF IMPACTS

Impacts are outcomes, effects, or consequences. They consist of significant social changes resulting from or spinning off from other changes. We are concerned here only with those technologically induced impacts that are directly linked to computer-mediated communication systems. Although impacts are frequently unanticipated consequences of other changes, we are attempting to predict them from present knowledge so as to be able to minimize or avert negative outcomes and maximize positive ones.

Impacts may be functional, dysfunctional, or neutral. The same change may have very different impacts on various subgroups, which need to be identified, and at different points in time.

Impacts are potential rather than predetermined, emergent rather than static, and conditional upon their context. They are dependent on the underlying social structure of the user groups and the design of the communication systems. "Groupware" is the configuration of group process and software, consisting of the use made of the system by individuals and groups plus the supporting and facilitating software. It refers to system design, or the presence or absence of specific system features, although some impacts are more design-sensitive than others. It also refers to the task or purpose of participation by different user groups, as well as the dynamics of the group context. The groupware variable raises such questions as: What are the effects on the user groups of different designs? Of different structures for organizing the flow of communication? Of different types of group process?

The larger constraining framework has been outlined by Hiltz and Turoff (1978b):

> The particular impacts to be found also depend on a complex interaction among at least four sets of factors:
>
> 1. What is being looked for, and how, and for how long. That is, choosing a level of impact and factors within it to focus on probably precludes finding other types of impacts. What is found in a study depends partly on how long it goes on; certainly, the behavior of users and the impacts of such use will be

much different after 5 years than after a 2–hour experiment . . . findings are going to be partially an artifact of the evaluation methodology chosen . . . .

2. Features and characteristics of the system itself, and its implementation. This includes the complexity, flexibility, and style of user interface of the system, as well as the print speed of the terminal used.

3. Application areas, that is, the kinds of groups that are using the system; for what purposes or services; and in what type of environment . . . .

4. Characteristics of the user and the immediate environment. Included here are user attitudes and motivation . . . ; user skills—reading and typing speeds, relative skill and preference for spoken rather than written communication; type of role played by conference moderators or other human facilitators on the system; and the total communication and work load of the user (pp. 261–262).

Impacts are also a function of factors both inherent in and extraneous to the electronic medium. They are dependent upon the cultural and social milieu, as well as the group and organizational context in which users are operating. Although it is not yet possible to anticipate all the antecedent and intervening variables which interrelate to determine or constrain impacts in specific situations, some additional factors that might affect the nature of observed impacts are access to the technology, communication needs, rewards or sanctions, and type of group membership (such as formal or informal, ascribed or achieved, compulsory or voluntary.)

PROCEDURE

A conceptual framework was constructed for studying the impacts of computer-mediated communication, recognizing that the development of a rigorous model was not a reasonable goal, given the current state of the art. We were willing to tolerate a certain amount of ambiguity or lack of conceptual rigor, aware that this is but a beginning. We began by identifying large areas of impacts and the systematic characteristics of usage under which they occur, after which specific impacts could be determined. As a consequence, we worked with a holistic methodology in which the emerging list of impacts generated the conceptual structure, which in turn created the awareness and consideration of additional impacts.

Literature reviews, findings from earlier studies, and the administration of data report instruments to evaluators provided the data with which we attempted to verify whether the hypothesized relationships did in fact exist. Verification sources thus included qualitative data (subjective impressions from observations, anecdotal data, and speculations) as well as quantitative data. Using experts within the field as the source from which to pool the results of myriad evaluations, we were one step removed from the actual subjects or users of these systems.

It was within these guidelines that we attempted to identify both past and future impacts of computer-mediated communication systems, while both nestling our conclusions in grounded data and speculatively peeking into the future. This was clearly an ex post facto, emergent and exploratory kind of methodology from which we believe testable hypotheses and controlled experiments will be derivable.

Table 4–1 shows the taxonomy of impacts within which the data were organized and examined.

Although the original plan was to divide each of these cells into immediate, short- and long-term impacts, superimposing the time dimension was not feasible for most of the impacts discerned. Similarly, it was decided at this point not to consider impacts according to specified systemic features or functions, but rather to explore computer-mediated communication systems as a whole. The refinement of this schema is one of the major needs of future research.

The impacts were divided into nine categories —by level (individual, group, and societal) and by type (cognitive, affective, and behavioral). Types of impacts were defined as follows:

Individual: Cognitive. Thinking and knowing (ideas, concepts, or information thought to be true or factual; values, opinions, or attitudes about things and ideas rather than about people).

Individual: Affective. Feelings (emotions such as sense of well being versus isolation, feelings of liking or disliking others); opinions, values, and attitudes about people.

Individual: Behavioral. Doing: individual communication styles and patterns; effectiveness of such communication or work patterns for individuals.

TABLE 4–1

Impact Categorizational Schema

Type of Impact	Cognitive	Affective	Behavioral
Individual	1	2	3
Groups, organizations, communities	4	5	6
Institutions and society	7	8	9

Group: Cognitive. Ideas, purposes, goals; group and intellectual resources; group norms and values; social definitions of truth.

Group: Affective. Informal structure (affective feelings of liking or disliking others); group cohesion; attitudes towards purposes and goals.

Group: Behavioral. Relationships with other groups, organizations, and the community; the nature and effectiveness of communication processes; and organizational features including formal and informal structure.

Society: Cognitive. Political; goals, purposes, values, and thoughts; basic ideas of society; knowledge, values to specify changes in societal and political ideas; skills, science and technology.

Society: Affective. Attitudes toward culture and goals; nature of life and society; feelings such as alienation; changes in intergroup relationships of liking and disliking; values and meanings about people (rather than about things or ideas).

Society: Behavioral. Political behavior such as lobbying or otherwise to influence the polity; economic; societal level of communication processes and outcomes; changes in social patterns and institutions.

In discussing observations and findings with evaluators, we realized that very few had any data on the societal level. Existing field trials and experiments have involved only relatively small numbers of users in a few organizations. Trying to project the findings of these small-scale studies to a situation in which most of a society is connected by computer-mediated communication systems is at this point a very speculative enterprise. Therefore, while recognizing that societal-level impacts will ultimately be the most important, we limited our survey to those levels for which there are existing data: the individual and group levels (cells one through six in Table 4–1).

A list of possible impacts, derived from the research literature and our collective experiences, was developed. The typology was refined and the questionnaire was written on line. The list was subsequently elaborated, refined, and categorized by "voting" on the cell in the taxonomy into which each impact best fit. Definitions of the cells were formed and modified in the process. It was then distributed as a data-gathering instrument to a group of experts for their validation, data, and comments.[1]

[1] They were asked to report findings for their studies as follows:
" + + ", strong supportive quantitative evidence;
" + ", weak quantitative evidence or only qualitative evidence;
"0", evidence was neither supportive nor refutive;
" − ", qualitative or weak quantitative refuting evidence; and
" − − ", strong refuting quantitative evidence.

One of several difficulties with the review of the existing literature is that it frequently does not distinguish between the type of methodology, the design of the system being used, the application areas, or the characteristics of the users and their immediate environment. Although the literature is fairly extensive, it is scattered, some is out of print, and much has not been formally published. Existing studies tend to be either application-oriented or conjectural discussions of potential impacts upon subgroups.

The list is by no means considered exhaustive. We are still unable to state many of the possible impacts with a comfortable degree of precision, while other impacts imply more than could be specified in simple questionnaire statements. Precise definitional and conceptual boundaries do not yet seem possible.

We hope that one of the future outcomes of this research will be the further structuring and categorization within each cell, beyond ordering the lists in terms of magnitude as was done here. For example, at the group level, it should be possible to arrange the impacts by effects on problem-solving activities, effects on group structures, and effects on group relationships, by time, and by the interrelationships among the impacts themselves.

COGNITIVE IMPACTS ON INDIVIDUALS

Impacts of computer-mediated communication systems upon individuals are categorized into cognitive, affective, and behavioral levels.

Cognitive impacts are those involving thinking and knowing. They consist of ideas, concepts, or information thought to be true or factual, as well as values, opinions, and attitudes about things and ideas rather than about people.

Below is the list of hypothesized cognitive impacts at the individual level which was submitted to our group of experts:

1. Computer-based communication systems create new perceived needs for information.
2. Continuing education and Computer Assisted Instruction (CAI) expand learning over a lifetime for many.
3. Learning occurs by the written word rather than through audio and visual media.
4. It requires new skills.
5. It discriminates in favor of the literate (writers, typists, etc.)
6. It increases the variety of ideas.
7. It may improve spelling and typing.
8. Literacy and information processing abilities improve.

9. Personal goals change with greater awareness of the global situation.
10. It expands "effective scope": the number of alternatives, pertinent stimuli, awareness of social and cultural horizons.
11. Users are able to deal with larger amounts of information more efficiently.
12. Because the volume of information can become overwhelming, it increases the possibility of information overload.
13. Because information overload requires periodic reassessment of goals and priorities, there is a reduced tendency to follow traditional patterns.

These items suggest that mental constructs undergo change as users become familiar with the medium. Communicating via computer impacts upon the ways in which people think. The greater the duration of exposure, the greater are the likelihood, frequency, and intensity of such impacts.

Discrimination in Favor of the Literate

Computerized communication discriminates in favor of the literate and educated, since it is grounded in writing and reading skills. Those already accustomed to dealing with words, ideas, and conceptual models will have a major initial advantage. Over time, as new generations begin to take computerized communication for granted, it will continue to act as an impetus into the world of ideas and away from the world of things. As an integral part of the communication-information age, computerized communication expands cognitive worlds.

The expert panelists who examined this impact found supporting evidence, with the exception of two studies which found no evidence one way or the other. COM reports strong quantitative evidence ("$+ +$"), whereas the others had weak quantitative evidence or qualitative evidence ("$+$") that this occurred in the predicted direction. The COM evaluator, Adriansson, found that more than 80% of both new and experienced COM users agreed with the statement that "Those who are good at written communication are favored." The CONFER evaluator comments that this is a tautology, and NLS has strong anecdotal data to support it. The JEDEC evaluators examined several components of literacy, however, and found no empirical support (Johnson-Lenz and Johnson-Lenz, 1980b:36–38).

Typing skills, as a component of literacy, produced comments. OICS reports that regression equations showed knowledge of typing to be an asset. The Devices for the Disabled group examined the impact but found no relationship ("0"), noting that although typing skill sometimes makes a difference, the data are not consistent. JEDEC also reports "0", with the finding that typing speed is an advantage not supported by the data.

Handling Larger Amounts of Information

Users are able to deal with larger amounts of information more efficiently. They can exchange far more information in a given time span than would be possible with conventional media (Vallee and Askevold, 1975:59; Turoff, 1972:163), and can sift through masses of information on complex issues. The individual's capacity to absorb and process information is greatly expanded (Bezilla, 1980a:1). The use of hypertext and various ways of structuring stored information can be greatly beneficial.

This hypothesized impact produced a mixed response from the panelists. OICS reports a " + + "; four others report " + " (General Systems, Hepatitis, CONFER, and NLS); two report a " − ", meaning that they studied the impact and found a moderate to weak negative relationship opposite to that described; and the Mental Workload group reports a stronger " − − ", meaning that there was strong quantitative evidence refuting the impact. The negative finding for the Devices for the Disabled group is attributed to information overload. The evaluator notes that it "seems to take a long time to learn how to deal with the amount of communications active users generally receive." The Legitech comment is similar: "Users were not used to the great amounts of information coming to them. Only a few seemed able to organize their offices in such a way as to develop a more efficient communication system to deal with the overload." This would suggest then, that for some users, efficiently dealing with larger amounts of information is a longer-ranged impact possibly learned by extended experience with the medium. Attributes of the medium itself are suggested by the NLS evaluator, whose " + " response is said to be "due to the unique capabilities of NLS to structure stored text (including messages)—'hypertext,' and the use of high-speed displays."

Although not responding to this item on the data report, the COM evaluation did include questions on two components of the ability to handle larger amounts of information. More than 80% of COM users agreed with the statements that "information is easier to disseminate" and "information reaches more people."

Learning via the Written Word

Learning occurs by the written word rather than through audio and visual media. This may be because written material can be more effective for communicating factual information, as a result of its precision and greater comprehension (Rice, 1980:24). Only two respondents reported studying this impact. General Systems Theory reports a confirming "+" with no comment. OICS has strong quantitative evidence of this impact, but appears to focus the response on learning the system itself rather than more general long-term learning. ("Training was leader-led instruction with hands-on administration. Physical and on-line user materials provided.") The respondents may have perceived more than one dimension in the question as stated.

New Information Needs

With easy access to remote resources, these systems may create new perceived needs for information. As geographic distance is removed as a major barrier to dialogue, access to both consultant and data base resources could become limitless (Johansen et al., 1979:20–21).

The findings of the OICS evaluation are especially illuminating since they contradicted the initial hypothesis that the disparity between perceived "information needed" and "information received" would decrease:

> There were a number of improvements between the pretest and the posttest in the perceived "information received." But the perceived "information needed" increased correspondingly. These findings suggest as access to information improved for the pilot group, expectations increased, as did perceptions of what was required (Tapscott, 1981:13).

Seven respondents to this item were in agreement, checking "+" or "++". McCarroll, commenting on the Devices for the Disabled group, says there is "qualitative evidence from discussions and comments— perceived need for information increases, upon realizing more is being done in the field than some individuals are aware of—primarily therapists and consumer groups affected this way." The only deviant data was from the Mental Workload group which reports a "− −" to indicate strong quantitative evidence of a negative impact.

Information Overload

New information sources are not without cognitive cost. The volume and pace of information can become overwhelming, especially since messages are not necessarily sequential and multiple topic threads are common, resulting in information overload (Vallee et al., 1978:123–124; Johansen et al., 1979:137–138). Information overload presents itself first as a problem, then as a constant challenge to be overcome. Intensive interaction with a large number of communication partners results in the mushrooming of the absolute amount of information and the number of simultaneous discussions, conferences, and other activities well beyond normal coping abilities. System features to enable users to effectively deal with this form of mental distress include filters, associations, keys, alarms, reminder files, word and text processing, user-defined functions, automatic collections, and search and retrieval capabilities. These are supplemented by learned habits and skills of individual users, who must periodically reassess goals and priorities, such as selectivity, organization, filtering, and time management. There is a drain on mental energy for those who do not succumb to overload and a mental expansion for those who meet the challenge.

Most of the panelists supported this impact with moderate to weak quantitative evidence or qualitative evidence (" + "). The Devices for the Disabled group notes that "Many users (were) not able to keep up with messages or conferences." Legitech points to user comments that this was a problem in messages and conferences; however, a filtering mechanism was established with Inquiry/Response software to ease information overload. The two respondents reporting conflicting negative findings (" − ") suggest the group-dependence of this impact. One was the Hepatitis group on EIES, which had relatively strong leadership and a specific task to accomplish, which in combination may have mitigated the problem of overload. The negative finding from NLS is attributed to factors specific to that system: hypertext, high-speed displays, and unique text structuring and storage capabilities.

Reduced Tendency to Follow Traditional Patterns

Because information overload requires periodic reassessment of goals and priorities, there is a reduced tendency to follow traditional patterns. The literature review did not include this issue, and of the five experts responding to this item, two (NLS and OICS) found no impact ("0"). Mental Workload reports a " + + " and both the General Systems Theory and Hepatitis groups report " + ", but with no comments. Although this coping mechanism may be a possible longer-range solution to the problem of information overload, the relatively short-term studies conducted thus far do not fully confirm it.

Improvement in Literacy

Literacy and information processing abilities improve. People can think more clearly without the pressure to respond immediately. With more control over the use of one's time and more information easily available, cognitive energies can be invested more efficiently. Housman

(1980:5) observes the "very powerful 'intellectual enhancement' effect made possible by such close linkage of minds . . . . Ideas get bounced around, criticized, and enhanced very rapidly and there is generally no hesitance to throw out a 'wild' idea or a severe criticism." Each of the four respondents to this item indicated agreement. OICS, however, qualifies this to refer to information processing abilities only and not literacy. And Bair of NLS attributes this impact to the unique features of that system.

Requirement of New Skills

Learning of new communication skills can become an unending process for users of computer-mediated systems (Vallee et al., 1978:157–159). Skills such as typing, spelling, and facility with the written language improve, as do conceptual abilities and intellectual work habits. Data indicate that skills increase directly with use of the system (Hiltz and Turoff, 1978a). Reporting the results of a set of laboratory experiments comparing face-to-face decision-making groups with computerized conferencing groups, Hiltz observes:

> In regard to gaining skill, users soon learn to take advantage of the unique pos-
> sibilities for presenting complex arguments or sets of information by using out-
> lining and indentations and by constructing directional diagrams with boxes and
> arrows . . . . They learn to very skillfully use the retrieval and editing capabilities
> of the computer to re-use and rearrange stored materials for new purposes (Hiltz,
> 1978b:13).

The respondents generally agreed, with the Devices for the Disabled group providing firm quantitative support. Other needed skills mentioned are understanding the logic of the system (Legitech) and learning to be comfortable while interacting on a computer terminal (CONFER). Only the Mental Workload group indicated a "0" for the absence of either supporting or refuting evidence.

Improvement in Spelling and Typing

Spelling and typing skills may be improved. However, we found no mention in the literature of this projected impact, and very mixed results in our panel: Two groups report " + ", two " – ", and two "0". Bair notes for NLS that it increases carelessness, which has also been observed on EIES. But the potential exists when perfect formal copy is needed, aided by built-in word processors and spelling correction programs.

Increased Variety of Ideas

Organizations and people learn more and more quickly of events of interest to them:

Computer conferencing provides a continuous, content-rich stream of useful information. Traditionally, people who receive a lot of information receive it in chunks: conferences, seminars, journals, papers, magazines, books, correspondence and occasional conversations. Users of computer networks, on the other hand, receive a steady stream of information, directed specifically at their interest, and often referred their way by peers or colleagues (Bezilla and Kleiner, 1980).

Martino and Bregenzer (1981) reporting on the impacts of the Futures group on EIES, state:

It was often startling to see the variety of views presented, and the vigor with which they were both attacked and defended. The conference probably made all participants much more aware than they had been previously of the variety of opinions held by Futures Researchers, on a great many topics (p. 361).

The panel of experts generally agreed. Each rated it with a " + " except for the Hepatitis group which accorded it a " + + ". The only exception again was the Mental Workload group which reports a " − − " for a finding in the opposite direction. Lamont explained Legitech's position: "By its inquiry/response structure, it increased the variety of responses to questions by calling on state/federal agencies not usually approached for answers."

Lifetime Learning

Continuing education (through computer-mediated communication systems) and computer-assisted instruction (CAI) could expand learning over a lifetime for many. Ideally, this involves embedding CAI systems within communication structures for interactive lessons, with built-in reinforcements and self-paced learning, connecting the student with both the teacher and peer group, and would most benefit the handicapped, incarcerated, and rural dwellers (Turoff and Hiltz, 1977:7; Hiltz and Turoff, 1978b). Although CAI and video education frequently have fallen short of expectations, combining the programmed individualization of the computer with the dynamics of video could produce exciting and innovative teaching methods (Bezilla, 1980b). Potentials include tailored learning experiences and individualized learning networks (Johansen et al., 1979:126–127). Demographic projections of shifting age, household, geographic, and economic characteristics also point to a possibly increased use of teleconferencing for CAI, given its advantages of cost, flexibility, and accessibility (Johansen et al., 1978b:43–65). Institutions of higher education will be better able to meet the continuing challenges of falling enrollments and older students returning to school, particularly if their flextime jobs require course offerings at a distance from the traditional centrally located campus. Individualized educational packages tailored to personal lifestyles and career aspirations will be possible (Scher,

1980). Only three evaluators responded to this item, possibly because it implies a future projection rather than a current reality. But two gave it a " + " and one a " + + ".

Expanded Effective Scope

Cognitive transmission and human memory are enhanced by the power of the computer to aid in organizing, synthesizing, analyzing, and presenting ideas. Improved cognitive retention and the ability to structure and precisely present complex ideas are made possible with the availability of a written modifiable transcript of the proceedings, the ability to search and retrieve past items, graphic capabilities, and asynchronous participation. The accuracy, efficiency, and timeliness of ideas and information are greatly improved (Turoff et al., 1978:46–47). There is not only more time for reflecting on ideas, but also the ability to revise, review, and edit previous entries, as users may be able to deal with larger amounts of information more efficiently. Positive support was obtained from the panel, with all rating it a " + ". Thus, "effective scope," or the number of alternatives, pertinent stimuli, and awareness of social and cultural horizons, is greatly expanded.

Change in Personal Goals

Personal goals can change with growing awareness of the global situation. A more enhanced world view can alter individual aspirations and expectations. The literature review gave no clue to this, but all the experts except one support it with a " + "; the exception was OICS which reports no relationship.

Summary

Advanced users of computer-mediated communication systems can take advantage of the processing power of the computer as an integral part of the communication process, by developing customized command interfaces, designing forms to collect and disseminate formulated information, writing adaptive text that permits the reader to indicate whether other material is desired, as well as by performing various processing computations on the information produced in these ways (Hiltz, 1978c:7). Such enhancements of the ability to seek, process, store, manipulate, and disseminate information increase the efficiency of intellectual work. For instance, about 80% of experienced COM users agreed that the "efficiency of work routines" increases. It also makes possible new forms of large-scale collaboration and cooperation in "knowledge work."

The development of new cueing mechanisms to replace the absence of nonverbal cues in the electronic medium has cognitive implications. Although the absence of nonverbal cues (such as smiles, gestures, and body language) is frequently perceived by new users as a troublesome barrier and although they complain of the lack of accuracy of their cueing perceptions and the seeming thinness of computerized communication compared with face-to-face communication, there are offsetting advantages. Communication may be asynchronous. And computer-mediated communication fully utilizes the computational, memory, and processing functions of the computer such that users have full control over both the spaces and times that are occupied at any given point or according to any self- or group-defined sequence. In an important sense, it is possible to be in more than one place at a time and to be in several times at one place (Kerr and Bezilla, 1979).

> The net effect may be described as a heightened sense of personal interaction. Not with a machine, but with a more rational, structured world where users possess greater control over multidimensional interactions that seem more efficient, more information-laden, more promising, less confining than those enjoyed through conventional media (Bezilla, 1980c:30).

As cognitive abilities expand, this may be a new threshold toward rationality. Certainly, more rational means for evaluating information are available (Bezilla, 1980a:1). Kochen (1981:148–150) includes problem solving, memory, information processing, and extended analytical reasoning abilities within the overall category of the amplification of cognitive abilities. Scenarios drawn by other futurists conflict in their visions of how these possibilities will be used.

Table 4–2 is a summary table which considers the amount of agreement or disagreement among the panel of experts, as well as the size of the sample from which the conclusion was drawn. Within cells, the impacts are ordered by the amount of consensus. For example, the expansion of effective scope produced unanimous agreement, whereas three of the panelists offered contradictory evidence to the hypothesized impact that users are able to more efficiently handle larger amounts of information. "Agreement" here signifies the absence of any dissenting votes. Those items appearing within the "disagree" category have at least one " – " from the panelists, but those at the top of this list tend most toward agreement.

The overall pattern suggests that the more socially significant cognitive impacts, such as those including conceptual skills and learning, generated support, whereas those which may be more trivial, such as spelling and typing skills, and those which are clearly negative in impact, such as information overload, are much lower on the list.

In terms of fruitful areas for further research, the top right and bottom

TABLE 4–2

Individual Cognitive Impacts

Many Studies[a]	Few Studies[b]
Agree	
Expands effective scope $(8+)$	Literacy improves $(1++;3+)$
Requires new skills $(1++;8+;1=0)$	Lifetime learning $(1++;2+)$
Discriminates in favor of the literate $(1++;7+;2=0)$	Learning via the written word $(1++;1+)$
Personal goals change $(5+;1=0)$	
Reduced tendency to follow traditional patterns $(1++;2+;2=0)$	
Disagree	
New information needs $(2++;5+;1--)$	
Increases variety of ideas $(1++;6+;1-)$	
Information overload $(2++;6+;1=0;2-)$	
Improves spelling and typing $(2+;2=0;2-)$	
Handling larger amounts of information $(1++;4+;2-;1--)$	

[a] 5 or more.
[b] Fewer than 5.

left cells are most promising. Impacts in the top left cell of the summary table are so solidly supported by a large number of studies that further work is not likely to add much to our knowledge. Those at the bottom left, where existing studies have yielded contradictory findings, might best be further explored with quasiexperimental or experimental designs that probe the conditions under which the sometimes observed impacts do or do not occur.

The numbers in parentheses summarize the observations. For example, "$1++;5+;1--$" means that one study reported a strong quantitative positive relationship; five reported a qualitative or weak positive relationship; and one had strong negative quantitative evidence. A notation of $2=0$ means that two studies found no relationship.

AFFECTIVE IMPACTS ON INDIVIDUALS

Computer-mediated communication can have significant consequences at the level of individual affect. Affective impacts upon individuals involve feelings and emotions, such as senses of well-being or isolation and liking or disliking others. Also included are opinions, values, and attitudes toward people. This is the list of hypothesized affective impacts administered to the panel of experts:

1. Computer-based communication systems have the potential for addiction.
2. As addiction and heavy usage increase, they create distance or isolation from close relationships outside the electronic medium.
3. Friendships can endure longer.
4. Terminated friendships will be more a function of changed interests than distance.
5. Friendship ties resolidify to counter residential mobility.
6. Computer-based communication can increase affective ties and sense of personal interaction.
7. However, participants sometimes feel a lack of group interaction and interpersonal feedback: Those who need or want immediate feedback might be frustrated, at least in the short run.
8. Computer-based communication increases the number and strength of support systems: kin, friends, the availability of professional help.
9. Computer-based communication supports self-presentation and emotional subtleties.
10. Computer-based communication introduces new sources of stress; for example, with more potential time together, family life might be strengthened or there might be more divorce and domestic violence; new sources of stress for individuals as work-day can expand, priorities change, and new social networks connect people in new ways.
11. Computer-based communication can enhance the candor of opinions.
12. Computer-based communication increases status relative to peers without access to it.

If the challenge of information overload is not dealt with, discomfort with the electronic medium and inability to cope with its output may produce avoidance of the system, manifested in infrequent, reluctant, or ineffective usage, or dropping out. Data accounting for this low level of participation are not yet available.

Because communication channels are restricted to the transmission of typed words and nonverbal cues are absent, the technology is often perceived initially as impersonal and cold. The possibilities for perceiving an absence of personal contact and group interaction (Ferguson and Johansen, 1975:39–40,56) and consequent felt remoteness from the group reduce the likelihood that the social and emotional needs of new or inexperienced users will be met and could permit reduced interaction, social isolation, or anomie. Two examples are quoted in a review of electronic mail systems:

> There can be a sense of remoteness . . . . People will sometimes feel a little lonesome and miss phone conversations (Lasden,1979:56).

> Every once in a while we have to tell our home workers to come in and rejoin society because their messages start becoming paranoid . . . they'll show increased levels of anxiety and misunderstanding (Lasden, 1979:58).

Offsetting evidence is offered by a full-time consultant on the EIES system:

> Sometimes I do miss the "coffee breaks" that would be a part of a normal office working environment. Because, yes, sometimes working this way is lonely. The tradeoff, however, is well worth it. My work literally spills over into the rest of my life . . . . Most people, including some of my friends, don't understand. To me, this is a far saner way of living than I've ever had before (quoted in Kleiner, 1980:535).

Potential for Addiction

Computerized communication systems have the potential for addiction. Because they can provide a steady source of needed information, links with those sharing common interests, rapid feedback, and an efficient use of time and energy, some users find themselves spending ever-increasing amounts of time on line, and this time is given increasing salience and priority over other activities.

Observations and interviews with users of a number of computerized conferencing and electronic messaging systems yielded descriptions of the compelling quality of the medium and the gradual non-debilitating addiction of some users. Addiction is defined as "returning to the terminal, more than . . . work or information needs alone would at first seem to justify," and may be "one of the first harbingers of change in attitudes and habits in the Information Age." Only qualitative evidence now exists:

> This list of addiction symptoms [was] "seconded" by a chorus of other users:
>
> 1. Signing on at least several times a day ("Maybe something is waiting").
> 2. Physical irritation when system is inaccessible.
> 3. Preference shown toward composing thoughts and writings on line.
> 4. Preference towards developing concepts on line.
> 5. Preference towards conducting collegial relationships on line.
> 6. Signing on "just one more time" before going to sleep.

> Many users first notice they are addicted when they have to pay or account for their own network connect time. Others notice when they find themselves staying late at the office to catch up on the work they missed because they were using the terminal. Others do not have to notice; they have co-workers, friends, spouses or children who notice for them, jealous of the time the user spends on the system . . . . But some users . . . only notice that they are addicted when the system goes down. "You know you've had it when your fingers start drumming on the tabletop," one user said (Bezilla and Kleiner, 1980).

The respondents generally supported this impact, with the exceptions of General Systems which found unspecified conflicting evidence and OICS which found no relationship in either direction. Comments from the nine reporting a positive relationship include observation of heavy usage, people missing the system when they could not access it, burn-out, and other anecdotal data.

Creation of Isolation

Heavy usage and possible addiction can create distance from primary relationships external to the electronic medium:

> While computer network addiction is not dangerous, it can create problems for the user. Spending so much of one's time with any medium . . . will certainly displace time from other activities. The two areas that are most likely to lose an addict's attention are working situations that are off the terminal, and friendships and personal relationships with those who are not on-line (Bezilla and Kleiner, 1980).

Bezilla and Kleiner predict that "this problem may resolve itself when most of an addict's work and personal life is accessible via terminals, and computer networks become just another communications tool, as ubiquitous and taken-for-granted as the telephone."

The experts were apparently less sure of this impact. The five responses were spread from " + " through " − ". Hepatitis and Mental Workload indicated " + ". A " − " is reported by the NLS group which commented that users denied this, and by OICS which notes that face-to-face communication remained at the same level. COM indicated very mixed responses to this item.

New Sources of Stress

Computer-mediated communication systems introduce new sources of stress as traditional lines are blurred, workdays expand, priorities change, and new social networks connect people in new ways. Family life might be strengthened with more potential time together, easier access to the extended family, and flexible schedules, especially for child care:

Telecommuting would enable the parent responsible for child care to have a flexible schedule. Since this is usually the wife, it would mean that women could work without the constant crisis of what to do if the school closes for holidays or the child is sick or the babysitter does not come. Moreover, with the main wage earner working in or near the home, he or she can spend more time with other family members, and conceivably perform a greater share of the household maintenance tasks (Hiltz and Turoff, 1978b:481–482).

Alternatively, there might be increased domestic strain, violence, and divorce. The ability to work from home could mean that family life would not be a refuge from office pressures. People could be more vulnerable to intrusions from co-workers via their terminals, or less so because they controlled the frequency of signing on line. New norms are likely to develop, analogous to the circumstances under which it is acceptable to phone people at home rather than at work.

Reactions of the spouses and children of current members of these systems to use of the terminal at home range from enthusiasm and supportive acceptance to jealous resentment and a major source of tension if they do not accept, or feel threatened by, the new networks (Hiltz, 1981: Chapter 5). These attitudes and their consequences can change over time. Qualitative observations and anecdotal information represent the only source of data in this area at the moment.

The experts generally supported this impact with four " + " responses, and only one " − " from the Futures group. NLS, although not examining this item, comments that "indications do suggest this."

Lack of Feedback Frustrating

Negative affect can change over time. New users are frequently frustrated by the absence of immediate feedback which accompanies asynchronous interactions (Vallee et al., 1978a:123; Johansen et al., 1978:94–95; Umpleby, 1980:5). But the data indicate that:

The desire to have truly synchronous conferences seems to almost totally disappear as experience is gained on the system. What seems to happen is that many new users like the immediate feedback and replication of face-to-face conversational conditions that the synchronous conference provides. Experienced users, however, find it most annoying to have to interact at a time and pace of somebody else's choosing! (Hiltz, 1979).

The panel of experts was asked if users sometimes feel a lack of group interaction and interpersonal feedback, such that those who need or want immediate feedback might be frustrated, at least in the short run. Positive responses were received from five of the EIES groups, with a sixth reporting no observed relationship. Representatives from the other systems surveyed were more mixed in their responses (one positive, one negative, one "0"), suggesting that system features may play a role in this impact.

Support of Self-Presentation
Enhancement of Candor of Opinions

The medium can support self-presentation and emotional subtleties, as well as enhance the candor of opinions (Vallee and Askevold, 1975), in part because users alone at their terminals may feel freer to express themselves (Hiltz and Turoff, 1978b:27–28). Day (1975:60) reports that anonymity permits the frank but less emotional discussion of issues: "This interpersonal forum removes some of the 'threats' associated with normal human interaction. Individuals try out 'dumb' ideas without fear of their judgment being questioned by superiors or subordinates." Turoff (1972:162–163) observes that pen names "could be quite useful when someone desires an uninhibited exploration of a touchy issue" and extends this to the possibility of sensitivity sessions. And Hiltz and Turoff (1978b:144) in applying this feature to managerial styles, suggest that while executives may be reluctant to introduce very new or different ideas into a face-to-face conference for fear of losing face or swaying decisions by virtue of rank, no such inhibiting factors need be present in the computerized conference. Adriansson's data on COM suggest that even within the same system, the medium can make some users feel more candid, but others do not have this reaction. Sixty percent of experienced COM users agreed that use of that system makes it "easier to express unconventional views." However, about 38% disagreed.

The panel of experts agreed with both issues. Three of four responding indicate that self-presentation and emotional subtleties are supported. Parnes, speaking for CONFER, comments that this is true for any written medium. Umpleby tempers his " + " finding for General Systems, saying that computerized communication does not prevent the impact, rather than actually supporting it. Bair reports an absence of a discerned relationship for NLS, but suggests that it is indicated and may be found in the longer run.

Seven of eight responding to the candor of opinion item indicate that it was enhanced with a " + ". Only the Hepatitis group offers conflicting evidence with a " – " answer.

Increased Status

Computer-mediated communication systems can increase status or prestige of users relative to peers who do not have access to the technology. Housman (1980:2) notes that at GTE, "It has become something of a status symbol for an executive to have his own terminal." Panko and Panko (1981) report increased status as one of the benefits cited by the users of an electronic mail system. And the JEDEC evaluation report included the observation that several questionnaire respondents "noticed the emergence of cliques of EIES users at JEDEC face-to-face meetings and that use of EIES conferred something of a special status not held by non-EIES users" (Johnson-Lenz and Johnson-Lenz, 1980b:70). The panel reports seven instances of positive relationships and one (CONFER) of a negative relationship.

Increased Affective Ties

Computerized communication can increase affective ties and the sense of personal interaction, and can allow some to bypass typical social protocols and become intimate more quickly. Johansen *et al.* (1979) quote Richard Bach's observation in a computer conference:

> We are convention bound to comment on the weather, current events, where do you live, what do you do for a living, et cetera. In computer conferencing I can say, and delight in it, 'M. Baudot, what for you is real?' ... You can draw preliminary conclusions about a person in minutes that take long times to draft face to face, occluded as face-to-face is with appearance, manner, speech patterns ... (p. 22).

Reviewing a number of systems, Kleiner and Davis (1979) note:

> Lots of electronic mail ends up being as personal as face-to-face talk. People form friendships, have arguments, crack jokes. Good writers and more literate people have the same social advantage that good-looking people have face-to-face (p. 118).

Hiltz and Turoff (1978b) add:

> There have been many cases observed or reported by the participants of the most intimate of exchanges taking place between persons who have never met face-to-face and probably never will. Revelations about personal inadequacies, deviant preferences, past love affairs, and serious personal problems that the sender may have told no one else except his/her psychiatrist have passed through the EIES system as private messages to "strangers" who were "met" on the system (p. 28).

Supportive evidence is also supplied by Spelt's evaluation of a computer conference held in preparation for a face-to-face meeting in which social messages predominated (Spelt, 1977:89).

The panel was unanimous in reporting ten positive findings. But the comments qualify this somewhat. Parnes, reporting for CONFER, says that "all communication media will do this," Bair for NLS says that it is "by virtue of some contact versus none as the alternative," and McCarroll of the Devices for the Disabled group points to the special applications for the disabled.

Longer-Lasting Friendships

Friendships can endure longer, or even resolidify to counter residential mobility, because it is simpler and less expensive to keep in touch with people at a distance (Hiltz and Turoff, 1978b:205–206), and because it is possible to maintain a strong sense of personal interaction (Vallee et al., 1978:123–124). Kleiner (1980) explains the process:

> Computer networks are best used for keeping in touch with people. Far away colleagues coordinate long-range projects, people with similar interests substitute computer networks for newsletters or telephone trees (and end up keeping in touch more personally as a result), and soul-searching friendships develop between those who have never met in person. Some members log on to get a sympathetic response in an emotional crisis. Others make long distance trips to meet in person those they've only seen on the network. There have been typed flirtations which developed into full-fledged romances and idle dreams which suddenly became high-commitment businesses (p. 534).

Although the nature of the friendships is real, there is sometimes a shock when relationships built up by teleconferencing have to deal with the complication of face-to-face interaction. The communication patterns are sufficiently different that people who have worked very well together electronically may be completely ineffective in the face-to-face mode (Theobald, 1980:17).

Three of the five groups responding report positive findings that friendships can endure longer; for two there is no empirical support.

Different Terminations of Friendships

In the future, terminated friendships could be more a function of changed interests than of distance, as people are able to maintain close contact despite geographical distance. Kerr (in Hiltz and Turoff, 1978b) hypothesizes that:

> 1. The mean duration of friendships will be longer in a "computer conference society" than at present.
> 2. Friendships terminated in a "computer conference society" are more likely to be a function of changed interests than distance (p. 206).

Only five experts responded to this item, again perhaps because it is more long-run than most of the other suggested impacts. Three groups (Futures, General Systems, and NLS) indicate " + " for support;

OICS reports neither empirical confirmation nor denial; and CONFER comments on the economic constraints ("Seems to be more a function of ability to pay for use of the system").

Resolidification of Friendship Ties

Friendship ties resolidify to counter residential mobility. This impact also is futuristic, and perhaps because of that could not be located in the literature. Only two panelists responded, both indicating agreement with " + ".

New kinds of personal relationships are made possible:

> One of the more popular computer-based conferencing forms is the "online cocktail party." This is used principally by new groups to practice use of conferencing and to establish personal ties much in the way conventional cocktail parties are used to initiate a personal gathering . . . . The form has reached its highest expression in annual New Year's Eve parties which enable some conferencers to toast in the New Year each hour from Maine to Hawaii (Bezilla, 1980a).

Strengthening of Support Systems

The communicatory proximity of physically dispersed family, friends, and professional help can increase the number and strength of support systems. The delivery of social services could be improved by regional and national coordination of services to clients receiving aid from multiple agencies, as well as data-base directories, referral services, and eligibility requirements for specific programs. On-line counseling would not only be more convenient, but might allow people to be more open and candid. Legal or accounting consultation could be delivered more rapidly and conveniently, as could other professional and paraprofessional services (Turoff et al., 1978:59–60; Hiltz and Turoff, 1978b:177–180,201–202).

There were seven responses to this item, five of which affirmed it with " + ". There was a "0" from NLS, which offers the comment that it is indicated but not yet supported by relevant data. Only the Mental Workload group produced " – – ", contradictory evidence.

Summary

The summary table, Table 4–3, again presents these findings by sample size and amount of agreement. Interestingly, the positive impacts tended to be supported by the panel, whereas the potential problems produced disagreement. Impacts at the level of individual affect are concerned with changes in the nature of social interactions. At the same time, there is the potential for new sources of stress to emerge.

TABLE 4-3

Individual Affective Impacts

Many Studies[a]	Few Studies[b]
Agree	
Increases affective ties $(10+)$	Friendship ties resolidify $(2+)$
Friendships endure longer $(3+;2=0)$	Friendships terminate differently $(3+;1=0)$
	Supports self-presentation $(3+;1=0)$
Disagree	
Potential for addiction $(1++;8+;1=0;1-)$	
Increases status $(1++;6+;1-)$	
Enhances candor of opinion $(7+;1-)$	
Lack of feedback frustrating $(2++;4+;2=0;1-)$	
Strengthens support systems $(5+;1=0;1--)$	
New sources of stress $(4+;1-)$	
Creates isolation $(2+;1=0;2-)$	

[a] 5 or more.
[b] Fewer than 5.

BEHAVIORAL IMPACTS ON INDIVIDUALS

Behavioral impacts on individuals refer to actions and doing. They include individual communication patterns and styles, and the effectiveness of such communication or work patterns.

These were the hypothesized behavioral impacts:

1. Computerized communication can blur the distinctions between work and leisure if users telecommunicate to work from home.
2. Computerized communication creates opportunities for flextime and changes in personal time management.
3. Changes in leisure time activities are possible with more time spent at home and less time watching television.
4. It creates the opportunity for communicating at the time of one's own choice.
5. It creates the opportunity to be "in the center of the action" without regard to geography.
6. Greater freedom of residence and a shift to rural areas are possible.
7. Computerized communication creates opportunities for communicating and joining groups without regard to sex, race, physical appearance, or other credentials.

8. It allows time for reflecting on the topic being considered.
9. It increases the degree of personal connectedness with others, in terms of expanding the status set, the number of social participations and the scope of social relationships; it leads to increased collegial contacts, an increase in the number of contacts that can be maintained, and creates the opportunity for regular connectedness with many people.
10. Computerized communication increases the quality of work and contact with others' work.
11. It increases the speed of interaction.
12. Because it is a written medium, it increases the explicitness of communications with more precise text.
13. Computerized communication can reduce travel.
14. It can reduce the need for paper files and change methods of filing output (more files in the short run but fewer in the long run with easier on-line searches).
15. Participants can get more deliberate responses to technical questions, backed by written facts and with less delay.

Choice of When to Communicate

Self-generated and self-paced participation rates create opportunities to communicate at the time and pace of one's own choosing rather than at the discretion of others:

> One participates . . . when convenience, need, and "mood" create optimum conditions. Because it is considered impolite to interrupt a speaker at a face-to-face meeting, other members are a "captive audience" . . . . How many participants in staff meetings . . . begin to exhibit signs of boredom, frustration, desire to get up and walk around? . . . Nonparticipation by group members . . . adversely affects group productivity. In computer conferencing no participant need sit through such tedium. He/she is free to make comments and contributions at any time; skip or only briefly skim entries in which there is no interest; get up and walk around or get a cup of coffee without being deviant (Hiltz, 1976:7–8).

Turoff (1974b) labels this "time dispersion":

> Since the conference dialogue is stored, it is not necessary for individuals involved to be on the computer terminals at the same time. A person may go to the terminal at a time that is convenient to him . . . . He may then receive any messages he had not previously seen, make his additional comments, and sign off. The next person to sign on will find these additional comments also, and anything else he had not seen previously. The individuals engaged in this random mode of conferencing may now control the use of their time to a much greater degree than is possible when a group must simultaneously meet for a discussion.

> The computer, therefore, not only allows a person to control his rate of interaction when he is participating in the conversation, but also when he wants to start or stop engaging and to trade that off with other demands on his time. He is no

longer a 'slave' to the demand of having a time for communication which corresponds with every other individual in the group (p. 136).

The panelists were asked about the opportunity for communicating asynchronously. All but one responded. Seven report " + " findings and five " + + ". More than 90% of COM users agree that the system increased their ability to "participate when it suits you best." This clearly is one of the most strongly supported hypotheses.

Increased Connectedness

Computer-mediated communication systems increase the degree of personal and social connectedness with others, in terms of expanding the status set, the number of social participations and the scope of social relationships. They lead to increased collegial contacts, an increase in the number of contacts that can be maintained, and create the opportunity for regular connections with many people.

Such systems increase connections by widening professional and social circles. Frequent users experience an exponential expansion of their contacts, with the intensification of relationships through continuous interaction, proliferation of new contacts, membership in new networks, and linkages with diverse people who otherwise would not have been known (Bezilla and Kleiner, 1980; Bezilla, 1979).

Public user directories function as cueing aids and substitute for the absence of nonverbal cues, as well as a means of connecting people for social and collegial contact. This is especially important as the size of the network expands. Using the directory, one can unobtrusively check those attributes of other users that they have chosen to enter. Shared statuses can then become the topic of introductory messages, and groups as well as ongoing conferences may be located. Directory searches can provide indirect cueing as users become aware of shared interests and perspectives (Kerr and Bezilla, 1979:6).

Vallee *et al.* (1978:111,115) report questionnaire data in which a majority of the respondents said that the ability "to keep in touch with others" was one of the major strengths of the medium.

Strong support for this impact was received from the expert respondents, eight of whom report " + " and one " + + ". Comments from users are cited to explain these findings. COM users with more experience using that system were more likely to agree than were less experienced users.

Opportunity to Be in the Center of Action

Computerized communication increases the opportunity to be "in the center of the action" without regard to geography, and affects with whom people work. Researchers significantly increased their contact with distantly located colleagues during the course of their computer conferencing (Johansen et al., 1978:54–61). Spelt (1977) found:

> A universally expressed benefit was the great motivation for small-college scholars to engage in conferencing . . . . In this period of reduced faculty mobility and the corresponding need to find other ways of communicating with scholars on remote campuses . . . the computer conference appears to provide a new alternative (p. 91).

Six report " + " findings and three, " + + " findings for this impact.

Speeded Interaction

The experts agreed, with two responding " + + ", six " + ", and two "0", that computer-mediated communication systems can increase the speed of interaction. The JEDEC participants indicated in response to a follow-up interview that the use of EIES resulted in decisions being made more quickly and that it accelerated exchanges in general (Johnson-Lenz and Johnson-Lenz, 1980b:64–65). Experienced users of the COM system were considerably more likely to agree with this than were inexperienced users. But the other comments to this item indicate that this is conditional upon other variables and therefore a potential more than a current reality. Depending on factors such as the regularity of signing on line, the task, and individual preferences for the various communication media available, computer-mediated systems can increase the speed of interaction but may not necessarily do so.

Ability to Join Groups More Freely

Computerized communication creates opportunities for communicating and joining groups without the intrusion of sex, race, physical appearance, or other irrelevant characteristics. This is especially likely in those systems which include the ability to send messages or enter conference or notebook comments with a pen name or anonymously:

> The pen name and anonymity features can counteract the tendency of conventional face-to-face meetings to be ruled by dysfunctional and irrelevant criteria. People can communicate in a computer-mediated meeting without distraction by . . . attributes, such as physical appearance or auditory quality. Ideas and achieved statuses become more relevant to the written exchange of issues, rather than ascriptive characteristics over which the individual has no control. Conferees can disguise cues irrelevant to professional and scientific dialogue which are influential in informal collegial communications, such as age, race, beauty, physical size, loudness of voice, body language, mannerisms, assertiveness, social class, and organizational position. Cues which could distract more than enhance the quality of group communications can be hidden (Kerr and Bezilla, 1979:8).

One of the many advantages of computerized communications over face-to-face meetings is the reduction of social inequalities as it affects groups such as minorities, women, and the handicapped. Users may elect to mask particular status cues. They may choose to reveal or hide, accentuate or ignore, certain personality, social, and cultural characteristics which would be readily apparent in communication by any other medium (Kerr, 1978:74).

The six panelists responding to this item all voted " + " or " + + ".

Reduced Travel

Computerized communications can reduce travel by replacing some face-to-face meetings and by providing a continuous link without the financial and human costs of travel. Some users, however, enjoy travel rather than feel overburdened by it, while others actually increase their travel to explore the new contacts and working relationships developed through the medium. Hiltz (1981) found that travel, whether for attendance at meetings of professional societies or for personal reasons, was as likely to increase as to decrease at all levels of system usage. "Anecdotal evidence suggests that among those who interact a great deal on line but have never met in person, there is a tendency for curiosity to prompt extensions to business or personal trips made for other purposes, in order to meet with one's on-line acquaintances." The substitution of communication for travel, then, appears to be dependent on a number of factors (Johansen et al., 1978a:74–75; Hiltz and Turoff, 1978b:235–236).

The panelists agreed, with three reporting " + + " strong empirical confirmation, four responding with " + ", and one "0". Kerr (1980) offers empirical data, with respondents to the post-use questionnaire saying that use of EIES for WHCLIS resulted in decreased travel.

Blurred Distinction between Work and Leisure

The distinction between work and leisure can blur as people telecommunicate rather than commute to work, from home, from neighborhood office centers, or from other flexible work locations. The automated office of the future may well be an office without walls or with very loose walls and flexible working hours, as the need for a central physical location is minimized or eliminated by access via terminals to information and communication. Possible benefits include the cost savings and efficiencies inherent in the reduction of travel time and energy consumption, changes in family interactions, and concomitant changes in lifestyles (Hiltz, 1976:24; Johansen et al., 1978a:66–67; Martino, 1979:99; Turoff et al., 1978:54–55; Vallee et al., 1975:134; Vallee et al., 1978:84–87; Winkler, 1975:2).

The six experts who examined this area each agreed with a " + " or " + + ". The OICS evaluator reports users taking terminals home with them on evenings and weekends.

Changes in Leisure Time Activities

Changes in leisure time activities are likely, with more time spent at home in active entertainment rather than passively watching television. Martino (1979) predicts:

> Telecommunications will invade the household . . . games . . . will be much more sophisticated than those in use today, incorporating a built-in computer . . . . CATV games will . . . permit individuals to play against a computer at the CATV head-end or against human opponents elsewhere in the service area of the cable system . . . . Since the same "software" will be owned by the CATV system, each user can have access to a far greater variety . . . . The potential for playing against other human opponents in different households will make possible the organization of tournaments and similar activities (p. 97).

In addition to games, the exchange of information about a variety of hobbies, interests, and other leisure-time activities is also likely. Turoff (1974b) suggests:

> Some day we should reach the point where the citizen can have the option of phoning from his home a catalog of on-going conferences and then dial and join a particular conference on a topic of interest to him—stamp trading, a new book, a group therapy session, marital problems, etc. When this happens people will have an efficient method for finding others of similar interests in the society. That type of capability will, in its own way, change and influence the very structure of the society itself. At the very least it would offer an active form of entertainment as opposed to the passive nature of broadcast (p. 142).

The panel of experts was less sure of this impact. Of the three responses, only General Systems reports " + ". Hepatitis has no supportive data, and OICS, which did not examine this factor at all, comments "Don't know yet!" This appears to be a futuristic impact now almost devoid of empirical support.

Freedom of Residence

Greater freedom of residence and a shift to rural areas are possible as people are no longer dependent upon a centrally located office. Greater variation in where people live and work is a projected impact. Moreover, the shift in population distribution from urban to nonurban areas since 1970 creates an increasingly dispersed population that seems well suited to use of the new media (Johansen et al., 1978b:48–50). Four of the experts confirmed this with "+" reports. Parnes of CON-FER observes that access to Telenet (and other network technologies) is a constraining factor, since ports are generally located only in populous areas.

Newly Created Opportunities for Flextime

Although it can create changes in when people work, including "flexibility in working hours, whether or not one must work simultaneously with others, and new ways to accommodate a heavy workload outside normal working hours," this was not consistently supported by data from users of the PLANET system (Johansen et al., 1978a:61–66). Edwards' (1977:99–100) study of NLS, however, found this to be one of the discerned impacts of that system.

More people may find themselves free from organizations as sources of employment, with the self-employed, consultants, and freelancers offering their services to a variety of geographically dispersed clients. The panel was asked if the medium can create opportunities for flextime and changes in personal time management. They responded positively, with five "+" and three "+ +".

Better Responses to Technical Questions

Users can obtain more deliberate responses to technical questions, with less delay and backed up by written facts (Vallee and Askevold, 1975). The availability of a written transcript permits explicit review of earlier discussions as well as skimming by those familiar with or not needing the information (Turoff, 1972:164). Again, the experts confirmed this impact, with six "+" and two "0" responses.

Increased Quality of Work

It increases the quality of work, in part because it increases contact with the work of others. By permitting rapid and relatively inexpensive access to remote resources, including colleagues, data bases, meetings, research in progress, and published works, the heightened speed of interaction permits people to keep both informed and connected.

An evaluation of the use of EIES for the development of standards by members of the Joint Electron Device Engineering Council found that it has "a positive effect on the quality and speed of decisions and on the effectiveness of JEDEC face-to-face meetings," as well as increasing the amount of information available for decisions (Johnson-Lenz and Johnson-Lenz, 1980a).

Qualitative evidence of increased productivity and job satisfaction has also been presented by Bezilla and Kleiner (1980) and Turoff and Hiltz (1980) who conclude that the quality of managerial and professional work, as measured by the accuracy, completeness, and timeliness of information brought to bear on decisions, as well as the morale of workers who experience increased autonomy, participation, and variety and challenge of their work, are likely to be positively affected by a well-designed computer-based communication system.

The medium evidently improves the self-assessed quality and quantity of work for some, but by no means all, of its scientific users. It seems to accomplish this both by yielding specific leads or information, and by increasing the general stock of ideas. It also changes their perceptions of the nature of their specialties and of the activities of other scholars within that specialty (Hiltz, 1979).

Such impacts of the EIES system upon individual productivity were measured by users' subjective responses to post-use questions probing the effects of EIES. The quality of work was somewhat more likely to be affected than the quantity, and by means such as increasing the stock of ideas, providing leads, and improving connectivity. The more time spent on line, the more likely were positive impacts (Hiltz, 1981).

The panel of experts was asked about the impact on quality of work and contact with the work of others, and the response was mixed. There are three " + + " reports, indicating strong quantitative evidence, from the Hepatitis group, WHCLIS, and OICS. The Futures group indicates a confirming " + ". Three groups (Devices for the Disabled, Mental Workload, and Legitech) explored this area but produced data which neither confirmed nor denied the impact ("0"). And NLS indicates a "-" negative finding with the comment that contact rather than quality increases.

More Time for Reflection

The quality of work is also positively affected by the medium's allowing time for reflection on the topic being considered before responding or after consulting off-line references (Vallee et al., 1978a:113; Ferguson and Johansen, 1975:12; Turoff, 1974b:135–136). The subjects of another study indicated that the computer conferencing experience increased the participants' ability to think about problems (Spelt, 1977:90). The respondents supported this impact, with two " + + "

and seven " + " votes. Only the Mental Workload group had refuting
" − − " evidence.

Increased Explicitness of Communication

Because computer-mediated communication is a written medium,
it increases the explicitness of communications with more precise text.
Davis (1971) compared face-to-face and teletype for the communication
of factual information, and found teletype to be the more effective
mode. Toussaint (1960), among others, found that comprehension is
improved with the written word. This may be because the written
channel allows the possibilities of rereading or checking difficult pas-
sages (Short et al., 1976:84). Four respondents checked " + " in agree-

TABLE 4-4

Individual Behavioral Impacts

Many Studies[a]	Few Studies[b]
Agree	
Choice of when to communicate (5 + +;7 +)	Freedom of residence (4 +)
Opportunity to be in the center of action (3 + +;6 +)	Changes in leisure time activities (1 +;1 = 0)
Increases connectedness (1 + +;8 +)	
Creates opportunities for flextime (3 + +;5 +)	
Able to join groups more freely (1 + +;5 +)	
Blurs distinction between work and leisure (1 + +;5 +)	
Speeds interaction (2 + +;6 +;2 = 0)	
Reduces travel (3 + +;4 +;1 = 0)	
Better responses to technical questions (6 +;2 = 0)	
Disagree	
Allows time for reflection (2 + +;7 +;1 − −)	
Increases quality of work (3 + +;1 +;3 = 0;1 −)	
Increases explicitness of communication (4 +;2 = 0;1 −)	
Changes filing methods (1 + +;1 +;2 = 0;1 −;1 − −)	

[a] 5 or more.
[b] Fewer than 5.

ment with this impact. Two (Devices for the Disabled and NLS) found no empirical support and indicate "0". Again, the "-" exception is for the Mental Workload group.

Changed Filing Methods

Computer-mediated communication can reduce the need for paper files and change methods of filing output, with more files in the short run but fewer in the long run as easier on-line searches become feasible. The literature made no mention of this area. And the expert respondents were very mixed in their replies. OICS reports " + + ", and CONFER " + ". "0" was checked by two groups (Devices for the Disabled and NLS). Hepatitis replied " − " and General Systems a firm " − − ". This impact, then, is very unsure. However, the comments indicate that it could be feasible in the long run, if the technology were made more reliable and storage space increased.

Summary

The behavioral impacts of computer-mediated communication systems upon individuals are summarized in Table 4–4. The dimensions encompass freedom of interaction, quality of life, and quality of work. Choices and opportunities are expanded and new lifestyles become possible.

GROUP IMPACTS

Groups, organizations, and communities constitute the second level at which impacts are investigated. Groups consist of sets of individuals who share some unifying relationship; organizations have functional and administrative structures; and communities represent larger less structured groupings. Each indicates some relationship or ordering among people and an underlying structure.

Relationships among geographically dispersed users of computer-mediated communication systems result in the creation of on-line groups, organizations, and communities. The individual users may already be members, or when linked electronically may become members of temporary or permanent groups or organizations. Included are groupings such as committees; professional, academic, research and development groups or organizations; interorganizational networks; and neighborhood community groups.

The word "group" will be used to represent all these various kinds of structures. A group may consist of all users, some users and some nonusers, or all nonusers, and may be created through the computer-based communication medium itself:

> The interpersonal structures, processes, and phenomena, some of which correspond to nonelectronic communications and some of which are unique to the electronic mode, are the foundation of a new social entity: electronic social groups. Computerized conferencing is an electronic technology from which a social system is emerging. Such electronic groups are theoretically and substantively very new social forms, rather than simply extensions . . . or replications of existing interactional patterns and processes (Kerr and Bezilla, 1979:3).

In addition, individuals may belong to more than one such electronic social group at a time.

COGNITIVE IMPACTS ON GROUPS

The group level of cognitive impacts refers to purposes and goals; ideas, information processing, and intellectual resources; and values about knowledge as well as social definitions of truth.

These were the hypothesized impacts:

1. Computerized communication creates group resources as individuals join on the basis of verbal output rather than traditional credentials.
2. It improves the quality of group decisions.
3. It increases understanding and appreciation of knowledge-based authority rather than hierarchical authority.
4. Greater awareness of the global situation changes organizational goals.
5. The creative process is more abstract.
6. Computerized communication provides a common framework and experience (a node for networks).
7. It creates opportunities to develop communities of interest rather than those based on geography, discipline, etc., and a redefinition of the meaning of "local."

Creation of Group Resources

Computer-mediated communication increases group resources as individuals join on the basis of verbal output rather than traditional credentials. There is a potential for increased access to both human and electronic sources of information. A group's available resources may be planned and intentional, including their members, consultants, and data bases, or unplanned and accidental, including locating new information sources as a byproduct of network membership.

Computerized groups are likely to be able to attract new members in part by the ongoing existence and activity of the group, rather than by more traditional devices. Movement in and out of conferences and groups on EIES has been largely based on interest in the topics under consideration. In some instances, people are offered membership based on their qualifications, and in others invitations are extended to those expressing an interest. The medium can, on the other hand, simplify the exclusion of potential group members when that is desired, since membership access is selective and the very existence of an electronic group can easily be kept secret.

The panel of expert respondents seemed to hesitate about this impact. There were only four responses. Two (General Systems Theory and OICS) report observing this impact in the predicted direction with a " + ". The Devices for the Disabled group indicates a "0" for the absence of empirical support. And Bair of NLS, while not studying this issue, observes that organizational roles, rather than verbal output or traditional credentials, determine membership.

Improved Group Decisions

Techniques such as the Delphi and nominal group processes have been developed to structure group communication processes so that it is efficient for a group to pool and coevaluate their knowledge about complex problems (Hiltz and Turoff, 1978b:18).

The medium can be a rich information environment, with interactive structuring tools providing groups opportunities to solve problems and make decisions. A full written transcript is available for reference. Voting mechanisms can be used for directing the agenda, reaching consensus, identifying divergent viewpoints, or collecting and displaying other feedback from participants. On-line questionnaires permit convenient, accurate, and relatively inexpensive data collection and feedback. The results of data base searches can be presented for consideration, broadening access to information resources (Johnson-Lenz et al., 1978:15–17).

Other structuring and decision support aids to increase a group's ability to reach consensus without sacrificing the quality of solutions can be included for problems such as budgeting resource allocations or contract negotiation. The computer can aid in gathering subjective estimates within a group and then facilitating the discussion necessary to focus on and resolve the differences that emerge (Turoff and Hiltz, 1980).

Turoff and Hiltz (1979) maintain that a larger number of options can be considered and that there is less pressure toward a forced consensus and more commitment to agreement when it occurs. Moreover:

> A new area, yet to be fully explored, is the incorporation of communication oriented games where individuals can play out the potential consequences of their decisions after agreement has been reached . . . . The interesting aspect of computer conferencing is that one can simulate real world communication conditions . . . . This is not possible in the usual co-located strategy, corporate planning, or war game without tremendous overhead investment in physical facilities and support people (p. 13).

Scher (1980) also argues that the medium can bring about more effective decision making. Elsewhere, he explains how the computer can be integrated into the decision-making process by continuously examining decision-making activities in the target application audience and identifying those activities the performance of which could be significantly enhanced through the introduction of interactive computer-based supportive tools:

> Our notion of support, however, is not restricted to the augmentation of existing processes, but is broad-based enough to include the capturing of additional processes which, when "blended" with the current processes yield positive, synergistic effect (Scher, 1979).

Controlled experiments on problem solving provide empirical evidence that groups can reach at least the same quality of solution utilizing this technology as they can with face-to-face discussions:

> Small groups of five individuals who were first time users of the computer conferencing technology were able to arrive at solutions that were just as good as the solutions arrived at by the face-to-face groups; they used only about one-third the number of words of communications (Turoff, 1980b; see also Hiltz et al., 1981.)

Lipinski et al. (1980:158–159) consider the task-focused communications required by groups involved in joint problem solving, and suggest that computer-based communication systems are appropriate in the structuring, evaluating, and documenting phases of problem solving, since time delays are acceptable, written responses are appropriate, and face-to-face contact is not essential. They believe that the implementing, searching, and conceptualizing stages of problem solving are less amenable to this technology. In another context, they maintain that the use of computerized conferencing for problem-formulation tasks allows a greater variety of perspectives with all members able to contribute their views equally, and that this broader scope of input improves quality. Problem formulation in a computer environment may encourage more precise and systematic contributions than in ordinary face-to-face sessions (Tydeman et al., 1980).

Johansen et al. (1979:21–22,131) reflect that although the increased number of perspectives provided with a large electronic meeting can provide more alternatives for untangling knotty problems and fuller support for the collective decision, it may also mean more conflict. They caution that a false sense of group consensus is possible, and that the failure to recognize and reconcile differences in perspectives may screen out divergent ideas and produce decisions of low quality.

The panel of experts was less sure of this potential impact and the votes are quite mixed. JEDEC offers strong empirical support with a " + + " and both the Hepatitis group and OICS report a " + ". On the other hand, the Mental Workload group votes " − − " for strong contradictory evidence, and the Devices for the Disabled group notes a "0" for the absence of confirming data. CONFER, although not examining this issue, indicates agreement.

Increased Knowledge-Based Authority

Computerized communication increases the understanding and appreciation of knowledge-based rather than hierarchical authority. This refers to orientation to the contents of communication rather than to the prestige or organizational position of the speaker. Although the evidence is inconclusive, and this issue could not be located in the literature, contact with peers external to the organization and awareness of other experts could under certain conditions reduce the automatic acceptance and deference to existing hierarchical structures.

This hypothesized impact elicited only three responses. General Systems Theory and OICS report a " + ", and Devices for the Disabled indicates a "0". There are no comments or explanations to clarify these views.

Greater Awareness of the Global Situation

Greater awareness of the global situation can change organizational goals since the volume of information exchanged is increased, the scope of knowledge is presumably broadened, and awareness is enhanced as people, groups, and organizations are electronically connected.

An evaluation of the use of the medium by legislative researchers concludes that the use of intelligent terminals and microprocessors "can further enhance policymakers' access to information about factual matters and about new approaches to the process of policymaking, as well as new ways of thinking about old (and new) problems" (Johnson-Lenz and Johnson-Lenz, 1980d:111).

There were only two responses to this item. OICS attributes a " + " to it. General Systems Theory reports a "0" for the absence of a discerned relationship and comments "not yet." This is an impact we may expect in the future, as use of the medium becomes more widespread and a larger number of groups and organizations gain familiarity with it.

More Abstract Creative Process

The creative process is more abstract. Large groups can work together and cooperate electronically far more easily than is feasible in face-to-face situations, and they can contribute more diversified and complex kinds of information. Remote, asynchronous interaction also allows more time for reflection and for referring to other sources of information. For example:

> An important facet of FORUM conferences lies in the ease with which the participants have access to services outside of the discussion itself: they can, for instance, submit a prepared statement to the rest of the group or insert parts of the discussion into a personal file. They can also draw responses from a database system and enter them into the general discussion. Clearly, the level of interaction thus reached is one not found in face-to-face meetings where experts are cut off from their files and personal notes (Vallee and Askevold, 1975:55).

Bair (1974:33–35) observes a sense of creative freedom and flexibility of both content and work rate among the users of NLS. He notes:

> Increased efficiency permitted the individual to exercise more control over the development of his own ideas on paper . . . . The subjects did state that their thinking was enhanced, that the structure added a new dimension to their thinking, and that the system provided mnemonic assistance (p. 76).

Remote coauthorship becomes feasible. The joint preparation of manuscripts by geographically separated authors is greatly simplified when the collaboration is electronic and with the use of word processing capabilities. Material is composed asynchronously in a joint notebook, disagreements are resolved in private messages, and the final document is produced on line.

Computer-based communication systems are unique in allowing a group as part of its communication process to modify, update, and reorganize what has transpired, with members automatically kept informed of such changes (Hiltz and Turoff, 1978b:38).

Price (1975) observes that:

> For the management of innovation, the stimulation of creativity, and the diffusion of innovations achieved, it would appear practical to augment the capabilities of . . . small organizations or organizational units by adding to their working equipment . . . computerized conferencing resources (p. 542).

In considering impacts upon institutional innovation, and specifically upon applications to organizational suggestion systems, Snyder (in Turoff et al., 1978) observes:

> A key factor in the success of suggestion systems . . . appears to be the process by which suggestions are approved for submittal and evaluated. Typically, productive suggestion systems flow rapidly, require no approval prior to submittal, and must be definitively assessed within a short period of time. A [computer conference] would be ideally suited to such a process . . . . Further, such a system would have the advantage of permitting a dialogue between the suggestor and the evaluators (p. 29).

This too is futuristic and essentially unconfirmed by the respondents. OICS reports an "0". Only NLS responds with " + ", attributing it to the unique structuring abilities, high speed displays, and hypertext features of that system.

Providing a Common Framework

Computerized communication provides a common framework and experience, or a node for networks. It can facilitate an electronically joined community of members whose ties grow beyond topic-oriented exchanges of information and who exhibit a high degree of personal interaction, group cohesiveness, and personal involvement. Members become committed to each other and to the purposes of the group (Johansen et al., 1978:34).

There can be a marked improvement in communications:

> The network becomes a "place" in the thought processes of those attached to each other via computer communications and this makes it possible to bring people together more frequently who are normally separated by travel time, time zones, and conflicting schedules (McKendree, 1978:14).

Thompson observes that the medium:

> Increases (virtually to infinity) the size of the common "information space" that can be shared by communicants (and provides a wider range of strategies for communicants to interrupt and augment each other's contributions).

> Raises the probability of discovering and developing latent consensus. (The enriched information base and heightened interconnectedness increase the chances that each conferee can receive unexpected and/or interesting messages.) (Gordon Thompson, quoted in Price, 1975:499–500).

Four groups responded, each indicating a " + " for agreement and the presence of weak quantitative or qualitative evidence. McCarroll comments for the Devices for the Disabled group that the "sense of community seemed to endure among many members."

Development of Communities of Interest

Computer-mediated communication systems create opportunities to develop communities of interest rather than those based on geography or discipline, and a redefinition of the meaning of "local." People are able to locate others with similar interests, including highly specialized groups who otherwise would be disconnected. Scientists located at small and isolated institutions or who have specialties not shared by their colleagues are able to communicate on a daily and routine basis with those who share their professional interests (Price and Kerr, 1978:20).

EIES users can browse through the membership directory to identify others with similar interests. In an informal environment conversations are easy to initiate and new relationships are frequently formed. "Local" can be defined as simply belonging to the same conferencing system. Networks with large and diverse memberships, and access of all users to each other, facilitate the formation of new friendships and the evolution of new temporary or enduring groups.

Kochen (1978:23) notes that "The current concept of 'community' may acquire a different meaning. Already people who do computerized conferencing daily want to establish contact in other ways."

A group located in the mid-Pacific islands, concerned with educational uses for computers, coordinated the use of EIES, PLATO, and the NASA PEACESAT satellite network to share information about current experiences, replacing slow and inefficient traditional methods:

> Educators located in institutions isolated by limited communications are using [these] techniques to meet with resource people and with each other to develop educational opportunities for island populations in areas of computer science. The potential for linking these islands . . . offers unanticipated opportunities for the island educators to introduce modern instructional methods to enhance educational opportunities for their students (Southworth et al., 1981).

Johansen et al. (1978a:56–60) found the impacts on those with whom people work to be inconsistent; some groups displayed an increase in contacts and others did not. They noted an increased and unplanned frequency of communicating among researchers in different disciplines, and conclude that the medium itself may not always facilitate new contacts; users must be motivated to communicate with other participants.

Seven panelists responded to this item, each indicating a " + " for agreement. Bair comments for NLS that this is "obvious from location of users." Those experiencing computer-mediated communication systems, then, are aware of and have experienced this positive feature.

Summary

Table 4–5 summarizes these impacts at the group cognitive level, which produced fewer strong agreements from a relatively large number of studies than did the impacts at the level of the individual.

TABLE 4–5

Group Cognitive Impacts

Many Studies[a]	Few Studies[b]
Agree	
Develops communities of interest (7 +)	Provides a common framework (4)
	Creates group resources (2 +;1 = 0)
	Increases knowledge-based authority (2 +;1 = 0)
	Greater awareness of the global situation (1 +;1 = 0)
	More abstract creative process (1 +;1 = 0)
Disagree	
Improves group decisions (1 + +;2 +;1 = 0;1 − −)	

[a] 5 or more.
[b] Fewer than 5.

AFFECTIVE IMPACTS ON GROUPS

The group affective level deals with the informal structure, including feelings of liking or disliking others, group cohesion, attitudes towards purposes and goals, and the group's general emotional tone toward persons, things, and ideas.

Two impacts were offered as hypotheses:

1. The use of surrogates in computer-based communication systems can inhibit levels of trust and security.
2. The absence of nonverbal cues and possible poor response to questions increases the attention paid to supportive, encouraging, or negative statements in both computerized conferencing and face-to-face meetings. This heightened understanding facilitates general social interaction.

Inhibition of Trust

The use of surrogates or shared membership slots can inhibit levels of trust and security, since some users allow subordinates to log in for them and retrieve messages or enter responses (Vallee et al., 1978:123–125). Since there is no way of knowing who has signed onto a specific account in the absence of voice identification, or who has actually read the communications, users may be concerned about the confidentiality of communicating sensitive issues, may be reluctant to make certain statements in writing, or may even develop a general insecurity and distrust of the medium itself (Bezilla, 1978).

Johansen et al. (1978a) offer these observations from the PLANET system:

> In a number of cases, secretaries or assistants actually typed in and retrieved messages for someone, though they often did so under the name of the indirect participant. This works quite well in many cases, particularly if a participant is very busy, has trouble accessing a terminal, or is simply not inclined to use keyboard devices. However, we saw several instances of confusion and frustration where other participants—not realizing that it was a surrogate and not the "real" participant—would enter private messages and not receive responses. (Sometimes the surrogate would become flustered or embarrassed and not know what to do in response to the message.) Such a situation can easily lower trust in a group (p. 50).

Johansen et al. (1979:11) add that this is generally a workable situation, but indicate that it can occasionally create some interpersonal problems. On the other hand, Tally (1981:3) found that the delegation of direct terminal interaction to subordinates proved advantageous in the experience of the group he observed, since "other staff members were able to share the experience and overcome some of the technical challenges of the system."

The dependence on technology can also impact upon group trust:

> Machines have been accused of choosing awkward moments at which to fail. And in electronic meetings, there are likely to be many potentially awkward moments. A broken connection during an emotional exchange might be devastating. At best, it would probably slow the whole communication process as group members restart and try to recover their momentum. At worst, a system failure might be interpreted as an intentional act—the slamming of an electronic door. Group trust would likely deteriorate (Johansen et al., 1979:24).

The panel did not confirm this impact. Only the General Systems and Hepatitis groups checked " + ". Mental Workload and USG-MSG responded " – " to indicate conflicting evidence. Two groups, OICS and Devices for the Disabled, replied "0" to show an absence of confirming data. The CONFER evaluator comments that this is "possible but no experiences as yet." Although the use of surrogates can lower the level of group trust, this evidently has not generally been experienced.

Perhaps awareness of the potential problem, plus communication among those sharing accounts, can prevent difficulty, although it is likely that this is also somewhat dependent on other variables such as the nature of the task and size of the group.

In addition to the use of surrogates, there may be the fear that recipients will show messages or information to those for whom they were not intended, or perhaps even that the system will misdirect private messages. For instance, more than a third of the COM users agreed with the statements that "information can come into the wrong hands" and "outsiders can see private messages." The majority did not agree and such fears were somewhat more prevalent among new users than more experienced users. Edwards' study of NLS found that privacy was a concern chiefly among those with supervisory responsibilities, and that 27% of the users did not use the system for work of a confidential nature (1977:49,91).

Facilitating Supportive Interaction

The absence of nonverbal cues and possible poor response to questions increases the attention paid to supportive, encouraging, or negative statements. This heightened understanding facilitates general social interaction both on and off line. This suggests that possible negative attributes inherent in the medium can in fact produce positive outcomes. Greater attention may be given to communications of an emotional or positive nature, producing greater group cohesion. This may be a longer-range impact than many of those already discussed.

Experienced users learn to communicate their personalities and emotions, sometimes by the use of pen names. The pen name capability may serve either as a cueing feature or as an identity mask. New role definitions and self-images can be assumed and acted out. The quality of the communications may undergo major alterations as the pen name assumes a unique personality over time. This personality may or may not reflect its human source, as users may allow aberrant or exaggerated dimensions of their personalities to emerge. Aspects of the self that one might be reluctant to expose to one's professional or social peers may be revealed because of the presence of the pen name option (Kerr, 1978:73–75).

Kerr and Bezilla (1979) report their observations of the use of pen names on EIES:

> Unlike personal and other telecommunication encounters, computerized conferencing allows its users to rapidly interchange ideas and cues according to context. As a result, frequently stultifying status sets are replaced by rich and diverse role sets that allow the user to participate in groups to the fullest extent of one's own innate abilities. The role can be defined by the user or group as appropriate to the context, and the interactive emission and reception of cues and roles by several will define a richer context (pp. 6–7).

The Futures research group on EIES engaged in a heated debate about energy. But Martino and Bregenzer (1980:7) observed that "One noteworthy feature of the discussion was a series of comments on the

TABLE 4–6

Group Affective Impacts

Many Studies[a]	Few Studies[b]
Agree	Facilitates supportive interaction $(3+)$
Disagree	
Inhibits trust $(2+;2=0;2-)$	

[a] 5 or more.
[b] Fewer than 5.

high level of decency, kindness, and respect shown for one another despite strong differences of opinion. Computerized conferencing did not seem to dehumanize people."

Only three panelists responded to this item, each voting " + ". Bair's comment for NLS that computerized communication "increases attention—yes, but social interaction merely approximates face to face" suggests that even his positive response is tempered.

Summary

For textual consistency, these results are summarized in Table 4–6. Clearly, more consideration of the group affective level is called for.

BEHAVIORAL IMPACTS ON GROUPS

Impacts at the group behavioral level include relationships with other groups, organizations, and the community; the nature and effectiveness of communication processes; and organizational features including formal and informal structure. The hypothesized impacts include:

1. Computerized communication increases cross-group communication.
2. It increases lateral network linkages among organizations.
3. It increases lateral network linkages within organizations.
4. Research communities become more open (rather than encapsulated) in the long run.
5. Communication links increase: computerized communication can promote communication among disseminated groups which may not otherwise communicate if the need to communicate is great enough.

6. Computerized communication may change social structures from pyramid or hierarchical to network-shaped.
7. It changes the centrality of members within groups.
8. It creates new demands (or reallocation) for institutional support funds within organizations.
9. It can increase the effective limits on the size of working groups, with as many as 50 people or more able to work together on a project.
10. It creates new kinds of social groups, clubs, activities.
11. It creates new ways for organizations to advertise and otherwise promote their goals.
12. The understanding of groupware (software + group needs) leads to new ideas about ways of structuring face-to-face meetings.
13. Computerized communication increases the need for strong and active leadership.
14. The emergence of a leader is different and less likely.
15. Computerized communication promotes equality and flexibility of roles; roles such as moderator, groupware designer, and user consultant carry over to other social situations.
16. It increases the potential for "electronic elites."
17. The increased use of organizational consultants indicates more flexible structures.
18. Computerized communication increases the possible span of control.
19. It increases the density of social networks and increases connectedness among disparate members of a user community.
20. It increases opportunities for decentralized communication.
21. The content threads of conversations increase.
22. Rapid communication reduces lag times. Organizations (and people) learn more and more quickly of events of interest to them.
23. Computerized communication may increase informal communication.
24. It changes who talks to whom.
25. Questions often go unanswered.
26. Groups take longer to reach agreement and consensus is less likely.
27. Computerized communication sometimes makes it difficult to focus discussions.
28. Regularity of individual participation is sometimes difficult to enforce.

29. There is a shift from hierarchical communication to fluid sets of teams.
30. There is greater equality of participation than in conventional media.
31. Kinship ties resolidify to counter residential mobility.

Increased Communication Links

Communication links increase since the medium can promote communication and cooperation among disseminated groups which might not otherwise interact, if the need to communicate is great enough.

Communication options expand, as users must choose which of their interactions will be conducted through computerized communications and which through more traditional channels such as face-to-face, telephone, or mail. Within the electronic medium, users can control their communications in terms of timing, intensity, and duration. They have choices which, depending on the design of the system, may include: synchronous or asynchronous mode; control over the readership of items written; entries with signature, pen name or anonymity; use of private or group messages, conferences or notebooks; conditional or delayed delivery of messages, serial routing, or routing with approvals incorporated; intra- or intergroup communications; self-defined commands; and alternative interfaces.

A significant growth in communication activities was observed among the operational trial groups on EIES:

> Their expanded use of the electronic information exchange system included establishing new computer conferences, increased use of existing conferences, expanded message traffic, the use of automated procedures to survey community members and to organize results, and joint authorship of papers. Research communities have also started inviting observers to participate in their conferences, thereby enhancing their discussions on particular items and providing wider exposure to electronic information exchange (Bamford and Savin, 1978:13).

Panko and Panko (1981) report that increased long-distance communication was the most strongly experienced benefit cited by the respondents to their study of an electronic mail system at DARCOM.

Teleconferencing applications seem especially suited to developing nations, in which the high rates and poor service of other communications media prevent researchers from interacting with their geographically scattered colleagues as easily as is done elsewhere (Ferguson and Johansen, 1975:12).

But the need and motivation to communicate must be present for this and most of the other impacts to occur:

Computer conferencing is a communications medium which must be activated by each user; there is no ringing telephone or other strong social demand. When a participant is so motivated, he dials an access point to a computer network and joins a conference. A person's need to communicate will influence the decision to join a conference, and a lack of group motivation will lead to sporadic attendance. As one user commented: "We had to depend on participants logging in regularly, but most didn't. For a person who is very busy, unless he has a great personal commitment to the conference, it's easy to ignore it" (Vallee et al., 1975:61).

Johansen et al. (1978a) point out that a strong perceived need to communicate is a prerequisite to a successful computer conference:

It is a strange medium to most people. While novelty effects may raise initial interests, the medium must become integrated with participants' workstyles if it is to have an impact. If the perceived need to communicate is not high, the medium is likely to go (pp. 86–88).

The provision of incentives for participation therefore appears to be one of the demands upon leadership.

The experts supported this hypothesized impact quite strongly, with seven checking " + " and two " + + ". The JEDEC evaluators comment that one of their subgroups had no existence off line and convened for special applications only electronically (Johnson-Lenz and Johnson-Lenz, 1980b:7).

Changes in Who Talks to Whom

Turoff and Hiltz (1980) observe that these systems are likely to change the patterns of communication within organizations, since the total amount of communication and the average number of persons with whom each user maintains regular communication are likely to increase. Continuous working relationships among geographically dispersed groups, contact with those in other disciplines, and the reduction of isolation caused by distance (Johansen et al., 1978a:54–61) indicate a change in patterns of interaction.

With the exception of the Mental Workload group which checked " − ", the respondents agreed with this impact. Two replied " + + " and six " + ". The only comment, made by Bair of NLS, was that the impact, "due mostly to exclusion of nonusers," suggests that the changes when they do occur may not necessarily be desirable or beneficial to the groups or organizations involved. The directions that this change can assume are unknown and represent a source of resistance to the technology.

Increases in Informal Communication

This impact is at least partially dependent on the design of the system, since it is possible to restrict interactions as well as monitor the content of exchanges. In an open democratically designed system, in which the privacy of items is protected, however, there are likely to be significant increases in informal communication accompanying the tasks of working groups. This has been frequently observed on both the EIES and PLANET systems. Umpleby (1980) reports an increase in informal communication ties for the General Systems Theory group on EIES. Informal communication can even be deliberately encouraged with devices such as the on-line "cocktail party."

This impact received the strongest support from the experts, with nine rating it " + " and two " + + ". The number of responses to this item was larger than for most.

Changes in Centrality of Members

Computer-mediated communication changes the centrality of members within groups. Comparing different communications media, Vallee et al. (1978:101–105) found that the leader in one may be a supporter in another, and concluded that the relative strength of individuals within organizations may be affected.

Hiltz and Turoff (1978a:20–21) hypothesize that if totally free communication is permitted, computer-mediated networks tend to be decentralized. Centrality is defined as the degree to which an individual, group, or organization within a network can control the communication of others or is free from such control. However, if free communication among members is restricted, the medium could support centralized or hierarchical networks.

Leadership within an ongoing conference may change over time, with different members assuming that role as the focus of the discussion shifts (McCarroll and Cotman, 1980).

Only four panelists responded to this item. Two (General Systems Theory and NLS) report a " + ". Hepatitis indicates "0". And the Mental Workload group disagrees with a " − − ". Bair comments that system knowledge rather than discipline knowledge is responsible for his positive vote, suggesting that the factors underlying changes in membership centrality may not necessarily be most functional to the group's goals, and that these factors may change over time.

Greater Equality of Participation

There is greater equality of participation than in conventional media, in part because everyone can be "talking" by typing or "listening" by reading at the same time.

Whereas face-to-face groups tend to be dominated by one person, who while not necessarily more intelligent or correct, leads the discussion and decision making, this is much less likely with computer-based communication. Since those who are slower to respond or less verbally assertive can more easily participate, it is possible that intelligence and correctness might be more highly correlated with the leadership and dominance processes. The larger the group size, the less likely is the emergence of a dominant leader (Hiltz and Turoff, 1978b:107; Hiltz et al., 1978:6–8).

A series of controlled experiments on EIES produced consistent empirical evidence that there is significantly more equality of participation in computerized communication than in face-to-face conditions (Hiltz, 1978a:11; Hiltz and Turoff, 1978a:14–15; Hiltz et al., 1978:28; Hiltz et al., 1980). And data from the FORUM studies indicate that participation is more balanced compared with other communication media (Johansen et al., 1976).

Turoff (1974b) observed that:

> Individuals communicating through such a system tend to develop a feeling of equality with the other group members. The resulting group atmosphere is very different from a committee meeting where some one individual usually takes control (even if only tacitly) for the purpose of sequencing the discussion (p. 136).

The evaluators of the PLANET system, however, found:

> While computer conferencing allows an equal amount of participation by all those involved, we have seen few examples where such equality has actually occurred. In practice, a few people usually make most of the entries — just as a few people generally dominate face-to-face meetings . . . . However, the equality of participation rates can vary considerably from group to group . . . some unevenness of participation rates appears normal in computer conferences (Johansen et al., 1978:47).

They also note, however, that synchronous conferences seem to encourage more equal distribution of participation rates than do asynchronous conferences.

The medium, then, appears to reduce the amount of inequality rather than producing true equality.

Applications of the technology to the handicapped and other disadvantaged have sought to use these features to broaden opportunity structures for those suffering mobility and communicatory restrictions, stigma, and exclusion from full societal participation, to bring them into the mainstream of society and their chosen careers. Computermediated communication systems can enhance the tools of rehabilitation by increasing social contacts, since users interact at their own pace with time and space boundaries minimized, and the suppression of nonverbal cues means they may interact equally. The interactive nature of the medium can foster social connectivity (Kerr, 1979; Kerr et al., 1979; Price and Kerr, 1978).

The panel of experts could not agree. Responses included one " + + ", three " + ", one "0", and two " − ". Although contributing one of the negative responses, Parnes of CONFER comments that "the same kinds of inequalities seem to hold in practice though in theory this is very plausible." Evidently, this is a potential which is dependent on a number of other unknown factors.

Increased Need for Strong Leadership

The nature of the medium, including the different kinds of group structures that emerge and the absence of pressure to sign on line and participate, create the need for strong and active leadership. The lack of adequate leadership is one of the factors sometimes responsible for conference failure; unless a moderator sets an agenda and keeps the group working toward its goal, nothing much will occur. But the presence of strong and active leadership does not guarantee the success of conferences. Leadership styles may need modification for the effective management of a group through this form of communication. Compared with traditional forms, leaders may feel more or less informed and in control of group activities. Vallee et al. (1978:153–155) maintain that "strong leadership is essential to the effective use of computer conferencing," and suggest that leaders will develop their own sets of organizing and facilitating skills. Edwards (1977:6) states that "to be fully effective, the use of this medium requires an active moderator or discussion leader."

Reporting the experiences of the Futures research group on EIES, Bregenzer and Martino (1980) indicate:

> Our disappointments could be summarized by saying that getting active, committed participation in a conference like ours is like pulling teeth. We do not blame the members. They are proven active, enthusiastic futures researchers. We

do not here blame the technology . . . . We blame the structure of the conference. Perhaps properly, it began in an informal manner without clearly defined goals or an agenda. Therefore members have been communicating as one would at a cocktail party . . . . But the focused, goal-directed type of communication is sorely missed by some of us, and also necessary to any group (p. 68).

Johansen *et al.* (1979) reach this conclusion:

> Computer conferencing provides potentially effective technical structures for controlling group interaction, but few of the familiar social structures. Training people to use the system will be technically easy but socially difficult. We believe it would be a mistake to rely on the technology to direct the communication process—either by imposing highly structured formats or simply using it as an open forum. Leadership is no less important in a computer conference than in face-to-face communication. Strong but subtle leadership appears most appropriate (p. 84).

Hiltz's study of the use of EIES by scientific groups produced conclusions consistent with this evidence:

> In observing the conferences from week to week, it could be seen that if a group leader went on vacation or otherwise disappeared for more than a week at a time, the conference activity tended to become disorganized and then drop off sharply. The group conferences needed a strong, active leader to keep the discussion organized and moving in a way that was satisfying to the participants. [The data] show an almost perfect rank order correlation between the leader's effort as measured by time on line and our measures of the overall success of the group (Hiltz, 1981:131).

There were six responses to this item. Hepatitis and Mental Workload report a " + + " and OICS a " + ". Both NLS and the Devices for the Disabled group have inconsistent evidence which produced a "0". CONFER had no data for this impact, but comments that it "depends on the conference and group goals. It really goes both ways." Perhaps there are circumstances under which the need for strong and active leadership is less than in others.

Difference in Leadership Emergence

The emergence of a leader is different and less likely in the typically unstructured environment of a computerized conference.

Hiltz *et al.* (1978:29–30) administered post-experimental questionnaires asking respondents to assign rankings on leadership behavioral dimensions. The computerized conferencing subjects were significantly less likely to be able to rank order the group than were those who operated in the face-to-face mode.

Multiple leaders, each specializing in and deferred to for a particular aspect of the problem or area of expertise, are more likely to emerge, because of the greater equality of participation and because the computer substitutes for many conventional leadership functions (Hiltz and Turoff, 1978b:107–108).

Umpleby (1980) relates his experience as leader of a group of general systems theory researchers on EIES:

> I for one began with the assumption that a computer conference should pretty much take care of itself. If a group of people with a common set of interests were given access to EIES, I expected that they could conduct their normal professional communication with enhanced speed and effectiveness. Alas, this was not to be . . . . User Consultants began [suggesting] that "strong leadership" was necessary for the success of a computer conference. I strenuously resisted this suggestion. Not only did it offend my democratic sentiments, it implied more work! But the evidence seemed to support the need for strong leadership. Hence I embarked on a strategy of delegation of authority. Surely several strong leaders were better than one . . . .
>
> It appears that an active moderator is necessary to keep the conference going but that as people get used to the system and initiate their own projects, several leaders begin to emerge (p. 56).

McCarroll (1980:74–75) indicates that the use of EIES by the multidisciplinary Devices for the Disabled group was successful in having individual members initiate and moderate a variety of both on-line and off-line activities.

The panel's reaction was quite varied, making it impossible to reach a firm conclusion. There was one " + + ", two " + ", one "0", two " − ", and one " − − ". This area clearly calls for future research.

Increased Network Density

Hiltz and Turoff (1978a:19–20) note a strong tendency for computerized conferencing networks to become increasingly dense or closely knit over time with many direct ties among members. Moreover, the links are multistranded in the sense of the different kinds of role relationships existing among the members of a network.

Quantitative data on this impact on interpersonal relationships emerged from the Social Network Community's experience on EIES (Freeman and Freeman, 1980). As one of the original operational trial groups, it was composed of interdisciplinary scholars studying social networks, or the patterns linking group or community members. A social relationship checklist was administered to the loosely knit members after an initial face-to-face meeting. Seven months later, the density of ties had increased significantly. They conclude that the computer conferencing experience impacted on the group's structure, with an increased density of ties, greater mutual awareness, and tight friendship cliques merging into larger structures.

Eight respondents checked " + " to this item. Only the Mental Workload group differed, with a " − " vote.

Promotion of Role Equality and Flexibility

Computerized communication promotes equality and flexibility of roles; roles such as moderator, groupware designer, and user consultant carry over to other social situations. Only preliminary and qualitative evidence internal to these systems now exists for this impact, as it implies a longer time frame to be actualized than many of those already examined. Vallee *et al.* (1975) have observed the roles assumed by different users on PLANET:

> We have found, for instance, that some persons tend to introduce many new ideas, while others are best at developing them, and still others function as synthesizers. The roles can vary greatly among persons and conferences, but we have noticed an apparent tendency for the "provocative" and "synthesizing" roles to be mutually exclusive. The "provoker" seems to push the discussion forward into new areas of thought, while the "synthesizer" ties the loose strands together (p. 9).

Cross-conference behavior on EIES produced these observations:

> The unique thing about EIES or similar conferencing systems is that the same person may play many different roles in many different conferences that involve different subgroups of people. In one, he or she may be an ordinary member. Since a person is free to browse through the Directory to find compatible groups conducting conferences in related areas, and to request admission to such conferences, a person is quite likely to have the role of outside expert in some conferences; and since every member has the privilege of setting up and acting as moderator of a temporary conference on any topic of his or her choosing, every member of the system has the opportunity to play the lead or moderator role in at least one conference. Thus, we have an extremely fluid social structure (Hiltz and Turoff, 1978b:121).

Although each of these roles is played in effective face-to-face meetings, the electronic medium requires that they be played more explicitly for maximum effectiveness (Price, 1975:550). Software has been designed to facilitate and support specific roles such as facilitator, coordinator, moderator, monitor, editor, gatekeeper, negotiator, and disseminator of information. While users may belong to multiple groups, they maintain separate identities while playing diverse roles.

There were only four responses to this item, two " + " from the Futures research group and General Systems, and a "0" from Hepatitis. Again, the Mental Workload group differed from the others with a "-" vote.

Shift from Hierarchy to Fluid Teams

There is a shift from hierarchical communications to fluid sets of teams. This impact appears to be derived from the relative equality of participation within the electronic medium. Users who had never before worked together have been observed forming temporary teams and small groups to cooperate on tasks for which they discovered a mutual interest.

The panelists supported this impact, with five of the six respondents reporting a "+". Only the Hepatitis group reported a "0" for the absence of either supporting or refuting data. This raises the question of whether the fluid sets of teams are more likely to be found in groups created in the electronic medium or whether they instead change previously existing organizational patterns.

Changed Meeting Structures due to Groupware

The understanding of "groupware" (software plus group needs) leads to new ideas about ways of structuring face-to-face meetings. (The concept of groupware is discussed in detail in Chapter 2.) This again is an idealistic potential rather than a currently documented phenomenon.

There were only three responses, but all were supportive. McCarroll offers this comment for the Devices for the Disabled group: "Have used EIES to plan and prepare for face-to-face meetings—found to be better prepared and further along by the time of the meeting. Also, agenda is usually different than if no computer conferencing beforehand." It appears that groups will need considerable experience using these new media before such groupware spillovers are widely realized.

There are, however, a number of potential problems at the behavioral level, or potentially negative consequences.

Increase in Content Threads

The content threads of conversations increase and multiple topics abound, since autonomous users determine their own participation rates and topics. Turoff (1974b) describes the process:

> One finds in such a discussion a number of separate discussion threads becoming interleaved, and . . . there is not the same pressure to restrict the discussion to a sequential flow with respect to the specific topic of the moment. Therefore, individuals who wish to think about what they will say on a particular matter may wait for a time before making their remarks, and the fact that some of the others in the conversation may have moved on to another topic does not detract from the ultimate impact of the comments. Furthermore, since the computer

assigns a unique sequence number to each message . . . a later message referring to an earlier one need only begin with "Ref. ms. #101." This is in sharp contrast to a verbal discussion where a typical comment referring back usually begins: "In regard to what John was saying awhile back about such and such . . ." A group communicating in this manner becomes accustomed to this oscillating form of communication . . . . Individuals quickly learn to refer back in their remarks to the specific earlier comment they are discussing and the written form fosters a degree of compactness on the remarks. Furthermore, the sorting capability of the computer could be used to regroup the discussion into its separate threads (pp. 135–136).

But there are consequent problems:

> With no norms about "sticking to the subject," participants tend to develop several different topics or ideas at once and reading the transcript can be confusing. A question may be asked in, say, statement number 119, and an answer may not appear until entry 130 or even 150 (Hiltz and Turoff, 1978b:29).

The transcript allows specific discussion topics to be tracked over time and labeled, although such ties are often implicit and difficult to follow (Vallee et al., 1975:9). A combination of software and leadership structuring can help maintain order. For example, a conference moderator may force a vote or a response to a particular item before allowing further action, or may delete items that are irrelevant to the topic.

There was mild agreement from the panel, with a " + + " response from Devices for the Disabled, " + " from three other EIES groups (General Systems, Mental Workload, and Hepatitis), and a "0" from OICS.

Difficulty in Focusing Discussions

It is sometimes difficult to focus discussions in computer-mediated systems, because multiple content threads abound as users participate at their own rates. Vallee et al. (1975:7; 1978:112) note the difficulty of compelling users to direct their comments and point out that "it is the price one pays for the flexibility of asynchronous communication." Leadership practices which emphasize clear organization and take advantage of some of the moderating control features offered by the computer, such as keywords, sequences of associations, or calling for a vote, can offset this problem and possibly lead to greater clarity than might be the case if single-issue discussions were enforced.

One user offered this comment:

> One problem with this week-long conference is that it often loses continuity. Everyone is busy and comes and goes. If four or five interested parties could all sit at the keyboard for the same two hours with a tight agenda, it might more

nearly approximate a brief conference (Cartter, quoted in in Ferguson and Johansen, 1975:39–40).

This issue appears as a tradeoff between single-issue clarity and a rich multiplicity of ideas.

The panel of experts responded with six " + " and one " + + " votes. There was only one dissenting " – " from OICS which included no explanatory comment, but suggests that either system features or leadership styles may offset this problem.

Irregular Participation

Regularity of individual participation is sometimes difficult to enforce (Vallee et al., 1978:112; Edwards,1977:6). This is a by-product of the self-pacing and asynchronous characteristics of the medium, since those whose work style is "interrupt-driven" will not participate much in the absence of scheduled time periods. Explicit expectations and deadlines can to some extent offset this, but at a cost.

Spelt (1977) found this to be characteristic of the conference that he evaluated, since:

> The activity carried little social pressure to participate, and was in addition to the regular duties of the participants. As a result, the degree of participation by the members ranged from very little to a lot . . . the normal constraints of time and space are largely eliminated, and participants are free to join and leave the discussion as their schedules permit. This freedom poses some problems for ongoing activity, because unless a participant chooses to activate his terminal and join the conference, there is no way for other conferees to reach him except by some other medium (pp. 87–88).

Johansen et al. (1978) include this as one of the problems of the medium:

> Organizers often suggest a minimum frequency of participation as a guideline, and this approach proves very useful. However, it may still be necessary to prod some participants further. While the problem may seem to be one of self-discipline, it may simply reveal doubts that a participant had about the purposes of the meeting in the first place. Those who participate frequently will become increasingly frustrated as others fall further behind. Once such a situation develops, it can easily get out of hand, with some participants getting so far behind that they have no hope of catching up. The conference organizer must keep constant readings on the participation of the various group members (p. 95).

Protocols, norms, and sanctions specific to participation in computerized communications media are likely to evolve over time to help the group and its leader more easily enforce expected levels of participation.

The respondents strongly agreed with this, responding with three

" + + ", six " + " and only one "0". Kerr (1980) documents the irregular patterns of participation within the WHCLIS group, and Lamont comments for Legitech that even minimum participation goals were difficult to meet.

Increase in Unanswered Questions

Questions often go unanswered. The asynchronous nature of the medium means that users can take as much time as needed or desired to read, contemplate, and formulate replies to questions. This advantage is counterbalanced by the reduction of the need for immediate responses to questions or other kinds of issues for which feedback is desired by other participants. It is easier to ignore comments or questions than when communicating face to face (Hiltz, 1976:5–6). A new source of frustration can emerge, as well as new challenges for leadership practices to deal with it. Vallee et al. (1975) observe:

> Freedom from the constraints of time and distance can naturally reduce the obligation to communicate. In computer conferencing, the balance between motivation and lack of demand to communicate is different from face-to-face interaction (p. 6).

The EIES groups supported this item quite strongly, with one " + + " and four " + ". But the three other respondents (CONFER, NLS, and OICS) each checked " − ". The comment from CONFER modified this somewhat: "True of any medium. But they often get answered as well. Depends on who is answering." If the EIES/non-EIES split is not spurious, there may be some unexplained system factors at work here. Clearly, more research is needed to explain the conditions under which this does and does not occur.

Decreased Likelihood of Consensus

Groups take longer to reach agreement and consensus is less likely. Controlled experiments conducted on EIES found that, compared with face-to-face groups, computer conferencing groups needed more time to reach a decision and were less likely to reach a unanimous decision for complex problems (Hiltz, 1978a:11; Hiltz et al., 1978, 1980, 1981). This difference in the ability to reach consensus is related to the likely absence of dominant leadership in the electronic mode. Voting routines can be used to facilitate consensus.

However, Siegel (1980) reports the successful experiences of the Hepatitis group on EIES, in which physicians utilized the system to validate and update by consensus the National Library of Medicine's Hepatitis Data Base. Controversial items were identified, discussed, and successfully resolved, and it is anticipated that other data bases will be added to this pilot study.

Similarly, the Joint Electron Device Engineering Council (JEDEC), an industry group for the standardization of hardware and software microprocessor products, developed definitions and standards on EIES in conjunction with quarterly face-to-face meetings. They found that supplementing the meetings with on-line communications sped the process of reaching consensus on decisions, whereas previously the component may have already become obsolete by the time the standard had been set (Johnson-Lenz et al., 1980).

The panelists were about as mixed as the literature review for this issue. The Mental Workload group and OICS supported the hypothesis that groups take longer to reach agreement and that consensus is less likely with " + + " and " + " respective responses. But both the Futures and Hepatitis groups had contradictory evidence and replied " − ". The Devices for the Disabled group studied this impact and found no significant impact ("0").

Reduction in Lag Time

Rapid communication reduces lag times. Group members can maintain constant communication with one another, on a daily or weekly basis and at their own convenience. Snyder maintains that "the replacement of a traditional institutional message system with [computerized conferencing] should substantially accelerate the pace of data flow and information mobilization within the organization" (quoted in Turoff et al., 1978:30).

McKendree (1978:14) notes that organizations can experience reduced turn-around time on urgent decisions or actions, ranging from one or two days in many cases, to one or two weeks. And it shortens the time required for all group members to be in the same place at the same time.

Martino and Bregenzer (1980) found that:

> The visits of two foreign Futures Researchers to the U.S. were greatly facilitated by private messages on the EIES system. Here it became evident that the system was better than the telephone because of its ability to overcome the problems of dealing with different time zones (p. 5).

The experts strongly agreed. With eleven responding, there were two " + + " and eight " + " votes. The Devices for the Disabled group checked "0" and reported inconsistent evidence. The medium will usually reduce lag times, but there evidently can be circumstances under which this is not the case.

Expansion of Group Size

Computerized communication can increase the effective limits of the size of working groups, with 50 or more people able to work together on a project, since all the participants can be "talking" or "listening" at the same time and it is impossible to interrupt. Hiltz and Turoff (1978b) describe the possibilities:

> Group size can be expanded without decreasing actual participation . . . . A single computer can accommodate from hundreds to thousands of users, whereas the mechanisms of finding a comfortable room and getting everyone together for a face-to-face meeting of such a group are expensive and discouraging (p. 9).

Turoff notes that it is possible to have 30 to 50 people engaged in a computerized discussion, comparing it with conference telephone calls which are cumbersome with more than five people participating (1972:163; 1974a:55). "We have had numerous examples on the EIES system of groups of up to 15 individuals jointly working on the same document and report preparation" (Turoff, 1980b). PLANET supports synchronous conferences of up to 36 people (Vallee et al., 1978:64).

Strong and positive agreement with this issue was obtained from the respondents, who checked one " + + " and six " + ". It is apparent even to new users. For instance, 70% of the less experienced COM users and 80% of its more experienced users agreed that "work in larger groups is possible."

Increases in Lateral Network Linkages within Organizations

It increases lateral network linkages within organizations:

> Inherently, these systems do encourage lateral communications. They make it possible for an individual to have a much larger number of people in regular and frequent communication than is otherwise possible. One can impose constraints on this freedom of communications but as yet there has been little experience with attempts at this sort of design. The experience in a number of organizations has been a greater tendency to increased coordination laterally on at least an informal basis (Turoff and Hiltz, 1980).

Housman (1980) describes a current application on GTE's Telemail electronic messaging system:

> In companies like GTE, which has subsidiaries spread out on a worldwide scale, terminals are appearing in many executive offices to coordinate corporate-wide activities and to maintain a continuous dialog with peers in other divisions (p. 2).

The OICS study found that "the time spent in communication among peers" increased, and that "the percentage of attempts to contact fellow workers that failed (e.g., from busy phone lines) decreased. Reductions in such shadow functions carry measurable cost-benefit implications" (Tapscott, 1981:12).

Increases in Cross-Group Communication

There are new opportunities to meet people with channels for electronic mobility and migration. An open system such as EIES includes a searchable directory, the ability to address messages to those who specify an interest in a topic as well as to individuals and groups, human user consultants for facilitation and connectivity as well as teaching system features, and public conferences including one in which private conferences open to new members are announced. This permits and encourages more cross-group communication than does a system such as PLANET which prohibits these kinds of introductions and interactions. People can discover each other's existence and connect on the basis of shared interests, rather than by job title, organizational purpose, or personal introduction (Price, 1975:514). Some managers or organizations may not want their members engaging in cross-group communication, however. For example, the Banker's Trust group on EIES instructed its members not to enter any information about themselves into the public directory.

Members of research communities have been observed joining the deliberations of other communities (Turoff, 1980b; Bamford and Savin, 1978). Bezilla (1979) labels this "a transitive network," allowing relatively free interactions among all members, rather than being restricted to either broadcasting or centralized communication paths.

The expert panelists, with the exception again of the Mental Workload group which voted " − ", agreed. Two reported " + + " and seven " + ". The comments here are widely dispersed, ranging from strong quantitative evidence to observations of group behavior.

Creation of New Kinds of Groups

Because people are able to find others with common interests, they can establish new groups and new kinds of activities not possible through other media. The electronic linkage of those who may never have met in person permits qualitatively different kinds of interactions and social forms.

Interaction within a viable social system results in the formation of qualitatively new kinds of primary and secondary relationships to supplement or replace traditional groups. The most frequent users of EIES, for example, report a strong sense of on-line community, with close friendships and collegial ties, as well as a sense of loss when unable to access the system.

Support was received from the panel, which reported four " + " and a "0" from OICS.

Increases in Lateral Network Linkages between Organizations

Open systems such as EIES promote or at least allow these kinds of cross-group interactions. Users are free to exchange messages with all others on line regardless of their group affiliations. They may be invited to join conferences established by other groups, either as participants or observers. A public conference in which all are free to read or contribute contains unrefereed papers on a variety of topics. And the public user directory permits members to discover others with shared interests and perhaps form their own informal or formal groups as a consequence.

Members of the EIES group exploring Devices for the Disabled have "expressed their appreciation for the contact this project has made possible with persons in other disciplines who can contribute to their work but with whom they previously had no available channel of communication" (McCarroll, 1980:76).

The evolution of Politechs-Topics on EIES illustrates a system created for a group of state legislative science advisors. Since the inquiries and responses range over a very diverse set of subjects and the activity is quite high, a filtering structure allows members to choose which topics they wish to track. Politechs is a system in which more than 50 individuals representing separate autonomous organizations share and exchange specialized knowledge and resources according to need (Turoff, 1980b; Johnson-Lenz and Johnson-Lenz, 1980d). Lamont's report (1980) on the group's experience concludes:

> The legislative researchers . . . have noted in particular the timeliness and quality of the responses they have received to their queries. Many have pointed out that the system has greatly increased their resource network with respect to other legislative researchers and the federal agencies. Most certainly the system has provided the opportunity to develop a more efficient communication system, eliminating duplication of research effort and enhancing the quality of information provided to legislatures (p. 461).

Simard and Miller (1980) report the use of NOTEPAD, by 64 United States utilities and several foreign utilities as well as technical advisory groups, for real-time information exchange related to the safety and licensing of nuclear reactors. A new crisis management tool has been created in the event of a major accident.

One respondent checked "+ +" for this impact, and five checked "+". The one dissenting "0" was from the General Systems group, and was accompanied by the comment that this is potentially the case.

Decentralization of Communication

Computer-mediated communication systems increase opportunities for decentralized communication because it is easier to keep all those concerned with the issues informed and up to date. Greater delegation of authority is possible with the capacity for accountability and reviewing decisions in a timely and orderly manner. Scheduling and action tracking facilities can be included for coordinating complex projects in which a change in one element must be reflected in others (Turoff, 1980b; Turoff and Hiltz, 1977:7).

> In some cases the technology is actively used at a peer group level to bring about agreement before raising the issue to a higher level of management. These systems also allow greater delegation of authority since they allow quick informing and review of potential actions as well as the accountability necessary for delegation of authority. The extent to which decentralization and delegation is desired should be a factor in both the design and the operational practices associated with these systems. One would suspect, for example, in organizations that thrive on competition among peer level managers that an open design might not be the most desirable or would not be very successful (Turoff and Hiltz, 1980).

The World Symposium on Humanity was a week-long event held simultaneously in London, Toronto, and Los Angeles in 1978. Rather than having a single headquarters from which decisions were dictated to other locations, a joint conference on EIES in which several people at each location participated enabled a decentralized decision-making process and daily sharing of information, problems, and issues. Decentralized control was possible because the medium provides the ability to coordinate actions and to establish accountability. "We know of no other way that a dispersed project team could have worked together with the same coordination of effort that can usually only be exhibited by a co-located team" (Turoff and Hiltz, 1979:10–12).

Hiltz and Turoff (1978b) predict that:

> The Home Office might become simply a supplier of services to relatively autonomous units of the organization . . . . If decisions are being made autonomously, at the local level, they might be made much more quickly and with a better understanding of the nature of the problem. For the corporate executive himself, his real power may be usurped by the local managers, and he may become reduced to serving as nothing more than a figurehead, like modern monarchs. On the other hand, executives who adapt to the new communications tool might find that they can become much better informed and much more able to try out controversial ideas than ever before. Computerized conferencing allows the lateral

coordination necessary for decentralization of authority with a speed and efficiency not possible with other communication systems. Ongoing transcripts of all conferences among middle managers permit monitoring of and/or intervention if an unwise decision seems imminent (p. 144).

The panel supported this impact with all eight respondents reporting "+".

Increases in Possible Span of Control

Computerized communication increases the possible span of control as a corollary of the possibilities of decentralization. Within organizations, it allows more centralized control over geographically dispersed units. Within more amorphous fields, such as scientific disciplines or invisible colleges, it expands the size of the groups which may be directed or influenced.

There were only three responses to this hypothesized impact, but all were positive. NLS reports a "+ +" and attributes it to increased vertical communication. Both OICS and the Hepatitis group responded with "+".

Increased Use of Organizational Consultants

The increased use of organizational consultants indicates more flexible structures. This is another long-range potential of the medium rather than an impact for which we have firm data. Johansen *et al.* (1979) offer these comments:

Teleconferencing provides an opportunity to organize groups in a nonparochial fashion, to tap resources that may be far away. Decisions about whom to consult or what information to use do not have to be constrained by what is closest. Distant experts can consult with a group more effectively: they can avoid tiring travel which may leave them less "expert"; and they can remain close to their own resources (pp. 20–21).

But they also point out that an overemphasis on the opportunities for easy access could encourage too narrow a view of experts. "The expert could become someone 'out there' who is available to solve all of the problems if only he or she could be reached. The expert's facts and figures might be viewed as the 'truth' when they are only limited truths at best; at worst, they might not even be accurate information" (Johansen *et al.*, 1979, pp. 20–21).

There were only two responses to this item, from the General Systems and WHCLIS groups, both of which reported "+". The White House Conference was able to utilize a number of consultants in the planning and coordination tasks that were conducted on EIES.

Changes in Social Structures

Given that varying group structures are simply accommodated or reflected in the medium, it could be used to revise conventional pyramid or hierarchical structures, at least experimentally, and possibly in the direction of the open democratic characteristics towards which these systems tend.

> Because EIES is dedicated to information exchange anyone on the system . . . is free to message anyone else on the system. It would certainly be possible in such a system to have set up restrictions on who could communicate with whom and even make these restrictions asymetric. Certainly, in some commercial systems being designed today, the assumption is that one will reflect the organizational structure in the message sending privileges (e.g., employees can only send to members of their own organizational unit and their immediate supervisor). Such designs could have the potential impact of further placing in concrete current organizational structures and inhibiting the possibilities for improved lateral communications that in turn could lead to new approaches to meeting organizational objectives (Turoff, 1979).

This item produced only a few positive responses, with one " + + " and three " + " votes.

New Ways to Promote Goals

New capabilities for advertising and promotion can reach more people, more selectively, and at reduced costs. Software for an information marketplace can be included within these systems so that recipients are protected against unwanted "junk mail," and so that equitable arrangements can be made for the exchange of goods, services, or information for either cash or barter (Turoff *et al.*, 1981). These features apply to commercial and nonprofit service groups and organizations, as well as to individuals.

There were five affirmative replies to this essentially futuristic impact, and the Devices for the Disabled group documented that this is already beginning to occur.

Creation of New Demands for Funds

Computerized communication creates new demands for reallocation of institutional support funds within organizations. There is as yet no material in the literature bearing on this impact. However, Vallee *et al.* (1978) outline some of the possible strategies that may develop for dealing with this kind of budgeting decision:

> The costs of computer conferencing can be charged in different ways. A conferencing budget may be established for each individual project, with the cost of

> terminals, computer usage, and support services charged to the project. Or all computer conferencing expenses may be viewed as part of general overhead, much like the telephone and letter correspondence are in many organizations. Of course, a halfway approach is possible, too: the cost of terminals, for example, may be charged to overhead while the computer usage costs must be covered by individual project budgets (p. 161).

The type of interorganizational communication made possible with regular working relationships among researchers at different institutions could challenge current administrative institutional structures for the allocation of research funds. Requests for alternative funding structures for work and resource sharing with remote groups would confront institutional barriers and possibly create new and independent group forms (Johansen et al., 1978a:106–107).

Six of the groups reported " + " findings for this issue, evidently reflecting their own experiences, since the comments attached refer to the problems experienced by their users.

Increased Potential for Elites

Computer-mediated communication systems increase the potential for "electronic elites." The realization of this impact would be ironic, since the EIES system in particular was designed in part to offset the exclusive nature of scientific communications. Prior to the development of computer-based communication systems, interaction could only occur by personal visit, telephone call, or use of the mails. The number of people who could simultaneously communicate was reduced usually to two except for meetings, or more with considerable difficulty or expense. Yet those with access to this new technology may emerge as a new elite precisely because their access better connects them to those with whom they need to communicate.

There were four " + " responses to this impact, and one " + + ", from the Mental Workload group, but OICS dissented with a " − ".

Increased Openness of Research Communities

Research communities become more open rather than encapsulated in the long run. This is the reverse possibility. The operational trials of EIES were formulated to test impacts on "invisible colleges" of eminent groups of scientists engaged in and dominating the resources of research specialties. These trials, sponsored by the National Science Foundation, hypothesized that members of such "colleges" would communicate more productively and efficiently, and in the long run be more open to new members (Hiltz, 1976:18–22).

Johansen et al. (1978a:60,82,102) recognize that the medium, on the other hand, could actually encourage more closed communication among a select group of people who form an electronic barrier between themselves and other potential participants, excluding them from their deliberations. Invitations to join a particular computer conference could become as prized as positions at prestigious institutions. But they also indicate that one of the outcomes of group usage has been the provision of more diverse contact for junior researchers who can gain status very quickly by building their own collegial networks.

This impact, then, will evidently depend on other factors such as group needs, values, and structures.

Most of the respondents agreed with the likelihood of this impact. COM responded with a " + + " and there were five supporting " + " replies. Only the Devices for the Disabled group had conflicting evidence leading to a " − " response. The comment was that users "may communicate more outside of their usual circles, but don't seem to become more open in their communications."

Resolidification of Kinship Ties

Kinship ties resolidify to counter residential mobility. This is another long-range hypothesized impact for which there is no support in the literature. Hiltz and Turoff (1978b) predict:

> Computerized conferencing can make it very easy to keep in touch with family and friends and colleagues who are located some distance away. A person could generate the equivalent of a "Dear Everyone" newsletter a few times a month, for instance, adding a few sentences at the beginning or end specifically directed to each person. In this manner, it would not be much of a time-consuming chore at all to keep in touch . . . computer conferencing provides a convenient and low-cost channel of communication for staying in touch . . . can enlarge the effective support network available to individuals (pp. 205–206).

This was the only listed impact which produced no responses at all from the panel of experts. In part, this may be because it now appears to have been incorrectly placed and perhaps should have been included among the impacts at the individual or group affective level. This also is clearly a factor that cannot yet be tested by data.

Summary

Table 4–7 summarizes these impacts at the group behavioral level by agreement and sample size. The dimensions unifying this section appear to be increased connectivity, changes in communication processes, and changes in the nature of social structures. Interestingly,

TABLE 4-7

Group Behavioral Impacts

Many Studies[a]	Few Studies[b]
Agree	
Increases informal communication (2 + +;9 +)	Changes social structures (1 + +;3 +)
Communication links increase (2 + +;7 +)	Groupware changes meeting structures (1 + +;2 +)
Decentralizes communication (8 +)	Increases possbile span of control (1 + +;2 +)
Expands group size (1 + +;6 +)	Increased organizational consultants (2 +)
Creates new demands for funds (6 +)	
New ways to promote goals (1 + +;4 +)	
Reduces lag time (2 + +;8 +;1 = 0)	
Irregular participation (3 + +;6 +;1 = 0)	
Increases lateral linkages within organizations (2 + +;5 +;1 = 0)	
Increases lateral linkages between organizations (1 + +;5 +;1 = 0)	
Fluid teams versus hierarchy (5 +;1 = 0)	
Content threads increase (1 + +;3 +;1 = 0)	
Creates new kinds of groups (4 +;1 = 0)	
Increases need for strong leader (2 + +;1 +;2 = 0)	
Disagree	
Increases cross-group communication (2 + +;7 +;1 = 0;1 −)	Promotes role equality and flexibility (2 +;1 = 0;1 −)
Changes who talks to whom (2 + +;6 +;1 −)	Changes centrality of members (2 +;1 = 0;1 − −)
Increases network density (8 +;1 −)	
Difficult to focus discussions (1 + +;6 +;1 −)	
Research communities become more open (1 + +;5 +;1 −)	
Increases potential for elites (1 + +;4 +;1 −)	
Greater equality of participation (1 + +;3 +;1 = 0;2 −)	
Consensus less likely (1 + +;1 +;1 = 0;2 −)	
Questions often unanswered (1 + +;4 +;1 = 0;3 −)	
Leadership emergence is different (1 + +;2 +;1 = 0;2 −;1 − −)	

[a] 5 or more.
[b] Fewer than 5.

the impacts which could be either negative or problematic produced disagreement among the panelists, whereas the positive impacts all appear within the two strong agreement cells. Those impacts in the bottom left cell, for which the data conflicted, represent the most pressing need for further research.

SOCIETAL IMPACTS

A list of impacts at the societal level was also generated. However, since we only have the most projective kinds of evidence for these impacts, we did not attempt to collect data for this level. They are presented below, however, both for completeness and for the beginnings of a list which will be capable of being documented sometime in the future.

Cognitive Impacts on Society

1. The shift from time-binding (traditional, religious) to space-binding (political, pragmatic, instrumental) societies continues.
2. Ease of communication brings news from greater distances, awareness of more events, increased cultural diversity, and new conceptual universes, leading to more complex world views and more humane social systems.
3. Libraries transcend current computerized discussions and past discussions from books and history.
4. Access to information becomes a political issue; for example, computerized information retrieval systems raise the question of paying for library services.
5. The growth of the information sector leads to the reexamination of economic policies; for example, reindustrialization policy.
6. Illiteracy is reduced.
7. Automated language translation creates norms for correct spelling.
8. Information becomes more culturally valued.
9. There are impacts on privacy, confidentiality, and anonymity.
10. Issues such as copyright, subpoena of computer message tapes, and liability change.
11. Pressure for unbreakable codes increases.
12. Better information for decision makers is available.
13. New jokes, cartoons, stories, plays, novels, music, art, etc., abound.

Affective Impacts on Society

1. There is a growth of shared metaphors for people in many walks of life.
2. Geographically defined communities decline as sources of identity, with increased attention to shared interest (including professional) affiliations.
3. The prestige of organizations changes.
4. Etiquette and social conventions change.
5. There is a greater preponderance of achieved versus ascribed statuses with a shift to judging people by ideas versus appearance, position, etc.
6. Use of computer conferencing by prisoners aids rehabilitation.
7. Electronic job mobility promotes the maintenance of communities.

Behavioral Impacts on Society

1. Governments attach tariffs (such as per character charges) to international data flow to prevent their telephone systems eliminating their telegraph systems.
2. New kinds of clandestine operations and covert warfare (e.g., international computerized conferencing combined with the electronic typesetting of newspaper copy) make it easier for the CIA or KGB to run propaganda, disinformation and destabilization campaigns in developing countries.
3. Sabotage of communication links is a countermeasure, as both subversive groups and the foes of revolution become more efficient.
4. Clever new ways of disseminating information and disinformation can be thought of as "information weaponry."
5. International contexts for teleconferencing lead to market preference for hard copy, since text is much easier to translate than is voice.
6. Cross-cultural dissemination of information increases, including impacts on third-world nations, as computerized conferencing is used to manage international projects.
7. International communication is easier for people with limited foreign language abilities, especially as computerized language translation becomes available.
8. It is simpler for governments to monitor communication traffic and message content if it is not encoded.
9. Social structures may be more fragile and vulnerable because

of the potential devastating effects of power failures, computerized support worker strikes, etc.

10. The potential for democratic capitalism is increased.
11. The potential for the centralization of power increases.
12. There is greater interagency collaboration and citizen participation in hearings, regulations, and legislation.
13. There are new ways to organize and operate political campaigns.
14. The rate of social change increases with more rapid dissemination of knowledge, higher quality of work, and less duplication of effort.
15. Contacts between scientists, businessmen, and government officials improve.
16. Unbreakable codes eliminate a major constraint to government and business use of public networks, resulting in fewer independent networks for the wealthy and more support for public networks.
17. There are increases in direct personal selling via electronic classified ads that can be searched automatically.
18. An increased share of family income is allocated to information goods such as terminals and connect time.
19. Reduced traffic lessens petroleum consumption and auto expenses.
20. The computer industry grows faster than the economy.
21. Electronic universities increase the number of faculty members who are either self-employed or employed at another university.
22. The publishing industry becomes an "output device" or summarizer of the computerized working media.
23. There is continued growth of software "cottage industry" and work-at-home programmers.
24. Neighborhood work centers fill the gap between working at home and office.
25. Needs for back-up power systems increase.
26. The opportunities for old people with knowledge and experience but reduced mobility are enhanced, but may not be realized until current users grow old.

CONCLUSIONS

A comprehensive literature review plus responses from a panel of experts provided the data from which we attempted to project cognitive, affective, and behavioral impacts of computer-mediated communication systems for individuals and groups. On the basis of projections from observed impacts at the individual and group levels, it is possible to make "informed guesses" about probable societal-level impacts. Such a list was generated by the participants in the project. However, until and unless these systems are in much more widespread use, it is not possible to test these societal impacts. Reviewing the summary tables presented in this chapter produces a picture of the current state of knowledge in this area.

The strongest support was achieved at the level of individual behavioral impacts, where 9 of the 15 or 60% of the hypothesized impacts produced unanimous agreement from a relatively large number of studies. The group behavioral level achieved the next highest support, with 47% strong agreement. The fact that behavioral impacts are more observable than are those at the cognitive or affective levels probably accounts for this.

Of the total of 79 hypothesized impacts, only 2 (at the group behavioral level) yielded disagreement from a small number of studies. Further research is called for in those areas producing either agreement from only a small number of studies or disagreement from a larger number of studies, since these are the impacts likely to be conditional upon such variables as the nature of the task, the design of the system being used, and the characteristics of the group.

The impacts were classified according to their desirability or positive attributes, rating them positive, negative, or neutral, and the results are presented in Table 4–8. An interesting pattern emerges in which the positive impacts of the medium exhibit much stronger support than do the negative ones. 25 of the 55 impacts classified as essentially positive produced solid support from a large number of studies. On the other hand, it is reassuring that 8 of the 9 impacts with undesirable consequences yielded disagreement from a large number of studies. For the most part, the negative outcomes appear to be conditional

TABLE 4–8

Impacts by Level, Consensus, and Desirability

	Positive	Negative	Neutral	Total
Many studies agree	25	1	6	32
Many studies disagree	15	8	5	28
Few studies agree	13	—	4	17
Few studies disagree	2	—	—	2
Total	55	9	15	79

upon other factors, since they are sometimes observed and sometimes absent.

These are clearly encouraging results. Further research should concentrate not only on the areas of disagreement, but on those conditions likely to enhance the positive impacts and reduce the negative ones.

CHAPTER 5

Appropriate Research Methodology

INTRODUCTION

This chapter reviews the various methodologies used in past studies of computer-mediated communication systems and explores the innovative methodological tools made possible by the electronic medium, in seeking to identify the most appropriate combination of research tools with which to examine this technology. In considering the kinds of evaluation methods appropriate to research on these systems, it is not possible to address the entire field of evaluation. Our goal is to review the nature and purpose of evaluating these systems and to give examples of appropriate methodologies which have been used.

Evaluation and feedback are integral to the development of computer-mediated communication systems. As James Bair has observed (in Uhlig et al., 1979):

> Ongoing assessment for at least the first two years of operation will provide management with feedback about the implementation performance permitting corrective action if performance is suboptimal. Implementation without a formal assessment is analogous to trying to navigate a mine field blindfolded (p. 252).

GOALS OF EVALUATION

In the quotation above, Bair is referring to what is termed "formative" evaluation. Evaluation of computer-mediated systems may include any or all of the goals of formative and summative research with applied or basic research aims.

Formative evaluation is used as a source of data about user reactions to be fed back to modify the system design or implement strategies to increase both system acceptance and desired outcomes. It may be discovered, for instance, that the interface is considered "unfriendly" or "awkward," that the documentation is inadequate, or that the system does not perform a function that would make it much more valuable for a specific application. For formative evaluation to be successful, the system designers must be receptive to implementing changes suggested by the data collection efforts. An example of an outcome from formative evaluation is given for HUB:

> Because HUB was a new and untested system, [formative evaluation] was extremely useful in locating problems and identifying ways in which the system could be improved. As a result of this feedback, a number of changes—some minor and some major—have been made in HUB over the course of the project. Some of these changes [were in system structure].
>
> Feedback from the first HUB trials indicated that users were becoming confused about the relationship of the system's modules. This led to a major revision of basic architecture of the system. In the initial version, HUB was essentially a central switcher for four separate subsystems—the conference, graphic, document, and program workspaces. Users had trouble visualizing this structure and had difficulty in moving from one module to another.
>
> In the new version, the conferencing facility was placed at the "center" of the system. The other services—the document, graphic, and program workspaces, and a new question workspace—were arranged around the central conference as auxiliary resources. This arrangement proved much more satisfactory, since sending and receiving conference messages is the simplest and most "natural" of HUB's services to use (Adler and Lipinski, 1981:444–445).

The concept of formative evaluation has been integrated into the very structure of the EIES system, which is designed as a continually evolving research and development test bed for computer-based communication research. The acquisition of data useful for improving the system's components and performance is an ongoing activity. Human user consultants are available for questions about the mechanics of using the system, complaints about its performance, and suggestions for its improvement. A file of these comments is periodically examined and changes are made in system features and capabilities accordingly.

Summative evaluation is concerned with the overall measurement of a system's costs and benefits and with the dissemination of this knowledge for guiding future implementations. The goals may very from the very "applied" decisions by a specific organization about whether or not to continue the use of a specific system, to the generation of knowledge about the impacts of these types of systems.

In the process of carrying out either formative or summative evaluation, basic rather than applied research goals may be adopted. For example, one may wish to develop a general set of principles of effective interface design for interactive computer systems in general, use the unique capabilities of the computer to develop new methodological techniques to conduct research in a variety of fields, or use the detailed kinds of information about human group interaction processes that can be gathered from the records on computer-mediated communication systems to develop general theories about communication or group processes.

The goals of formative, summative, basic, and applied research are not necessarily contradictory. Although different "stakeholders" in the evaluation process are likely to have differing priorities about their relative importance, a comprehensive evaluation can achieve multiple goals. Neither are the various methodological approaches described below mutually exclusive; on the contrary, they are generally much better used in combination than as single data collection techniques. For instance, the evaluation of the EIES field trials by Hiltz (1981) was a cross-group investigation conducted by using a series of questionnaires, interviews, participant observation, and monitor data. It was a formative evaluation since the results were fed back to the system designer and implementors for the evolution of system features to meet the expressed needs of users. Users were queried in detail about their reactions to such system features as the information brochure, user's guide, protocols, and alternative interfaces. It was a descriptive and analytical evaluation which addressed some basic research questions in that specific hypotheses about the impact of the medium upon scientific research specialties were systematically investigated. A quasi-experimental design involved a time series of measurements of the information-seeking, communication, and productivity related behavior of the users. And it was a summative evaluation since comparable cross-group data were collected for generalizations about the group characteristics or conditions associated with various degrees of successful or unsuccessful use of the medium.

STAKEHOLDERS

Stakeholders who initiate and fund the evaluation, as well as those who carry it out, are concerned with its outcome. A detailed description of the various stakeholders in system development and evaluation is provided by Rice and Danowski (1981), whose observations are summarized:

1. *Funders* may be a private or public organization financing the development of a computer-mediated communication system. As controllers of the resources, they frequently determine access and subsidization, as well as the level of funding and evaluation requirements.
2. *Activists* are those concerned with the social uses and effects of the medium, as proponents, technological forecasters, or social planners.
3. *Designers* are concerned with products and markets. Issues for them include the tasks to be supported by the software and the human factors to be addressed by the design.
4. *Content providers* influence the flow of information with supply, training, regulation, feedback and distribution. Libraries are likely to play an increasing role as electronic information exchange brokers, as are news services and on-line data bases.
5. *Administrators* include program and system directors, programmers and support staff, and facilitators.
6. *Users* of these systems are also to be counted among the stakeholders. Rather than being concerned with the outcome of evaluation, they are concerned with its costs to them, in terms of time demands to participate or intrusions on their privacy.

DATA COLLECTION AND ANALYSIS METHODS

Most evaluations rely heavily on the primary methods of data collection used in other social science research: surveys, participant observation, content analyses, and controlled experiments. These methods, to be used most fruitfully, should be modified to take into account the special circumstances and unique possibilities offered when the interaction being observed is captured in an electronic form. In addition, there are methods made possible only by the nature of the systems themselves, such as automatic monitoring of user activity and social network analysis of user groups based on who-to-whom data generated by message traffic. We will review the nature of each of the major data collection methodologies, describe the adjustments and cautions that should be observed when applying them to evaluation of computer-mediated communication systems, and provide some examples of their use in previous evaluation studies.

User Surveys

Questionnaires and structured interviews are the traditional research tools most frequently applied to evaluation of this medium. Ideally, they are administered in a time series to study patterns of change in attitudes and behavior over time. For instance, during the EIES operational trials, questionnaires were administered to all users before they first signed on line, 3 to 6 months later, and after 18 to 24 months of use. With this "panel" design of repeated measures over time, changes in attitudes and needs as a function of experience in using such systems can be traced, patterns of cause and effect that produce impacts on the users can be discerned, and it can be learned how to build a system meeting the needs of both new and very experienced users.

The survey is the main source of quantifiable data which can be subjected to multivariate analysis so as to untangle often complex webs of causality. It is important that surveys be designed and analyzed by experienced research professionals. Designing a set of questions which are clear, unbiased, and interesting requires considerable experience: A questionnaire put together by an amateur is liable to yield a low response rate and invalid data. It is also important that the research design (choice of variables to be included, methods and timing for collecting the data, and analysis) be done by someone very familiar with this area, lest important variables be omitted or incorrect conclusions drawn. Unless multivariate methods are used which rely on knowledge both of the findings of previous studies of communication-information systems and of a variety of statistical techniques, spurious correlations can easily be accepted as "effects." An example is the simple bivariate correlation between typing ability and acceptance of NLS observed by Edwards; when she introduced overall preuse attitude toward the system as a control variable, there was no relationship (Edwards, 1977). Typing ability was being used as a socially acceptable excuse by those who were negatively disposed toward the system. An inexperienced evaluator would probably stop at the observed two variable relationship and incorrectly conclude that only good typists will use such systems.

Although the survey used in a multiwave or panel design serves as the "backbone" of most evaluation efforts, other data collection techniques are needed to fill out this skeletal information into a rich, full body of knowledge about an implementation effort.

The timing of surveys and other data collection is of major concern. Since the consequences of the system cannot yet, if ever, be fully anticipated, preuse measures of existing communication patterns and behavior that might be affected need to be gathered. But user opinions prior to gaining experience on these systems are often misleading, and frequently difficult to obtain, as they are not yet aware of new opportunities or needs. A normative approach of asking what communication processes are needed and then designing a system to encourage those processes is both superior to and more difficult than simply attempting to make current patterns more efficient (Turoff, 1980b). And response rates are often disappointingly low on preuse surveys. As Johansen et al. (1978) point out:

> There was a real reluctance to participate in pretests before the usage period began. Questionnaires sometimes had the effect of "scaring away" potential participants and less obtrusive methods (e.g., observation of communication patterns) were either very difficult to arrange or would have been perceived as a violation of group privacy (p. 49).

Automated Surveys

Structured interviews and questionnaires can be automated for administration on line. This has clear advantages over the traditional application of these methods. Respondents can query the researcher directly requesting clarification of questions, complex branching of questions is greatly simplified, and there are options for multiround Delphi studies with feedback to participants. The instruments are not subject to interviewer variation, response bias, and other common sources of error. Moreover, accuracy and response rates may well be greater, and delays and costs reduced, since reminder notes can be automatically distributed at predetermined intervals, interviews are not individually administered, and respondents can participate at their convenience.

> A poll or survey conducted over computerized conferencing could very conceivably have the questions sent out, answered, and automatically tabulated and reported back by the computer within a single day's time. One could even imagine designing a set of questions in the morning, pretesting them in a period of an hour or so, and later conducting the full-scale survey, all in the same day. There is no need, for instance, to wait for typing and photocopying of survey instruments. They can be composed, corrected, revised and sent out on line in a matter of hours (Hiltz 1978c:11–12).

Participant Observation

With this method, the evaluator both observes and participates in the on-line activities (with the knowledge and permission of the groups involved, of course), gaining a qualitative grasp of the nature of the interaction, and specifically with the factors associated with the success or failure of different groups using the same system. Unless one is quite confident ahead of time of which variables to study and precisely how to measure them, it is crucial to include participant observation among the data collection methods.

There are, however, two dangers: "going native" and role conflict. The first refers to involving oneself in the group to the extent that objectivity is lost. Role conflict can mean a dilemma between the goals of the group and those of the evaluation. Being a "complete observer" who takes no active part in the group being observed is likely to make the subjects feel self-conscious or resentful, and unlikely to confide in or trust the observer with private information about their experiences. For both methodological and ethical reasons, it is preferable for the participant–observer to actually find a useful but unobtrusive way of participating in the group. Hiltz (1981) describes the role she played and the problems of losing objectivity as follows:

> These qualitative observations have been useful in providing an understanding of what the user groups actually did on the system. The role played might be described as "observer as participant"; the scientists knew that the author was observing for evaluational purposes. As a form of reciprocity, the observer offered to be of assistance whenever possible. A passive role was played, with comments entered by the participant observer generally only in response to a direct request for information or an opinion. Many participants also shared their reactions to the system in private messages to the evaluator, and played the role of informant, describing or calling attention to activities and exchanges on the system which they thought would be of interest in the study.
>
> The most severe of the methodological problems, of course, is the problem of "going native." In order to understand the use of EIES and its evolving electronically based social system, and to remain in communication with the subjects, it was necessary to spend a great deal of time on line. More than 3000 hours on line have been logged in the course of this study. Thus, the objectivity afforded by "outsider" status was long ago lost.
>
> The main solution to the "going native" problem is that the data presented and interpretations made stay as closely as possible to objective evidence supplied by the participants themselves . . . . (p. 30).

Kerr, in studying the WHCLIS group on EIES, played the dual role of evaluator and facilitator. As she points out, awareness of the situation can help:

> Although the role of the researcher as both group facilitator and evaluator posed some potential methodological dilemmas for participant observation, this in fact was not a major problem because of awareness of the situation, because the two efforts were separated in time segments, and because the relevant statistics were collected and presented separately (Kerr, 1980:788).

An example of the unique value of participant observation in studying the frequently unanticipated outcomes of use of this new medium is provided by Martino and Bregenzer (1981):

To a very great extent, the observed behavior of the group departed from our expectations. We do not fully understand the reasons for this. However, the results were quite clearcut. Some behavior that we expected to see was absent or nearly so. Conversely, some behavior we had not anticipated did take place. The effect of this departure from expected behavior was that many of the measurements we had planned to make turned out to be impossible. Instead, we found that analysis of what actually took place in the conference required sensitivity to interpersonal behavior rather than objective measures of small-group activity. Fortunately, the presence of a social scientist as "assessor" made it possible to carry out this type of analysis instead of the "count-and-measure" type of analysis we had originally planned (p. 360).

Controlled Experiments

Controlled experiments have been conducted to explore specific characteristics of the medium as both independent and dependent variables, using laboratory studies to investigate such variables as media variation, decision-making time and quality, consensus, and satisfaction (Hiltz, 1978a; Hiltz et al., 1978, 1980, 1981). There are ethical questions here concerning the randomization of these controls, with unpredictable consequences for assignment to the computerized communication versus alternative treatment group. Truly randomized control groups are not possible using this technology, and experimental conditions and designs can only be approximated. Other issues include the duration of the experiments and the nature of the user populations, since results obtained from college students as experimental subjects are at best only suggestive of other applications.

Controlled experiments can be most useful for obtaining reliable answers to specific questions, such as the relative effectiveness of face-to-face versus computerized conferences for different kinds of tasks (Hiltz et al., 1980), or of alternative styles of interface or error messages (see Shneiderman, 1980, for a review of experimental approaches to system design).

An example of an experimental study is one conducted by Hiltz et al. (1981) to determine the effectiveness of alternative means of structuring computerized conferences. It used a survival problem called "Lost in the Arctic" (Eady and Lafferty, 1975), which requires group members to individually rank order the relative importance of 15 items to survival in the subarctic. The group's task then is to reach consensus on a single rank-ordered list. This problem is representative of the class of managerial decisions in which a group must reach agreement on the relative importance or priority of a number of options.

The arctic problem has a correct or criterion solution, provided by experts (Royal Canadian Mounties trained and experienced in subarctic rescue). The quality of decision reached by face-to-face versus computerized conferencing groups can then be compared, and a quantitative index of consensus computed. Since some groups begin with members who are better informed than others, the measure of interest is the amount of improvement in the final group and final individual decisions compared with the decisions generated by the individuals before discussion.

The selection of a formal group leader constituted the first structuring of the interaction. Groups in this "human leadership" condition were asked to choose a group leader whose responsibilities were to focus discussions, suggest specific ranking changes to reach consensus, and summarize progress.

The alternative condition was using the computer to compile, analyze, and feed back to the group information on the distribution of rank orderings at different points in time. An updated table listing the members' rankings was periodically printed. Subjects could rerank items at will. In this "computer feedback" condition, a second table was generated, listing the items in terms of their mean ranking by all group members, displaying the individual votes on each item, and reporting two measures of agreement, so that the group could follow its progress toward consensus. Technically, this experiment was a two-by-two factorial design.

Analysis of the results showed that human leadership or computer feedback had a significant effect on the group's ability to reach consensus. But there was a strong interactive effect: As compared with unstructured conferences, either a human leader alone or the computer feedback tables alone aided consensus. But together they conflicted or canceled each other's effects.

The quality of the decision was measured by the percentage improvement of the final group decision compared with the individual decisions before group discussion. The groups did well in all conditions, improving about 35 percent. But when the large differences among the groups were taken into account, there were no significant differences in quality of decision.

The experimenters had assumed that the most effective structure would be combining human leadership with computer feedback. Only with a controlled experiment could the nature of the kinds of interactive effects observed be discovered. But controlled experiments also have limitations. One cannot, for example, maintain complete control over conditions for long periods of time in natural rather than somewhat unreal conditions. We feel that the controlled experiment is best used for testing a few hypotheses emerging from data gathered by other means, such as surveys or participant observation.

Using Computer-Mediated Communication
as a Laboratory Tool

Although the controlled experiment for group problem solving is a venerable methodological tool, the computer itself can be used to advantageously introduce new refinements to traditional experimental procedures.

Human experimenters are subject to error, producing a source of unwanted variation in the research design. It is very difficult to give the same instructions in exactly the same way each time. Particularly with complex designs such as that described above, where there were four conditions, each with its own special set of instructions, tired humans will err. The manner in which instructions are given can vary by the experimenter's mood, or by using more than one person to conduct the experiment, each presenting different appearances and personalities to the subjects.

By totally automating the experiment, one can eliminate these sources of error and the confounding of results. In the experiment described above, for instance, the entire process was automated; after the experimenter set the condition, all instructions were automatically delivered to each participant by the computer at the correct point in the sequence of events. Moreover, all data were automatically collected by the computer and could be analyzed without rekeying.

In the section below, we will explore data collection methods which represent not merely variations made possible by the presence of a computer, but sources of data and analysis that would not be possible without it.

NEW METHODOLOGICAL TOOLS

Some tools are made possible specifically by the computerized nature of the medium and can be readily adapted for evaluation purposes. Hiltz and Turoff (1978a) outline the potential:

> Methodologically, the unique feature of computerized conferencing is that the totality of the interaction among the members of the social system can be captured. The actors in the social space can be seen as leaving electronic trails . . . . Complete and accurate measures of both the structure of network ties at any one point in time, and the process by which they change over time, can potentially be generated (p. 16).

Measuring instruments can be incorporated directly into the communication process itself. The fact that the data collection is automatic and essentially error-free, low cost, and rapid permits greater research flexibility and potential productivity than do traditional methods.

Transcripts and Content Analysis

A written transcript is maintained of conference proceedings. This is a characteristic of the medium in general and a feature of each of the specific systems. It functions as a substitute for minutes, heightens accuracy, and fosters a collective group memory. Although it can make new users somewhat self-conscious, it is generally regarded as a major advantage. The transcript is a complete record of what has transpired, but unlike audio or video recordings of face-to-face meetings, it may be modified to reflect changes in opinions and the deletion of erroneous, inappropriate, and outdated material. A malleable group record is thus produced, and the evaluator can trace changes in structure, function, and process as they occur.

The transcript may be subjected to a variety of content analyses for the study of group processes. Statistical manipulations can be performed on the data derivable from the transcript, such as participation rates and the length and timing of entries (Kerr, 1980, Table 1). Automated content analyses can be incorporated, since the data are always current and in machine-readable form (Danowski, 1981). Descriptive analyses of specific conferences may be undertaken by following the sequence of item associations and keywords to trace topics or functions over time. These applications of the transcript are of course dependent upon the context and purpose of the evaluation, which may be internal to the nature of a specific group or conference, or seeking comparative conclusions across groups, conferences, or systems.

Monitor Statistics

User statistics can be automatically collected by a monitor program to capture all interactions and patterns of usage for individuals, groups, or an entire system. They can be defined and aggregated according to such variables as member, group, amount of system experience, time, item length, and item type. Comparative data can be gathered, as well as changes over time. This can be used for tracing interactions among members or groups, mapping sociograms, doing general network analyses, and studying specific network applications within or among groups. It may be used by the system designer or evaluator for measuring changes in system facility, knowledge, and sophistication as a function of experience on line. Reports can be automatically generated and stored with formatting and statistical calculations incorporated.

The EIES statistical monitor currently generates monthly and cumulative data for each user, group, and the overall system, to track the frequency, amount, and type of use. Included are the number of times signed on; time spent on line; number and length of messages, conference comments, and notebook pages both sent and received; and the number of messages sent and received within and outside the group. Users may access data about themselves, and the group coordinator and evaluator may access information about groups. The raw data are collected and stored so that statistical profiles may be easily generated.

Message traffic patterns among users may be collected with statistics showing "who-to-whom" exchanges. Names can be removed or encoded to preserve privacy and confidentiality.

Ethical questions, especially about the potential for invading privacy, are implied in all these measures, but are of greater concern for private message traffic than for the somewhat more public group conferences. The subjects must be aware of the research being conducted and consent to the collection of the data. The power of the computer can be employed to help guard confidentiality, since content analyses can be programmed and automatic, and identities encoded, to protect privacy while studying communication patterns. It is probably best if the contents of private messages are never examined, even with permission, since they would too likely be contaminated by the awareness of being observed. Privacy concerns include the subjects' informed consent to the accessing of their individual data and the presentation of all reports in the form of aggregated group statistics and anonymous quotations.

Each of these methods has the advantage of allowing unobtrusive measures of participation and behavior. Although the ethics of research dictate that the users be aware of the evaluation, the flow of communication is not disrupted by the measuring instruments. Moreover the manual coding and data manipulations typical of more traditional research tools are eliminated, permitting greater accuracy and speed of data collection at a reduced cost.

The kinds of questions most typically addressed by these new tools include those from network analysis and system evaluation, as well as those examining the changing characteristics of groups interacting with this medium. Substantive and process changes can be traced. The "electronic migration" of users to other groups and their different behaviors in those new contexts can be observed. And the contrasting leadership styles that emerge in this medium can be analyzed for their impacts and effectiveness.

CONCLUSIONS

The methodological opportunities and innovations inherent in the computerized medium may well represent breakthroughs in the tools of research. But at the moment they remain potentials. Methodological weaknesses of the existing research need to be noted.

The medium has been limited to a relatively small number of users and groups, typically highly educated male professionals, for limited periods of time, so that generalizations to a situation of widespread usage are probabilistic and dependent upon some known and some unknown variables. Even their usage has been atypical of projections, since it was for the most part subsidized, limited to only a small percentage of their interactions, and certainly influenced to some degree by the novelty of the technology.

The subjects' knowledge that they were being studied in some way influenced their behavior, both on line and in response to direct research instruments. This "Hawthorne Effect" can only be overcome with completely unobtrusive measuring instruments.

Clearly what is needed to answer the questions raised here is the continued refinement of available research instruments and the systematic development of new tools made possible by the medium. A multimethod multilevel approach, integrating systematic empirical research with theoretical underpinnings, should be more feasible and more closely linked to the research questions being explored than has generally been possible with more traditional research. Answers to both quantitative and qualitative questions should be derivable from the integration of the research tools into the processes being studied.

This is not to say, however, that the researcher can proceed directly to precise studies testing specific hypotheses, since these systems are typically used in unforeseen ways and with unanticipated consequences. There is a continued need for exploratory field research and unstructured participant observation, in conjunction with controlled laboratory experiments and structured field experiments. The participation of the researcher in the groups and medium under investigation allows the refinement of hypotheses and data collection instruments, with qualitative data used to modify hypotheses and refine measuring instruments.

CHAPTER 6

Summary and Conclusions

SUMMARY

Twenty-one designers and evaluators of computerized conferencing, electronic mail, and office support systems helped to build a common conceptual framework and reported their findings and conclusions in terms of that framework. Topics included are the importance of various software design features, determinants of user acceptance, six types of impacts (cognitive, affective, and behavioral impacts upon individuals and user groups), and evaluational methods.

We have attempted to synthesize the current state of research on computer-mediated communication systems. This raises a large number of questions and suggests some of the directions to be taken by future research. With a wealth of frequently conflicting evidence it is difficult to reach firm conclusions, much less predict the future with any certainty. The following is a very brief summary of our tentative conclusions.

1. In terms of system software, such characteristics of all interactive systems as accessibility, humanization, and responsiveness are most highly rated. Text-editing capabilities are also rated by system designers as extremely important. There is disagreement about the relative importance and desirability of many of the software features

unique to computer-mediated communication systems, such as system evolution and communication richness.

2. There is sparse evidence about many of the determinants of acceptance of computer-mediated communication systems. The two best predictors, based on available evidence, are preexisting communication networks which can create the demand for enhanced communication among group members, and the nature of the leadership provided to the on-line group. Attitudes (expectations about the system and its potential usefulness), some previous experience with computer terminals, having one's own terminal, and the degree of geographic dispersion of the group are also predictors that have held across many studies.

3. The behavioral impacts of computer-mediated communication systems upon individuals encompass freedom of interaction, quality of life, and quality of work. Choices and opportunities are expanded and new lifestyles become possible. The dimensions underlying these group impacts appear to be increased connectivity, changes in communication processes, and changes in the nature of social structures.

4. There is a need for continued refinement of available research instruments and the systematic development of new tools made possible by the medium. The methodological opportunities and innovations inherent in the computerized medium may well represent breakthroughs in the tools of research. A multimethod, multilevel approach, integrating systematic empirical research with general theories, should be more feasible and more closely linked to the research questions being explored than has generally been possible with more traditional research tools.

REFLECTIONS ON THE DELPHI PROCESS

At an early stage of research in a new area, a Delphi type of procedure is probably the best way to accelerate a synthesis of the emerging findings, compared with the 5 years or more that it might take if the researchers spontaneously found each other's results, compared them, and reached conclusions. However, the Delphi procedure is not an easy one occurring without much effort by a study director, nor was this study without its problems (see Hiltz and Kerr, 1981, for a fuller description of difficulties than is provided here). It is also not a quick process. If the group of experts is used to generate and review the framework, review the derived questionnaire and respond to it, complete at least a second round, review the results of the questionnaire and have an opportunity to change their responses, and review the draft manuscript, the minimum reasonable time frame when relying on the mails is probably a year.

Another disappointment was the low rate of active participation for the second round of the Delphi process. Although all respondents were requested to review their initial responses to the data report forms, compare them with others and change their responses or estimates where appropriate, only two or three actually did so for each module. We do not know whether this means they neglected to review and reconsider their responses or if they did not have any additions or changes to offer.

Systematic feedback from the active participants was obtained through a questionnaire probing the benefits derived from the project and suggestions on how to "do it better next time." One assumption of the Delphi technique of pooling expert opinions is that the participants learn from and benefit from the process, as well as contributing to it. This seems to have been the case for this project. Most did find new ideas for future research, get some fresh ideas for completing current research projects, become more familiar with the work of others, and become more connected to the emerging "invisible college" in this area of research.

In sum, we feel that both we and the participants learned a great deal. Hopefully, the results were worth the effort expended.

CONCLUSIONS

The experiences of many of the groups reported here have been experimental, in terms of both the evolution of system facilities and the nature of the individuals and groups using them. Compared with future users, these pioneers probably exhibit greater technical curiosity and are more intellectual, innovative, and task oriented. A large number have had their usage subsidized through government grants or their employing organizations. In addition, we know that usage patterns change markedly over time, while user profiles have not yet been collected for more than 4-year periods.

Our findings represent a mixture of largely unreplicated quantitative and qualitative evidence. Yet we are, tentatively and with a consciousness of the extrapolative considerations, attempting to project them onto a broader future universe of users so as to maximize positive outcomes and avoid or minimize negative ones.

A good deal of future research is called for, to provide firm answers to the questions raised in these pages and to new questions which will emerge with more widespread use of these systems. It is crucial that these studies be undertaken by professionals in the field who are familiar with these systems and who have been trained in the methodology of social science research. We strongly recommend employing professional researchers for ongoing assessment and evaluation, especially in the early stages of implementing these systems when feedback to the designer and implementors can provide significant increases in both system acceptance and positive impacts upon its users.

We conclude that although the current systems have not always lived up to all the hopes of their designers, these systems are apparently here to stay and will affect larger and larger proportions of white-collar workers in the future. The majority of people do seem to learn to use them and to accept them as a new communication and information tool. Most of the impacts appear to be positive rather than negative.

The theme of the 1981 annual meeting of the American Sociological Association was the assessment of "social inventions for solving human problems." We see computer-mediated communication systems as such a "social invention," designed to improve communication and ultimately white-collar productivity. As Whyte (1981) points out:

> The first model of a mechanical invention almost never measures up to the hopes of its inventor, and technological progress would be impossible if inventors stopped their work upon the failure of the first model. Unfortunately, in social life many potentially important inventions are considered discredited when the first model fails to achieve its promised results. In such cases, the sociologist can perform an invaluable service in discovering the flaws in the initial model which, when corrected, might make the invention viable, or in discovering the particular conditions of the socioeconomic and material environment into which the social invention must be fitted if it is to achieve its promise (pp. 2–3).

We have attempted to synthesize the results of studies of the early versions of computer-mediated communication systems. Our goal has been to provide a conceptual framework in the form of an inventory of critical variables which are related to the success of this particular social invention, and a summary of methodological considerations. We hope that this can provide the starting point for conceptually strong and well designed research to explore the many unanswered questions about the acceptance of and impacts of these systems. It remains for future case studies employing these variables in a systematic fashion to understand the interactions among all of these factors, and to further "perfect the invention." We believe that the challenge is not primarily in further perfecting the computer and telecommunication technology, which is already here, but in the "social engineering" problem of fitting the technological possibilities within particular social contexts.

Background Information on the Systems and Studies[1]

COM

Jacob Palme
Senior Research Officer
Swedish National Defense Research Institute
S-10450 Stockholm, Sweden

Number of Participants
   About 375 using the system once a month or more; 240 once a week or more. Some results based on smaller subgroups.

Population
   61% below age 40; 17.9% are bosses; 54% have academic education. Most are researchers at various technical institutes.

Period of use
   Between 1 month and 2 years. Mean experience is about 80 sessions.

Reports
   Palme, J. (1979). "Teleconference-Based Systems—Implementation

---

[1]Supplied by the system designers and evaluators named.

Manual." Swedish National Defense Research Institute, Stockholm.

Palme, J. (1980). "COM Teleconferencing System—Continuation Manual." Swedish National Defense Research Institute, Stockholm.

Palme, J. (1980). "COM Teleconferencing System—Implementation Manual." Swedish National Defense Research Institute, Stockholm.

Palme, J. (1981). "Experience with the Use of the COM Computerized Conferencing System." Swedish National Defense Research Institute, Stockholm.

Palme, J., and Enderin, L. (1979). "COM Teleconferencing System—Concise Manual." Swedish National Defense Research Institute, Stockholm.

Palme, J., Arnborg, S., Enderin, L., Meyer, C., and Tholerus, T. (1980). "The COM Teleconferencing System—Functional Specification." Swedish National Defense Research Institute, Stockholm.

The following are available in Swedish only (English translations may be forthcoming):

Adriansson, L. (1980). "Group Communication through Computer: Initial Social Psychological Studies of the COM System." Swedish National Defense Research Institute, Stockholm.

Adriansson, L. (1980). "Group Communication through Computer: Social Psychological Studies of Attitudes to and Experience with the Effects of the COM System on the Work Environment." Department of Psychology, University of Gothenburg, Gothenburg, Sweden.

Palme, J. (1978). "Computerized Conferencing Systems." Swedish National Defense Research Institute, Stockholm.

General System Characteristics

Hardware
Four DEC system. Ten computers at different institutes in several cities. Each computer has own conferencing system; some exchange made through computer network with automatic transfer of information between systems. Same computers used for large number of other tasks; on the largest, the conference system uses 18% of terminal hours.

Software
Assembler for DEC system 10; some utility programs in Simula.

Pricing
1. Charge: Typical hourly cost for local university users = $7; nonlocal universities = $14. Lower charges for evenings and weekends.
2. Billed: Universities and public research institutes.

CONFER

Robert Parnes
Advertel Communication Systems, Inc.
1030 Fountain
Ann Arbor, Michigan 48103

Number of Participants
Over 1500.

Population
Wide variety of students, staff, and faculty at two universities. Many not-for-profit research organizations.

Period of Use
5 years.

Reports
Parnes, R., Hench, C., and Zinn, K. (1977). Organizing a computer-based conference. *Transnat. Assoc.* **10,** 418–422.

Zinn, K.L. (1979). Computer-aided communications: New directions for higher education. *In* "Proceedings of the 1979 Annual Conference" (A. Martin and J. Elshoff, eds.), Abstract. ACM, Detroit, Michigan.

General System Characteristics

Hardware
Amdahl U8 at University of Michigan; Amdahl U6 at Wayne State University.

Software
Nonportable version of FORTRAN IV with many calls to assembler subroutines. Implementation of CONFER requires that system be running under MTS.

Pricing
1. Charge: Depends on academic status of user and user site. Most costly: WSU nonacademic commercial use: $0.20/minute (excluding Telenet), with small disc storage charge (few cents daily).
2. Billed: Organizations, individuals, groups on grants, some commercial use.

Capacity
1. Number of users: No effective limit; each conference can accommodate up to 960 users.
2. Simultaneous users: Through Telenet, presently 14 (soon to increase to 64). By direct dialing, up to 200.

3. Average storage: As much as user needs and is willing to pay for.

Equipment

CRT, nonintelligent; hard-copy, nonintelligent; intelligent or specially equipped terminal.

CONFER runs as special-applications program on a large time-sharing system under MTS. In addition to CONFER, users may easily access large number of other computing facilities including text processors and data bases. Also have access to tape storage, quality output on Xerox 9700, etc.

DEVICES FOR THE DISABLED

Jane H. McCarroll
Innovative Systems Research, Inc.
P.O. Box 18590
Cleveland Heights, Ohio 44188

Number of Participants
About 65.

Population
Involved R & D of devices for physically disabled persons. Included rehabilitation engineers, manufacturers, therapists, clinicians, disabled persons.

Period of Use
About 2.5 years.

Report
McCarroll, J.H. (1980). EIES for a community involved in R & D for the disabled. *In* "Electronic Communication: Technology and Impacts" (M.M. Henderson and M.J. MacNaughton, eds.), pp. 71–76. AAAS Sel. Symp. 52, Westview Press, Boulder, Colorado.

EIES (Electronic Information Exchange System)

Murray Turoff
Computerized Conferencing and Communications Center
New Jersey Institute of Technology
323 High Street
Newark, New Jersey 07102

Number of Participants
1000 (approximately).

Population
Varied.

Period of Use
Varies.

Reports
There have been about 17 research reports published by the Computerized Conferencing and Communications Center, including:

Turoff, M., and Hiltz, S.R. (1978). "Development and Field Testing of an Electronic Information Exchange System: Final Report on the EIES Development Project." Res. Rep. No. 9. Computerized Conferencing and Communications Center, Newark, New Jersey.

Hiltz, S.R., Johnson, K., Aronovitch, C., and Turoff, M. (1980). "Face-to-Face versus Computerized Conferences: A Controlled Experiment." Res. Rep. No. 12. Computerized Conferencing and Communications Center, Newark, New Jersey.

Hiltz, S.R. (1981). "The Impact of a Computerized Conferencing System on Scientific Research Communities." Final Report to The National Science Foundation. Res. Rep. No. 15. Computerized Conferencing and Communications Center, Newark, New Jersey.

See also:

Hiltz, S.R., and Turoff, M. (1978). "The Network Nation—Human Communication via Computer." Addison-Wesley, Reading, Massachusetts.

General System Characteristics

Hardware
Perkin-Elmer 7/32, 8/32, and the complete 3220 series.

Software
FORTRAN, INTERACT, ASSEMBLY

Pricing
1. Charge: Class 1: $75/month membership, plus $7.50/hour Telenet or $7/hour Uninet. Class 2: $8 per hour with a $25/month minimum, plus Telenet or Uninet.
2. Billed: Organizations, individuals, groups on grants, foundations.

Capacity
1. Number of users: 1500.
2. Simultaneous users: 64.
3. Storage: Unlimited messaging plus 100 57–line pages of up to 132 characters per line; additional storage is $0.10/page per month.

Facilities
Messaging, conferencing, personal notebooks, word processing, and specialized communication structures.

Equipment
Hard-copy, nonintelligent (typical); intelligent or specially equipped terminal (optimal).

FUTURES (Futures Research Group)

Joseph P. Martino and John Bregenzer
University of Dayton
300 College Park Avenue
Dayton, Ohio 45469

Number of Participants
About 30.

Population
All futures researchers, mostly academics.

Period of Use
2 years.

Reports
Bregenzer, J., and Martino, J.P. (1980). Futures research group experience with computerized conferencing. *In* "Electronic Communication: Technology and Impacts" (M.M. Henderson and M.J. MacNaughton, eds.), AAAS Sel. Symp. 52, pp. 65–70. Westview Press, Boulder, Colorado.

Martino, J.P., and Bregenzer, J. (1980). "Report on an Experiment with an Electronic Conferencing System within a Scientific Community." Final Report to the National Science Foundation, Washington, D.C.

Martino, J.P., and Bregenzer, J.M. (1981). A trial of computerized conferencing among a group of futures researchers. *In* "Studies of Computer-Mediated Communications Systems: A Synthesis of the Findings" (S.R. Hiltz and E.B. Kerr, eds.), pp. 352–385. Final Report to the National Science Foundation. Computerized Conferencing and Communications Center, Newark, New Jersey.

GST (General Systems Theory)

Stuart A. Umpleby
Department of Management Science
George Washington University
Washington, D.C. 20052

Number of Participants
  About 60.

Population
  Almost all academics.

Period of Use
  Varied, to 2.5 years.

Report
  Umpleby, S.A. (1980). Computer conference on general systems theory: One year's experience. *In* "Electronic Communication: Technology and Impacts" (M.M. Henderson and M.J. MacNaughton, eds.), AAAS Sel. Symp. 52, pp. 55–63. Westview Press, Boulder, Colorado.

HEPATITIS

Elliot R. Siegel
Senior Scientist
Lister Hill National Center for Biomedical
  Communications
National Library of Medicine
8600 Rockville Pike
Bethesda, Maryland 20014

Number of Participants
  13.

Population
  Physicians engaged in clinical research on viral hepatitis.

Period of Use
  2 years.

Report
Siegel, E.R. (1980). Use of computer conferencing to validate and update NLM's hepatitis data base. *In* "Electronic Communication: Technology and Impacts" (M.M. Henderson and M.J. MacNaughton, eds.), AAAS Sel. Symp. 52, pp. 87–95. Westview Press, Boulder, Colorado. A Final Report is in preparation.

HUB

Hubert Lipinski and Sara Spang
Institute for the Future
2740 Sand Hill Road
Menlo Park, California 94025

Number of Participants
About 80.

Population
Telecommunications managers and consultants; corporate planners; computer scientists in an academic setting; computer analysts in a military setting.

Period of Use
Varies in length: 3 days to 2 1/2 years.

Reports
Lipinski, H., Spang, S., and Tydeman, J. (1980). Supporting task-focussed communication. *In* "Communicating Information: Proceedings of the 43rd ASIS Annual Meeting" (A.R. Benenfeld and E.J. Kazlauskas, eds.), pp. 153–160. Knowledge Industry Publications, White Plains, New York.

Adler, R.P., and Lipinski, J.M. (1981). HUB: A computer-based communication system to support group problem solving. *In* "Studies in Computer-Mediated Communications Systems: A Synthesis of the Findings" (S.R. Hiltz and E.B. Kerr, eds.), Final Report to the National Science Foundation, pp. 436–447. Computerized Conferencing and Communications Center, Newark, New Jersey.

General Systems Characteristics

Hardware
PDP-10 or PDP-20.

Software
PDP-10/20 ASSEMBLY language; TOPS-20 Operating System.

Pricing
1. Charge: No royalty charged for use. Each individual or group pays for own communication and computer costs. Different rates dependent on group. NALCON group using ARPANET and ARPA computer at ISI is free; Speakeasy group using BBN computer pays $15–25/ hour.
2. Billed: Each group makes own arrangements with host computer.

Capacity (Research applications have not tested this)
1. Number of users and number of simultaneous users: As many as host computer can hold; HUB does not constrain.
2. Average storage: Storage allocated per group and dynamically used. Most groups have upper limit of 250 pages (1 page = 2560 characters).

Equipment
Hard copy, nonintelligent.

JEDEC (Joint Electron Devices Council)

Peter and Trudy Johnson-Lenz
695 Fifth Street
Lake Oswego, Oregon 97034

Number of Participants
77 people had EIES accounts; 58 used the system at least once; 34 baseline questionnaires were returned; 52 follow-up interviews were completed.

Period of Use
20 months.

Reports
Johnson-Lenz, P., and Johnson-Lenz, T. (1980). "JEDEC/EIES Project: Standardization in Minicomputer/LSI Products via Electronic Information Exchange." Final Report to the National Science Foundation, Washington, D.C.
Johnson-Lenz, P., and Johnson-Lenz, T. (1981). JEDEC/EIES project— Use of electronic information exchange in developing standards in the electronics industry. *In* "Studies of Computer-Mediated Communications Systems: A Synthesis of the Findings" (S.R. Hiltz and E.B. Kerr, eds.), Final Report to the National Science Foundation, pp. 406–435. Computerized Conferencing and Communications Center, Newark, New Jersey.

LEGITECH

Valarie C. Lamont
c/o Participation Systems, Inc.
43 Myrtle Terrace
Winchester, Massachusetts 01890

Number of Participants
   24.

Population
   State legislative researchers.

Period of Use
   Varied from approximately 6 to 18 months.

Reports
   Lamont, V.C. (1980). Computer conferencing: The LegiTech experience. *In* "Teleconferencing and Interactive Media" (L.A. Parker and C.H. Olgren, eds.), pp. 457–461. Extension Center for Interactive Programs, University of Wisconsin, Madison.

   Johnson-Lenz, P., and Johnson-Lenz, T. (1980). LegiTech/EIES: Information exchange among state legislative researchers. *In* "Electronic Communication: Technology and Impacts" (M.M. Henderson and M.J. MacNaughton, eds.), AAAS Sel. Symp. 52, pp. 103–111. Westview Press, Boulder, Colorado.

   Johnson-Lenz, P., and Johnson-Lenz, T. (1981). "The Evolution of a Tailored Communications Structure: The Topics System." Res. Rep. No. 14. Computerized Conferencing and Communications Center, Newark, New Jersey.

   Stevens, C.H. (1980). Many-to-many communication through inquiry networking. *World Future Soc. Bull.* **14,** 31–35.

MACC @MAIL

Dave Brown
Network Services Manager
University of Wisconsin
Madison Academic Computing Center
1210 West Dayton Street
Madison, Wisconsin 53706

Number of Participants
   200.

Population
Professional programming staff, administrators and researchers in a major university and educational services (Educom) environment.

Period of Use
3 years.

Reports
Landweber, L. (1979). Theory net: An electronic mail system. *In* "Proceedings of the 1979 Annual Conference, ACM" (A. Martin and J. Elshoff, eds.), Abstracts, pp. 29–31. ACM, Detroit, Michigan.

Roberts, A. (1980). MACC'S computer mail system—Its features, usage statistics, and costs. *In* "Teleconferencing and Interactive Media" (L.A. Parker and C.H. Olgren, eds.), pp. 472–481. Extension Center for Interactive Programs, University of Wisconsin, Madison.

General System Characteristics

Hardware
UNIVAC 1100/82 computer. 21 remote job entry stations. 120 timesharing terminals.

Software
NUALGOL: An Argol compiler. 96% of code kept in high-level block-structured language to allow easy maintenance.

Pricing
1. Charge: Run priced as sum of resources used. Mail session costs $0.05/access to file. Typical message cost: $0.50. Per hour cost approximately $10.
2. Billed: Organizations, individuals, groups on grants.

Capacity
1. Number of users: Less than 2000.
2. Simultaneous users: 100.
3. Average storage: Unlimited; user pays for amount used.

Equipment
CRT, nonintelligent; a few intelligent terminals are starting to be used.

MENTAL WORKLOAD

John Senders
Keneggy West
Columbia Falls, Maine 04623

Number of Participants
 About 40.

Population
 Human factors, engineering psychologists interested in theoretical and practical problems of Mental Workload and in testing the notion of an "Electronic Journal" on that topic.

Period of Use
 1.5 to 2 years.

Report
 Guillaume, J. (1980). Computer conferencing and the development of an electronic journal. *Can. J. Inf. Sci.* **5**, 21–29.

NLS (On Line System—Augment)

James Bair
BNR, Inc.
355A East Middlefield Road
Mountain View, California 94943

Number of Participants
 37 split into experimental and control groups. 17 NLS users.

Population
 Knowledge workers (engineers, computer programmers, managers, human factors psychologists) and 2 clerk/secretary/administrators. Mostly male civil servants. Nonrandom subject selection based on formal organization (2 similar departments).

Period of Use
 1 year.

Reports
 Bair, J.H. (1974). "Evaluation and Analysis of an Augmented Knowledge Workshop: Final Report for Phase I." Rome Air Force Development Center, RADC-TR-74,79. Griffiss Air Force Base, New York.
 Edwards, G.C. (1977). "An Analysis of Usage and Related Perceptions of NLS—A Computer-based Text Processing and Communications System." Bell Canada H.Q. Business Development, Montreal.

OICS (Office Information Communication System)

Don Tapscott, Manager
Morley Greenberg, Systems Staff Member
BNSR 522 University Avenue
Toronto, Ontario, Canada

Number of Participants
  Original Pilot Group = 19; Control Group = 26.

Population
  Managers, professional and technical, administrative.

Period of Use
  8 months.

Report
  Tapscott, D. (1981). Investigating the office of the future. *Telesis* **8**, 2–6.

General System Characteristics

Hardware
  PDP-11/70–real time clock KW11–P; FP11 Smaller PDP-11/03 connected to communications network (Datapac); CPU connected via Massbus to high-speed peripherals and by UNIBUS to low-speed peripherals; 4 RM03–disk packs; TWE16–EA tape drive; high-speed line printer; letter-quality printer; Two DZ11–E and a DH11–AD; DR11–B connected 11/70 to 11/03.

Software
  "C"

Pricing
  1. Charge: Log-in per hour: $8; Storage: $0.08 per block.
  2. Billed: Each group billed (may be internal, or external to company).

Capacity (512 kb MOS main memory)
  1. Number of users: Approximately 150–175.
  2. Simultaneous users: 25.
  3. Average storage: Approximately 1000 blocks per user.

EQUIPMENT
  VT100

PANALOG

Edward M. Housman
Manager, Information Services
GTE Labs
40 Sylvan Road
Waltham, Massachusetts 02154

Number of Participants
  More than 100.

Population
  All walks of life: teenagers, scientists, hearing-impaired persons, artists, secretaries, technicians, executives, professors, managers, information scientists.

Period of Use
  Varies, up to 3 years.

Report
  Seabrook, R.H.C. (1978). PANALOG: Shaking the foundations. *Bull. Am. Soc. Inf. Sci.* **4,** 21.

General System Characteristics

Hardware
  IBM 3033

Software
  VS APL under TSO

Pricing
  1. Charge: No charge to participants. Experimental testbed system.
  2. Billed: Research project bears all costs.

Capacity
  1. Number of users: Unsure; have not hit maximum (at 100 +).
  2. Simultaneous users: Conference Subsystem = 1; Electronic Mail Subsystem = 50 + (undetermined)!
  3. Average storage: No measure kept.

Equipment
  CRT, nonintelligent; hard copy, nonintelligent; intelligent terminal; any ASCII or APL terminal, also 3270 type.

PLANET

Richard Miller
Infomedia Corporation
530 Lytton Avenue, #303
Palo Alto, California 94301

Reports
   Johansen, R., DeGrasse, R., Jr., and Wilson, T. (1978). "Group Communications through Computer." Vol. 5, Rep. R-41. Institute for the Future, Menlo Park, California.
   Johansen, R., Vallee, J., and Spangler, K. (1979). "Electronic Meetings: Technological Alternatives and Social Choices." Addison-Wesley, Reading, Massachusetts.
   Vallee, J., Lipinski, H., and Miller, R. (1974). "Group Communication through Computers." Vol. 1, Rep. R-32. Institute for the Future, Menlo Park, California.
   Vallee, J., Johansen, R., Randolph, R., and Hastings, A. (1974). "Group Communication through Computers." Vol. 2, Institute for the Future, Menlo Park, California.
   Vallee, J., Johansen, R., Lipinski, H., Spangler, K., and Wilson, T. (1975). "Group Communication through Computers." Vol. 3, Rep. R-35. Institute for the Future, Menlo Park, California.
   Vallee, J., Johansen, R., Spangler, K., and Wilson, T. (1978). "Group Communication through Computers." Vol. 4, Rep. R-40. Institute for the Future, Menlo Park, California.

General System Characteristics

Hardware
   DEC (Digital Equipment) PDP-10 processor (CPU) under TOPS-2+, TOPS-10, TENEX, TYMEX (Proprietary to Tymshare, Inc.)

Software
   DEC MACRO Assembly

Pricing
   1. Charge: On basis of connect time, CPU utilization, on-line disk storage, and number of participants, and includes telecommunication costs. Average: $40/hour.
   2. Billed = Client organization; billing breakdowns by individual or group available.

Capacity
1. Number of users: Can accommodate within one client account an unlimited number; within one conference, 127.
2. Simultaneous users: No limit on number using one account; 36 may use conference.
3. Average storage: 1000 bytes per user within an account.

Equipment
CRT, nonintelligent; hard copy, nonintelligent.

USC-MSG
(MSG and LINK on TENEX at the Educational Computing Laboratories, University of California)

James Danowski
School of Journalism and Mass Communication
University of Wisconsin
Madison, Wisconsin 53706

Number of Participants
38.

Population
Retirement community residents in a test of computer communication and the elderly.

Period of Use
9 hours over 3 weeks.

Report
Danowski, J.A., and Sacks, W. (1980). Computer conferencing and the elderly. *Exp. Aging Res.* **6**, 125–135.

WHCLIS (White House Conference on Library and Information Services)

Elaine B. Kerr
Computerized Conferencing and Communications Center
New Jersey Institute of Technology
323 High Street
Newark, New Jersey 07102

Number of Participants
41.

Population
Staff (8), Advisory Committee Members (21), observers (12). It was a well-educated, older, egalitarian group, with a wide variety of professional backgrounds.

Period of Use
7 months.

Reports
Kerr, E.B. (1980). Conferencing via computer: Evaluation of computer-assisted planning and management for the White House Conference on Library and Information Services. *In* "Information for the 1980s: A Final Report of the White House Conference on Library and Information Services, 1979" pp. 767–805. US Govt. Printing Office, Washington, D.C.

Kerr, E. B. (1981). Evaluating the role of computer conferencing in planning the White House Conference on Library and Information Services: A case study in uneven results. *In* "Studies of Computer-Mediated Communications Systems: A Synthesis of the Findings" (S.R. Hiltz and E.B. Kerr, eds.), pp. 386–405. Final Report to the National Science Foundation. Computerized Conferencing and Communications Center, Newark, New Jersey.

WYLBUR @MAIL SYSTEM

Clifford Lynch
Manager, Computing Resources
Division of Library Automation
186 University Hall
University of California
Berkeley, California 94720

Number of Participants
About 120, including occasional users and some outside users.

Population
DLA staff: programmers, managers, administrative support.

Period of Use
8 months.

Report
Lynch, C.A. (1980). Practical electronic mail through a centralized computing facility. *In* "Communicating Information: Proceedings of

the 43rd ASIS Annual Meeting" (A.R. Benenfeld and E.J. Kazlauskas, eds.), pp. 34–37. Knowledge Industry Publications, White Plains, New York.

General Systems Characteristics

Hardware
IBM 370 or compatible (OS/360)

Software
Group of extensions to Stanford WYLBUR coded in IBM 370 assembler language.

Pricing
1. Charge: No charge for computer time internally.
2. Billed: This is an internal system and use is not billed. Resources allocated based on user needs and DLA organizational priorities.

Capacity
1. Number of users: At least 300.
2. Simultaneous users: Over 50, currently.
3. Average storage: Varies; from 10 Up to 1000 tracks (not used solely for mail) 1 track = 13K bytes.

Equipment
CRT, nonintelligent; hard copy, nonintelligent.

REFERENCES

Adler, R.P., and Lipinski, H.M. (1981). HUB: A computer-based communication system. *In* "Studies of Computer-Mediated Communications Systems: A Synthesis of the Findings" (S.R. Hiltz and E.B. Kerr, eds.), Final Report to the National Science Foundation, pp. 436–447. Computerized Conferencing and Communications Center, Newark, New Jersey.

Adriansson, L. (1980). "Group Communication through Computer: Social Psychological Studies of Attitudes to and Experience with the Effects of the COM System on the Work Environment." Department of Psychology, University of Gothenburg, Gothenburg, Sweden.

Bair, J.H. (1974). "Evaluation and Analysis of an Augmented Knowledge Workshop: Final Report for Phase I." Rome Air Development Center, RADC-TR-74,79. Griffiss Air Force Base, New York.

Bamford, H.E., and Savin, W. (1978). Electronic information exchange: The National Science Foundation's developing role. *Bull. Am. Soc. Inf. Sci.* **4,** 12–13.

Bennett, J.L. (1972). The user interface in interactive systems. *Annu. Rev. Inf. Sci. Technol.* **7,** 159–196.

Bezilla, R. (1978). "A Discussion of Selected Aspects of Privacy, Confidentiality, and Anonymity in Computerized Conferencing." Res. Rep. No. 11. Computerized Conferencing and Communications Center, Newark, New Jersey.

Bezilla, R. (1979). Computerized communication systems: An overview. Presented at the Association for Computing Machinery, Detroit, Michigan.

Bezilla, R. (1980a). Computer-based conferencing—A system approach to the 'officeless office'. Presented at the Information Management Conference, New York.

Bezilla, R. (1980b). The impacts of new technologies upon children in the 1980s. Presented at the National Council for Children and Television, Princeton, New Jersey.

Bezilla, R. (1980c). Online messaging and conferencing systems. Presented at the Online 1980 Conference, San Francisco, California.

Bezilla, R., and Kerr, E.B. (1979). The culture of an electronic society. Presented at the Annual Meeting of the American Anthropological Association, Cincinnati, Ohio.

Bezilla, R., and Kleiner, A. (1980). Electronic network addiction. Presented at the National Computer Conference, Anaheim, California.

Bregenzer, J., and Martino, J.P. (1980). Futures research group experience with computerized conferencing. In "Electronic Communication: Technology and Impacts" (M.M. Henderson and M.J. MacNaughton, eds.), AAAS Sel. Symp. 52, pp. 65–70. Westview Press, Boulder, Colorado.

Danowski, J.A. (1981). An evaluation methodology for computer conferencing: An illustration with a CBBS conference. In "Studies of Computer-Mediated Communications Systems: A Synthesis of the Findings" (S.R. Hiltz and E.B. Kerr, eds.), Final Report to the National Science Foundation, pp. 448–480. Computerized Conferencing and Communications Center, Newark, New Jersey.

Danowski, J.A., and Sacks, W. (1980). Computer conferencing and the elderly. Exp. Aging Res. **6**, 125–135.

Davis, M.A. (1971). Communication effectiveness as a function of mode. M.A. Thesis, University of Waterloo (unpublished).

Day, L. (1975). Computer conferencing: An overview. In "Computer Communication: Views from the ICCC '74" (N. Macon, ed.), pp. 53–70. International Council for Computer Communication, Washington, D.C.

Eady, P.M., and Lafferty, J.C. (1975). "The Subarctic Survival Situation." Experiential Learning Methods, Plymouth, Michigan.

Edwards, G.C. (1977). "An Analysis of Usage and Related Perceptions of NLS—A Computer-based Text Processing and Communications System." Bell Canada H.Q. Business Development, Montreal.

Ferguson, J., and Johansen, R., eds. (1975). "Teleconferencing on Integrated Data Bases in Postsecondary Education." Institute for the Future, Menlo Park, California.

Freeman, L.C., and Freeman, S.C. (1980). A semi-visible college: Structural effects on a social networks group. In "Electronic Communication: Technology and Impacts" (M.M. Henderson and M.J. MacNaughton, eds.), AAAS Sel. Symp. 52, pp. 77–85. Westview Press, Boulder, Colorado.

GMD (1979). KOMEX: An experimental system for computer conferencing. Presented at WFSC, Gessellschaft fur Mathematik und Datenberarbeitung, Institut fur Planungs, Bonn, Germany.

Guillaume, J. (1980). Computer conferencing and the development of an electronic journal. Can. J. Inf. Sci. **5**, 21–29.

Hammond, K.R., Stewart, T.R., Brehmer, B., and Steinman, D.O. (1975). Social judgment theory. In "Human Judgment and Decision Processes" (M.F. Kaplan and S. Schwartz, eds.), pp. 271–311. Academic Press, New York.

Hare, A.P. (1976). "Handbook of Small Group Research." Free Press, New York.

Hiltz, S.R. (1976). Computer conferencing: Assessing the social impact of a new communications medium. Presented at the annual meeting of the American Sociological Association, San Francisco, California.

Hiltz, S.R. (1978a). Controlled experiments with computerized conferencing. Bull. Am. Soc. Inf. Sci. **4**, 11–12.

Hiltz, S.R. (1978b). Social and psychological aspects of teleconferencing. Presented at the annual meeting of the American Association for the Advancement of Science, Washington, D.C.

Hiltz, S.R. (1978c). Using computerized conferencing to conduct opinion research. Presented at the annual meeting of the American Association for Public Opinion Research, Roanoke, Virginia.

Hiltz, S.R. (1979). The social effects of human communication via computer. Presented at the Irvine Conference on Social Issues and Impacts of Computing, Irvine, California.

Hiltz, S.R. (1981). "The Impact of a Computerized Conferencing System on Scientific Research Communities." Final Report to the National Science Foundation. Res. Rep. No. 15. Computerized Conferencing and Communications Center, Newark, New Jersey.

Hiltz, S.R., and Kerr, E.B. (1981). "Studies of Computer-Mediated Communications Systems: A Synthesis of the Findings." Final Report to the National Science Foundation. Computerized Conferencing and Communications Center, Newark, New Jersey.

Hiltz, S.R., and Turoff, M. (1978a). Electronic networks: The social dynamics of a new communications medium. Presented at the annual meeting of the American Sociological Association, San Francisco, California.

Hiltz, S.R., and Turoff, M. (1978b). "The Network Nation—Human Communication via Computer." Addison-Wesley, Reading, Massachusetts.

Hiltz, S.R., and Turoff, M. (1981). Office augmentation systems: The case for evolutionary design. Presented at the 15th Hawaii International Conference on System Sciences, Honolulu, Hawaii.

Hiltz, S.R., Johnson, K., and Agle, G. (1978). "Replicating Bales Problem-Solving Experiments on a Computerized Conference: A Pilot Study." Res. Rep. No. 8. Computerized Conferencing and Communications Center, Newark, New Jersey.

Hiltz, S.R., Johnson, K., Aronovitch, C., and Turoff, M. (1980). Equality, dominance, and group decision making: Results of a controlled experiment on face-to-face versus computer-mediated discussions. Presented at the Int. Council for Comp. Comm, Atlanta, Georgia.

Hiltz, S.R., Johnson, K., and Turoff, M. (1981). The quality of group decision making in face-to-face versus computerized conferences. Presented at the annual meeting of the American Sociological Association, Toronto, Canada.

Housman, E.M. (1980). Online communication by computer conferencing and electronic mail. Presented at the 4th Online Meeting, London, England.

Johansen, R., Vallee, J., and Palmer, M. (1976). Computer conferencing: Measurable effects on working patterns. Presented at the National Telecommunications Conference, IEEE, Dallas, Texas.

Johansen, R., DeGrasse, R., Jr., and Wilson, T. (1978a). "Group Communications through Computer." Vol. 5, Rep. R-41. Institute for the Future, Menlo Park, California.

Johansen, R., McNulty, M., and McNeal, B. (1978b). "Electronic Education: Using Teleconferencing in Postsecondary Organizations." Rep. R-42. Institute for the Future, Menlo Park, California.

Johansen, R., Vallee, J., and Spangler, K. (1979). "Electronic Meetings: Technological Alternatives and Social Choices." Addison-Wesley, Reading, Massachusetts.

Johnson-Lenz, P., and Johnson-Lenz, T. (1980a). "Case Study: JEDEC/EIES Project-Use of Electronic Information Exchange in Developing Standards in the Electronics Industry." (Submitted to the National Science Foundation.)

Johnson-Lenz, P., and Johnson-Lenz, T. (1980b). "JEDEC/EIES Project: Standardization in Minicomputer/LSI Products via Electronic Information Exchange." Final Report to the National Science Foundation, Washington, D.C.

Johnson-Lenz, P., and Johnson-Lenz, T. (1980c). Groupware: The emerging art of orchestrating collective intelligence. Presented at the 1st Global Conference on the Future, Toronto, Canada.

Johnson-Lenz, P., and Johnson-Lenz, T. (1980d). LegiTech/EIES: Information exchange among state legislative researchers. In "Electronic Communication: Technology and Impacts" (M.M. Henderson and M.J. MacNaughton, eds.), AAAS Sel. Symp. 52, pp. 103–111. Westview Press, Boulder, Colorado.

Johnson-Lenz, P., and Johnson-Lenz, T. (1981). "The Evolution of a Tailored Communications Structure: The Topics System." Res. Rep. No. 14. Computerized Conferencing and Communications Center, Newark, New Jersey.

Johnson-Lenz, P., Johnson-Lenz, T., and Scher, J.M. (1978). How groups can make decisions and solve problems through computerized conferencing. Bull. Am. Soc. Inf. Sci. 4, 15–17.

Johnson-Lenz, P., Johnson-Lenz, T., and Hessman, J.F. (1980). JEDEC/EIES computer conferencing for standardizing activities. In "Electronic Communication: Technology and Impacts" (M.M. Henderson and M.J. MacNaughton, eds.), AAAS Sel. Symp. 52, pp. 97–102. Westview Press, Boulder, Colorado.

Kerr, E.B. (1978). Identities and role definitions in computerized conferencing. In Bezilla (1978, pp. 72–84).

Kerr, E.B. (1979). Computer-mediated communications with the mobility-limited aged and cerebral palsy children: An application of the Electronic Information Exchange System. Presented at the Conference of the World Future Studies Federation, Berlin, Germany.

Kerr, E.B. (1980). Conferencing via computer: Evaluation of computer-assisted planning and management for the White House Conference on Library and Information Services. In "Information for the 1980s: A Final Report of the White House Conference on Library and Information Services, 1979" pp. 767–805. US Govt. Printing Office, Washington, D.C.

Kerr, E.B., and Bezilla, R. (1979). Cues and clues: The presentation of self in computerized conferencing. Presented at the National Computer Conference, New York.

Kerr, E.B., Hiltz, S.R., Whitescarver, J., and Prince, S. (1979). Applications of computer conferencing to the disadvantaged: Preliminary results of field trials with handicapped children. In "Information Choices and Policies: Proceedings of the ASIS Annual Meeting" (R.D. Tally and R.R. Deultgen, eds.), pp. 149–158. Knowledge Industry Publications, White Plains, New York.

Kleiner, A. (1980). Life on the computer network frontier. In "The Next Whole Earth Catalog" (S. Brand, ed.), pp. 534–535. Rand McNally, New York.

Kleiner, A., and Davis, W. (1979). Personal computer networks: Better than the next best thing to being there. Coevol. Qu., Summer, 114–119.

Kochen, M. (1978). Long-term implications of electronic information exchanges for information science. Bull. Am. Soc. Inf. Sci. 4, 22–23.

Kochen, M. Technology and communication in the future. J. Am. Soc. Inf. Sci. 32, 148–157.

Kowitz, A.C., and Knutson, T.J. (1980). "Decision Making in Small Groups." Allyn & Bacon, Boston, Massachusetts.

Lamont, V.C. (1980). Computer conferencing: The LegiTech experience. In "Teleconferencing and Interactive Media" (L.A. Parker and C.H. Olgren, eds.), pp. 457–461. Extension Center for Interactive Programs, University of Wisconsin, Madison.

Landweber, L. (1979). Theory net: An electronic mail system. In "Proceedings of the 1979 Annual Conference, ACM" (A. Martin and J. Elshoff, eds.), Abstracts, pp. 29–31. ACM, Detroit, Michigan.

Lasden, M. (1979). Will you love electronic mail or hate it? Comput. Decisions 2, 47–60.

Linstone, H.A., and Turoff, M., eds. (1975). "The Delphi Method: Techniques and Applications." Addison-Wesley, Reading, Massachusetts.

Lipinski, H., Spang, S., and Tydeman, J. (1980). Supporting task-focussed communication. *In* "Communicating Information: Proceedings of the 43rd ASIS Annual Meeting" (A.R. Benenfeld and E.J. Kazlauskas, eds.), pp. 158–160. Knowledge Industry Publications, White Plains, New York.

Lynch, C.A. (1980). Practical electronic mail through a centralized computing facility. *In* "Communicating Information: Proceedings of the 43rd ASIS Annual Meeting" (A.R. Benenfeld and E.J. Kazlauskas, eds.), pp. 34–37. Knowledge Industry Publications, White Plains, New York.

McCarroll, J.H. (1980). EIES for a community involved in R & D for the disabled. *In* "Electronic Communication: Technology and Impacts" (M.M. Henderson and M.J. MacNaughton, eds.), AAAS Sel. Symp. 52, pp. 71–76. Westview Press, Boulder, Colorado.

McCarroll, J.H., and Cotman, L. (1980). "Evaluation Report on a Trial Application of Computer Conferencing by the Placement Trainers Consortium." Innovative Systems Research, Cleveland, Ohio.

McKendree, J.D. (1978). Project and crisis management applications of computerized conferencing. *Bull. Am. Soc. Inf. Sci.* **4**, 13–15.

McQuillan, J.M. (1980). A retrospective on electronic mail. *SIGOA Newsl.* **1**, 8–9.

Mailman, F., Hubbard, D., and Canache, P. (1981). "A Computer Conferencing Directory." American Society for Cybernetics, Washington, D.C.

Martin, J. (1973). "Design of Man–Computer Dialogues." Prentice-Hall, Englewood Cliffs, New Jersey.

Martino, J.P. (1979). Telecommunications in the year 2000. *Futurist* **13**, 95–103.

Martino, J.P., and Bregenzer, J. (1980). "Report on an Experiment with an Electronic Conferencing System within a Scientific Community." Final Report to the National Science Foundation, Washington, D.C.

Martino, J.P., and Bregenzer, J.M. (1981). A trial of computerized conferencing among a group of futures researchers. *In* "Studies of Computer-Mediated Communications Systems: A Synthesis of the Findings" (S.R. Hiltz and E.B. Kerr, eds.), Final Report to the National Science Foundation, pp. 352–385. Computerized Conferencing and Communications Center, Newark, New Jersey.

National Science Foundation (1976). "Program Announcement: Operational Trials of Electronic Information Exchange for Small Research Communities." NSF 76–45. National Science Foundation, Division of Science Information, Washington, D.C.

Neisner, U. (1964). "MAC and Its Users." Proj. MAC, Memo. MAC-M-185.

Open Systems (1981). Case history, into the wild blue yonder. *Newsletter* **2**(1), 6–7.

Palme, J. (1979). "A Human–Computer Interface for Noncomputer Specialists." FOA Rep. C 10128–M3(E5,H9), Swedish National Defense Research Institute, Stockholm.

Palme, J. (1981). "Experience with the Use of the COM Computerized Conferencing System." FOA Rep. C 10166E-M6(H9), Swedish National Defense Research Institute, Stockholm.

Palme, J., Arnborg, S., Enderin, L., Meyer, C., and Tholerus, T. (1980). "The COM Teleconferencing System Functional Specification." FOA Rep. C 10164–M6(H9), Stockholm.

Panko, R.R. (1980). "Electronic Message Systems: A Survey." Working Paper 80–03. College of Business Administration, University of Hawaii, Honolulu.

Panko, R.R., and Panko, R.U. (1981). A survey of EMS users at DARCOM. *Comput. Networks*, March.

Parnes, R., Hench, C., and Zinn, K. (1977). Organizing a computer-based conference. *Transnatl. Assoc.* **10**, 418–422.

Parsons, T. (1951). The Social System. Free Press, New York.

Price, C.R. (1975). Conferencing via computer: Cost-effective communication for the era of forced choice. *In* "The Delphi Method" (H.A. Linstone and M. Turoff, eds.), pp. 497–516. Addison-Wesley, Reading, Massachusetts.

Price, C.R., and Kerr, E.B. (1978). Electronic 'connectedness': Its meaning for personal and social disabilities. *Bull. Am. Soc. Inf. Sci.* **4**, 19–20.

Reichwald, R. (1980). New office systems and acceptance problem. *Telecom Rep.* **3**, 5–8.

Rice, R.E. (1980). Computer conferencing. *In* "Progress in Communication Sciences" (M. Voigt and B. Dervin, eds.), Vol.2, Ablex, White Plains, New York.

Rice, R.E., and Danowski, J. (1981). Issues in computer conferencing evaluation and research. *In* "Studies of Computer-Mediated Communications: A Synthesis of the Findings" (S.R. Hiltz and E.B. Kerr, eds.), Final Report, Computerized Conferencing and Communications Center, Newark, New Jersey.

Roberts, A. (1980). MACC's computer mail system—Its features, usage statistics, and costs. *In* "Teleconferencing and Interactive Media" (L.A. Parker and C.H. Olgren, eds.), pp. 472–481. Extension Center for Interactive Programs, University of Wisconsin, Madison.

Scher, J.M. (1979). Distributed decision support systems: An overview. Presented at the Joint Meeting of the Operations Research Society of America and the Institute of Management Sciences, Milwaukee, Wisconsin.

Scher, J.M. (1980). Higher educational and managerial–organizational uses of computer-based human communication systems: Some futures and opportunities. *In* "Through the 80s: Thinking Globally, Acting Locally" (F. Festher, ed.), pp. 317–322. World Future Society, Washington, D.C.

Seabrook, R.H.C. (1978). PANALOG: Shaking the foundations. *Bull. Am. Soc. Inf. Sci.* **4**, 21.

Shaw, M.E. (1976). "Group Dynamics: The Psychology of Small Group Behavior." McGraw-Hill, New York.

Shneiderman, B. (1980). "Software Psychology: Human Factors in Computer and Information Systems." Winthrop Computer Systems, Cambridge, Massachusetts.

Short, J., Williams, E., and Christie, B. (1976). "The Social Psychology of Telecommunications." Wiley, New York.

Siegel, E.R. (1980). Use of computer conferencing to validate and update NLM's hepatitis data base. *In* "Electronic Communication: Technology and Impacts" (M.M. Henderson and M.J. MacNaughton, eds.), AAAS Sel. Symp. 52, pp. 87–95. Westview Press, Boulder, Colorado.

Simard, R., and Miller, R. (1980). Computer conferencing to enhance nuclear reactor safety. *In* "Communicating Information: Proceedings of the 43rd ASIS Annual Meeting" (A.R. Benenfeld and E.J. Kazlauskas, eds.), pp. 161–162. Knowledge Industry Publications, White Plains, New York.

Southworth, J.H., Flanigan, J.M., and Knezek, G.A. (1981). Computers in education: International multimode node electronic conferencing. Presented at the Pacific Telecommunications Conference, Honolulu, Hawaii.

Spelt, P.F. (1977). Evaluation of a continuing computer conference on simulation. *Behav. Res. Methods Instrum.* **9**, 87–91.

Stech, E., and Ratcliffe, S.A. (1976). "Working in Groups: A Communication Manual for Leaders and Participants." National Textbook Co., Skokie, Illinois.

Sterling, T. (1974). Humanizing computerized information systems. *Commun. ACM* **17**.

Sterling, T. (1975). Humanizing computerized information systems. *Science* **190**, 1168–1172.

Stevens, C.H. (1980). Many-to-many communication through inquiry networking. *World Future Soc. Bull.* **14**, 31–35.

Tally, R. (1981). An experiment in computer conferencing. Presented at the ASIS Continuing Education Program, New Techniques in Communication, annual meeting of the American Society for Information Science, Washington, D.C.

Tapscott, D. (1981). Investigating the office of the future. *Telesis* **8**, 2–6.

Theobald, R. (1966). Cybernetics and the problems of social reorganization. In "The Social Impacts of Cybernetics" (C.R. Dechert, ed.), pp. 39–69. Simon & Schuster, New York.

Theobald, R. (1980). The communications era from the year 2000. *Natl. Forum* **60**, 17–20.

Toussaint, J.H. (1960). A classified summary of listening: 1950–1959. *J. Commun.* **10**, 125–134.

Turoff, M. (1972). 'Party line' and 'discussion' computerized conferencing systems. In "Computer Communication—Impacts and Implications" (S. Winkler, ed.), pp. 161–170. International Conference on Computer Communication, Washington, D.C.

Turoff, M. (1974a). Computerized conferencing: Present and future. *Intellect* 54–57.

Turoff, M. (1974b). Computerized conferencing and real time delphis. *Proc. Int. Conf. Comput. Commun.*, pp. 135–142.

Turoff, M. (1979). On the design of human systems—or confessions of a designer. Presented at the National Computer Conference, New York.

Turoff, M. (1980a). The designer's view. In "Electronic Communication: Technology and Impacts" (M.M. Henderson and M.J. MacNaughton, eds.), AAAS Sel. Symp. 52, pp. 113–120. Westview Press, Boulder, Colorado.

Turoff, M. (1980b). Management issues in human communication via computer. Presented at the Stanford Conference on Office Automation, Stanford, California.

Turoff, M., and Hiltz, S.R. (1977). Computerized conferencing: A review and statement of issues. Presented at the NATO Telecommunications Symposium, Bergamo, Italy.

Turoff, M., and Hiltz, S.R. (1978). "Development and Field Testing of an Electronic Information Exchange System: Final Report on the EIES Development Project." Res. Rep. No. 9. Computerized Conferencing and Communications Center, Newark, New Jersey.

Turoff, M., and Hiltz, S.R. (1979). Information and communication in international affairs. Presented at the International Studies Association, Toronto, Canada.

Turoff, M., and Hiltz, S.R. (1980). Structuring communications for the office of the future. Presented at the National Computer Conference Office Automation Conference, Atlanta, Georgia.

Turoff, M., Hiltz, S.R., McKendree, J., Panko, R., Snyder, D., and Wilcox, R. (1978). "Research Options and Imperatives in Computerized Conferencing." Res. Rep. No. 10. Computerized Conferencing and Communications Center, Newark, New Jersey.

Turoff, M., Whitecarver, J., Leurck, A., Howell, J., Moulton, T., Voyce, B., and Chinai, S. (1981). On the design of an information marketplace. In "The Information Community: An Alliance for Progress—Proceedings of the 44th ASIS Annual Meeting" (L.F. Lunin, M. Henderson, and H. Wooster, eds.), pp. 193–195. Knowledge Industry Publications, White Plains, New York.

Tydeman, J., Lipinski, H., and Spang, S. (1980). An interactive computer-based approach to aid group problem formulation. *Technol. Forecasting Soc. Change* **16**, 311–320.

Uhlig, R.P. (1977). Human factors in computer message systems. *Datamation*, May, 120–126.

Uhlig, R.P., Farber, D.J., and Bair, J.H. (1979). "The Office of the Future: Communication and Computers." North Holland Publ., Amsterdam.

Umpleby, S.A. (1980). Computer conference on general systems theory: One year's experience. In "Electronic Communication: Technology and Impacts" (M.M. Henderson and M.J. MacNaughton, eds.), AAAS Sel. Symp. 52, pp. 55–63. Westview Press, Boulder, Colorado.

Vallee, J. (1976). There ain't no user science—A tongue-in-cheek discussion of interactive systems. Proc. ASIS Annu. Meet. 13.

Vallee, J., and Askevold, G. (1975). Geological applications of network conferencing: Current experiments with the FORUM system. In "Computer Networks and Chemistry" (P. Lykos, ed.), pp. 53–65. Am. Chem. Soc., Chicago, Illinois.

Vallee, J., Lipinski, H., and Miller, R. (1974a). "Group Communication through Computers." Vol. 1, Rep. R-32. Institute for the Future, Menlo Park, California.

Vallee, J., Johansen, R., Randolph, R., and Hastings, A. (1974b). "Group Communication through Computers." Vol. 2, Institute for the Future, Menlo Park, California.

Vallee, J., Johansen, R., Lipinski, H., Spangler, K., and Wilson, T. (1975). "Group Communication through Computers." Vol. 3, Rep. R-35. Institute for the Future, Menlo Park, California.

Vallee, J., Johansen, R., Lipinski, H., Spangler, K., and Wilson, T. (1978). "Group Communication through Computers." Vol. 4, Rep. R-40. Institute for the Future, Menlo Park, California.

Walker, D.E. (1971). "Interactive Bibliographic Search: The User/Computer Interface." AFIPS Press, Montvale, New Jersey.

Warfield, D.E. (1976). "Societal Systems: Planning, Policy, and Complexity." Wiley, New York.

Whyte, W.F. (1981). Exploring the frontiers of the possible: Social inventions for solving human problems. Program, 77th Annu. Meet., Am. Soc. Assoc. pp. 2–3.

Winkler, S. (1975). The quiet revolution. In "Computer Communication: Views from the ICCC '74" (N. Macon, ed.), pp. 1–4. International Council for Computer Communication, Washington, D.C.

Zinn, K.L. (1979). Computer-aided communications: New directions for higher education. In "Proceedings of the 1979 Annual Conference" (A. Martin and J. Elshoff, eds.), Abstract. ACM, Detroit, Michigan.

Author Index

Subject Index